Roads & Kingdoms presents

PASTA, PANE, VINO

Also presented by Roads & Kingdoms

**RICE, NOODLE, FISH
GRAPE, OLIVE, PIG**

PASTA, PANE, VINO

Deep Travels Through Italy's Food Culture

—

MATT GOULDING
DESIGNED BY DOUGLAS HUGHMANICK
EDITED BY NATHAN THORNBURGH

AN ANTHONY BOURDAIN BOOK

PASTA, PANE, VINO

HarperCollins books may be purchased for educational, business, or sales promotional use.
For information, please e-mail the Special Markets Department at SPsales@harpercollins.com.

Parts of this book have been adapted based on material previously published at roadsandkingdoms.com.

FIRST EDITION

Designed by Douglas Hughmanick

Cover photographs © kivoart/iStock/Getty Images (Pasta); DanielBendjy/iStock/Getty Images (Bread);
© igorr1/iStock/Getty Images (Wine)

Library of Congress Cataloging-in-Publication Data has been applied for.

ISBN: 978-0-06-265509-7

18 19 20 21 22   OV/LSCC   10 9 8 7 6 5 4 3 2 1

For the nonne, *who have taught the world so much about eating*

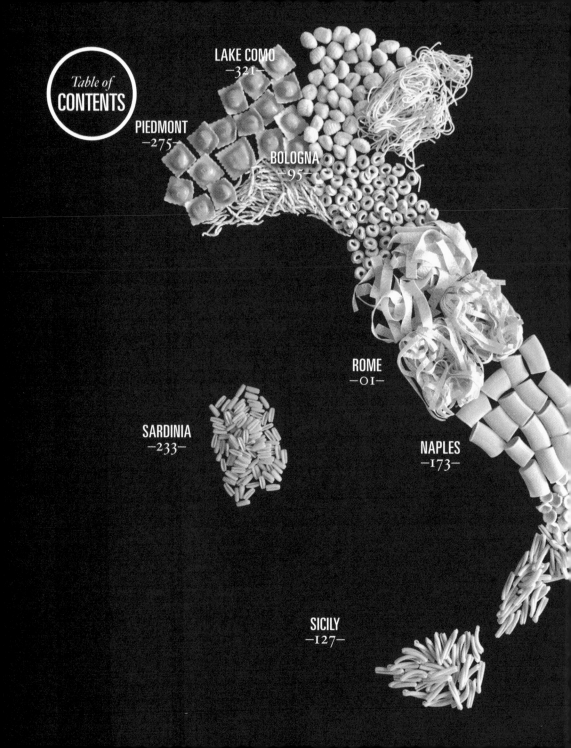

Table of
CONTENTS

ROME
PUGLIA
BOLOGNA
SICILY
NAPLES
SARDINIA
PIEDMONT
LAKE COMO

PUGLIA
—51—

IN CORRESPONDENCE WITH BOURDAIN:
How This Book Was Born

Dear Tony,

I'm in a tough spot. Of all the people I know, I'm guessing you're the one who will best appreciate my predicament. I write to you from Savigno, just outside Bologna, a town surrounded by sweet pignoletto vines and truffle-studded forests. Today is Easter, a day of liberation for the Italians, and splayed before me are the bones of half a dozen courses: ragù streaks, gnawed lamb ribs, pistachio dust. My blood runs with a mix of rendered pork fat and bitter spirits, six months in the underbelly of Italy's food world hitting me down to the marrow. But it's not my lipid profile I worry about; it's the table full of grandmas and couples and new friends around me. Let me explain.

When I first left New York in 2010 in search of a new start, I set my coordinates for Emilia-Romagna. There I would find a hilltop town, not unlike Savigno, powered by egg-rich pastas and slow-simmered sauces and single women with a penchant for lost Americans. Only a stopover in Barcelona and a fateful cerveza with a young Catalan I now call my wife kept me from my al dente destiny.

Granted, my vision was far from original. Most of the world dreams of Italy—of the pinup landscape porn, the cumulus clouds of cappuccino foam, the meals that stretch on like radioactive sunsets. It was those same dreams that drove me back here, that have me itching to capture this magic on the page. But lately I've been having nightmares about Italy. Nightmares about what the Italians will think about another foreigner's take on their traditions.

Nightmares about getting it wrong—about mistaking Parmesan for pecorino, pancetta for *guanciale*, spaghettini for spaghettoni. I don't mean nightmares in the figurative sense; I mean nightmares in the cold-sweat-and-sleepless-nights sense.

Nobody takes food more seriously than the Italians. I've seen family feuds break out over pasta shapes and grape varietals. No doubt you've been caught in the crossfire before. But these aren't the petty beefs of food snobs—these cut to the core of what it means to be Italian. More than anywhere else in the world, food carries the full weight of Italy's heritage: the pains and joys of its history, the depth of its ingenuity. Politicians are corrupt, democracy is fragile, borders are porous, but *la cucina italiana* is eternal.

At the end of the day, these are the people I want to surround myself with—the type who won't hesitate to spit in my vino if I ask for Parmesan with my spaghetti alle vongole. But they are also the ones I fear I will inevitably disappoint.

Does the world need another book about Italian food? Am I walking into a trap?

Yours,
Matt

🌱 🍇 🍷

Dear Matt,

The path you have chosen is indeed fraught with peril. The overwhelming instinct of Italophiles like you and me is to romanticize, oversentimentalize, and generally follow the well-worn tradition of soft-edged food porn when writing about Italy.

What is charming to us is often a frustration and even an affliction to Italians. The same political and cultural paralysis that keeps this beautiful collection of city-states "real" also traps its citizens in a reality that often approaches the tragically surreal.

But one can be forgiven, I hope, for finding great joy, even epiphany, in a bowl of pasta vongole (though not with cheese) and a bottle of rustic wine, the simple things that seem the birthright of the average Italian.

Careening through Rome late at night in a taxi, half-swacked on Negronis, listening to Mina, remains magic. To lay eyes on a bowl of *cacio e pepe*, a plate of *trippa*, *agnolotti*, urchins in season, porchetta—that's some powerful shit.

The mysteries of Italian parking, law enforcement, hand gestures, dress, family relationships, superstitions, dialectal differences, slang, and physical contact are unknowable yet enticing in that unknowability.

I'm still trying to figure it all out. It sounds like you are, too.

Tony

🌿 🍇 🍷

Ciao Tony,

I will leave the mysteries of law enforcement and hand gestures to the locals, though I've been on the receiving end of both throughout my time here.

But I have been trying to solve a few mysteries of the kitchen, namely what makes Italian food so damn delicious. A wise man in Kyoto once told me: Western cuisine is about addition; Japanese cuisine is about subtraction. But I think he overlooked a kinship between Japanese and Italian cooking—both built around exquisite product, both guided by a type of magical math best described as addition by subtraction: $3 - 1 = 4$.

And like Japanese cuisine, Italian food is driven by a set of rules and beliefs established over hundreds if not thousands of years, and embraced by a citizenry that largely rejects the notion of people fucking with their food. But Italian cuisine is not a statue in a museum; it's not some intractable monument to the past. It lives and breathes and bleeds like any good culture does.

I thought I could come here, eat a ton of *tagliatelle*, soak my bones in vino, and pay gentle tribute to the traditions of this wondrous place. I thought I would write a book about *nonna*, but everywhere I turn, I find granddaughters and grandsons writing the next chapter in their family history: three young brothers in Puglia expanding the essence of mozzarella and burrata in a deeply conservative culinary corner of Italy; a father-daughter team in the Piedmont who cast off the yoke of Barolo's staid history to produce some of the most poetic and controversial wines in the world; a class of next-generation *pizzaioli* in Naples wood-firing a path to a new understanding of the planet's most popular food.

In the end, it's not a book about grandmas and their sacred family recipes (though they have a few delicious cameos); it's a book about a wave of cooks, farmers, bakers, shepherds, young and old, trying to negotiate the weight of the past with the possibilities of the future.

I know how you feel about Italian cuisine. I know you don't want some young hotshot turning pasta alla carbonara into performance art. You don't want your cappuccino with condescension. I'm with you. But after a few hundred meals here, I'm starting to see just how important

—

this chapter is in the story of Italian cuisine, and I think it might make a worthy addition to this little series we have working.

What do you think?

Saluti,
Matt

Matt,

My response to you—and this sort of improvisation, innovation, expansion on traditional Italian regional specialties is entirely emotional—is a blind, unthinking, instinctive hostility. I hate it. I hate the thought. I am a curmudgeon when it comes to all things Italian.

I do not doubt there are delicious new takes on pizza, even that beloved carbonara. It is possible. It is, I guess, only right that new generations of Italian chefs are flexing their creative minds and their skills in the interest of moving things forward.

But I hate the idea in a way that only a non-Italian, newly besotted with an over-romantic view of that country, can be. Italians complain that their country doesn't work, that it is stuck, mired in the corruption and incompetence and antiquated attitudes of another time—that nothing ever changes. Which is exactly what I love in so many ways about the country. That state of paralysis. If it worked, it would change. And I don't want it to change.

I go to a place in Rome every time I'm there. And there's another place in Turin. The waiters are the same as they were twenty years ago. The owner who buzzes you into the locked door is the same. The menu is tiny (when there is one) and that never changes, either. Simple. Unpretentious. Handmade pastas, a few simple sauces. *Polpette*. Constant. A true friend.

To me, after thirty years of cooking, of garnishing, of torturing and manipulating food into being pretty enough or "interesting" enough to sell to an ever-fickle dining public, another two decades of experiencing every type of culinary genius or frippery, there is a deep satisfaction and joy in food made with enough confidence and love to take three or four good ingredients, cook them right, and dump them unceremoniously on a plate. Better yet is if the cook feels good enough about the food to serve it with a rough, not particularly good, local wine.

That makes me happy.

You are right, there is something almost Japanese about Italian food at its best. But Italian food is much, much, more emotional. One should experience it like a child, never like a critic, never analytically.

I am hopelessly compromised on this issue.

It is personal for me.

I cannot be trusted.

But I am right.

Still, if you ignore my advice and write this book, I'll read it. If it's good, I might even publish it.

Good luck,
Tony

Chapter One

ROME

Long after the sun has set behind the Palatine Hill, after the sands of the Colosseum have been swallowed by shadows, after the tint of the Tiber has morphed from *acqua minerale* to Spritz to dark vermouth, you come upon a quiet piazza down a meandering cobblestone street where a beaming restaurant owner—"Tonight is your lucky night," he says, Italian accent clinging to his English like a coddled egg to a carbonara—ushers you to a checkered-table-cloth table and asks if he might be allowed to read you the daily specialties while you settle into the evening, and by the time he's finished explaining the brilliance of the braised oxtail and the two types of sea-

sonal ravioli, made by hand every morning, a basket of bread and a carafe of wine have nestled in next to your elbows and you're just about ready to write home and tell your loved ones that all bets are off.

At the next table over, two Barolo-bellied men, teeth stained purple with Chianti, argue about Serie A soccer, the proper cutoff hour for a cappuccino, whose mother makes a better ragù. Every so often, a couple wanders out of the shadows and into the light of the restaurant, only to be turned gently away by the owner ("Try again tomorrow!"), making this moment just a bit more delicious. On the way to the bathroom, you catch a glimpse of a grandma in the kitchen, forearms coated in a fine layer of semolina, moving between the pasta bench and her seat next to the stove. The food dispatched from her kitchen perch will be the first and last thing you tell everyone about back home.

The wine keeps coming long after you stop ordering it. The owner makes the rounds, shaking hands and proffering glasses of his sticky homemade limoncello as the low purr of conversation rises with the moon. And as you slide your spoon through the last ripple of cocoa-laced mascarpone and savor the final drops of a bittersweet espresso and the night feels suspended in some blissful state of animation, you lean back in your chair and wonder: *Wow, so it really is like this?*

🌱 🍃 🍷

Only it's not really like this. Those tables filled with gesticulating Italians are actually filled with slow-blinking Americans and Brits and Japanese. That impossibly cheap and delicious house wine is an unholy mix of wounded soldiers left behind from nights past. Those flickering lights are in fact electric candles bought at the new IKEA. And that grandma with rivers of time running through her fingers, lost in the kneading of fresh *tonnarelli*, is actually an underpaid cook from Cairo, bringing his own traditions to the table.

Italian cuisine is the most famous and beloved cuisine in the world for a reason. Accessible, comforting, seemingly simple but endlessly delicious, it never disappoints, just as it seems to never change. It would be easy to give you, dear reader, a book filled with the al dente images of the Italy of your imagination. To pretend as if everything in this country is encased in amber. But Italian cuisine is not frozen in time. It's exposed to the same winds that blow food traditions in new directions every day. And now, more than at any time in recent or distant memory, those forces are stirring up change across the country that will forever alter the way Italy eats.

That change starts here, in Rome, the capital of Italy, the cradle of Western civilization, a city that has been reinventing itself for three millennia—since, as legend has it, Romulus murdered his brother Remus and built the foundations of Rome atop the Palatine Hill. Here you'll find a legion of chefs and artisans working to redefine the pillars of Italian cuisine: pasta, pizza, espresso, gelato, the food that makes us non-Italians dream so ravenously of this country, that makes us wish we were Italians, and that stirs in the people of Italy no small amount of pride and pleasure.

If you know anything about Italy, you know change doesn't come easily here. More than any other cuisine on Earth, Italian is one imbued with a sense of timelessness and immutability, the recipes not slowly evolved over millennia of high times and hardship but bestowed upon the people through an act of divine intervention. The food comes with a set of rules, laws so sacred and unbreakable they may as well be etched on stone tablets. *Thou shalt not overcook pasta! Thou shalt not mix cheese and seafood!* Break them at your own peril. How dangerous is it to offend Italians over

matters of the stomach? Just ask Nigella Lawson, domestic goddess of the British Isles, who innocently added cream to her carbonara recipe and watched the entire country rise up against her. Wrote one excitable defender of Italian heritage: "Nigella you are a wonderful woman but your recipes are the DEATH of Italian recipes, literally!"

If you need further proof of just how perilous the culinary waters can be in Italy, log on to Facebook or Twitter and search for the innocent prey of pasta zealots lurking in the e-shadows. The great Twitter account Italians Mad at Food documents the incensed reactions of the country's eaters to the injustices perpetrated on their cuisine. A representative sampling: *If you dare to serve that shit in Italy, you will be legally prosecuted and locked up in jail for life . . . Every time you put cream in a sauce, an Italian chef dies . . . We're not just offended, we're actually vomiting.*

But the wrath is not felt only by foreigners. When Carlo Cracco, one of Italy's most celebrated chefs, went on television and suggested adding garlic to *amatriciana*, the tomato-based pasta from the town of

Amatrice in Lazio, an article appeared in *La Repubblica*, Italy's largest newspaper, decrying the chef's transgression. The polemic was dubbed the "garlic war" and took on the same sharp tenor typically reserved for political scandals. The mayor of Amatrice took to Facebook to deride Cracco's blasphemous interpretation and reestablish the true recipe of *amatriciana*: "The only ingredients that compose a true *amatriciana* are *guanciale*, pecorino, San Marzano tomatoes, white wine, black pepper, and chili."

Yes, other great cuisines come with their own unspoken rules, but no one is going to send you death threats if you dump wasabi in your soy sauce or put ketchup on your New York hot dog. In Italy, these are deeply personal matters. The offended employ not just words of shock or displeasure but violent imagery to articulate their outrage: the raping and pillaging and murdering of Italian culture.

Yet not even Italians can agree on the details of their most famous dishes. There is no one true recipe for any of Italy's totemic regional plates: *tagliatelle al ragù,*

agnolotti al plin, risotto Milanese, *orecchiette alle cime di rapa, pasta con le sarde*—all inspire endless debates about the "right way," when in fact the right way is a series of choices—pancetta or *guanciale*, Parmesan or pecorino—not a fixed reality. But that doesn't stop the defenders of Italian regional cuisine from passionately protesting every perceived transgression. Which, in its own way, is a beautiful thing. The fact that people—not chefs or food writers but your average Italian—care this much about details the rest of the world would dismiss as trivial is exactly what makes this cuisine so damn great. Allow cream into the carbonara, and next thing you know the barbarians will be feasting on your loved ones.

Of course, it's not just the food. It's cultural heritage, identity, history, and a boundless source of pride for everyone from the granite peaks of Piedmont to the sugared shores of Sicily.

The central figure at the heart of our understanding of Italian cuisine is *la nonna*, the battle-tested grandmother who for centuries has made tiny miracles out of the hands dealt to her by history and circumstance. In times of feast and famine, she always found a way to feed her family the fruits of the season, always found a way to make food special. It was *la nonna* who established the rituals and recipes of the Italian kitchen, who turned it into one of the world's great cuisines, who helped perfect a formula that, in many minds, leaves little to no room for improvement. "In Italy, no cook is better than your grandmother." It's a sentence I hear so often that I begin to wonder if it doesn't appear in Italian school textbooks. Italian food culture exists primarily at home, in the comfort of the family kitchen, but for those of us who don't have a drop of Italian blood, we look for the next best thing: a sweet old woman in the back of the restaurant, making history with her hands.

If *la nonna* is the best cook, who needs a chef? If Grandma's heirloom *polpette* are the best, who needs a modernized version? But what, then, happens when the grandmas are gone?

The easy answer is that a new generation of grandmothers will rise up and take their place at the crux of Italian culture, but women born after the war were raised in an entirely different Italy. Broadly speaking, these aren't women who spent their formative years simmering sauces and mashing mortars and making pasta by hand; these were women making the gears of the Italian economy churn, who were lucky enough to make it home in time for dinner, let alone spend all day making it.

Cuisine, like all culture, is alive, and it's always finding new ways to express its DNA. *La cucina della nonna* isn't dead, but to define Italian food by what the oldest and most traditional practitioners cook is to deny the work being done across the country by thousands of ambitious cooks, young and old, female and male. From the mountain villages of Sardinia to the craggy coastline of Le Marche, everywhere you turn in Italy you see examples of a cuisine in a moment of great change—perhaps the greatest this country has seen since the aftermath of World War II, when a scarcity

CUCINA TIPICA ROMANA
FRESH EVERY DAY

WE ARE AGAINST WAR AND TOURIST MENU.

ITALIAN CUISINE IS NOT FROZEN IN TIME; IT IS NOT ENCASED IN AMBER.

of resources forced cooks to find new ways to feed their families.

These aren't radical changes, mind you. This isn't Ferran Adrià working a Bunsen burner on the Costa Brava, changing food on a molecular level. To be sure, wildly inventive cuisine has found its way to certain corners of Italy—most famously with Massimo Bottura in Modena and Carlo Cracco in Milan—but the more enduring change is the slow, steady progression of a cuisine that neither needs nor wants a dramatic shake-up.

The tension between past and future is the through line that defines all modern Italian culture, and it's the key to understanding the changes under way in the country's cuisine. Individually, the cooks and creators behind this change have established outposts that blend tradition and innovation in a way that will help inform the future of Italian food. Collectively, the work they do is a resounding reminder to traditionalists and innovators alike that food is a living, breathing, constantly morphing organism. No one can stop its evolution, not even *la nonna*.

Marcus Gavius Apicius was a man of many appetites. He ate with relish the swollen liver of pigs fattened on diets of dried figs. Lamb crusted in exotic spices from far-flung worlds. Crests of roosters boiled directly from their still live heads, red mullet bathed in a fermented sauce made from its guts. Born around the time of Christ, he became the foremost foodie of the Roman Empire during the reign of Tiberius.

His cookbook, *De Re Coquinaria*, considered the world's first, has become an important artifact for understanding Roman culture during the height of the empire. Apicius's Rome was a place where exotic tastes from across the empire converged. Where extravagant feasts were blunt expressions of wealth and status. Where a nascent brand of experimental gastronomy pushed the limits of food and its role at the center of a global empire.

He embodied the most extreme expression of the ancient Roman appetite: a love of spice, of sauces and condiments, of products from the far reaches of the empire. He also embodied one of its most infamous qualities: boundless gluttony. In his final and most notorious act, the bankrupt Apicius decided to take his own life rather than go on without the wealth it would take to live the grandiose and exuberantly delicious life he craved—an eerie foreshadowing of the gluttony that would eventually bring the empire crumbling down three centuries later.

But beyond the extravagance of Rome's wealthiest citizens and flamboyant gourmands, a more restrained cuisine emerged for the masses: breads baked with emmer wheat; polenta made from ground barley; cheese, fresh and aged, made from the milk of cows and sheep; pork sausages and cured meats; vegetables grown in the fertile soil along the Tiber. In these staples, more than the spice-rubbed game and wine-soaked feasts of Apicius and his ilk, we see the earliest signs of Italian cuisine taking shape.

The pillars of Italian cuisine, like the pillars of the Pantheon, are indeed old and sturdy. The arrival of pasta to Italy is a sub-ject of deep, rancorous debate, but despite the legend that Marco Polo returned from his trip to Asia with ramen noodles in his satchel, historians believe that pasta has been eaten on the Italian peninsula since at least the Etruscan time. Pizza as we know it didn't hit the streets of Naples until the seventeenth century, when Old World flat-bread met New World tomato and, eventually, cheese, but the foundations were forged in the fires of Pompeii, where archaeologists have discovered 2,000-year-old ovens of the same size and shape as the modern wood-burning oven. Sheep's- and cow's-milk cheeses sold in the daily markets of ancient Rome were crude precursors of pecorino and Parmesan, cheeses that literally and figuratively hold vast swaths of Italian cuisine together. Olives and wine were fundamental for rich and poor alike.

But many of the dishes now seen as archetypal Italian cuisine didn't come to the table until much later than we might believe—many are decades, not centuries or millennia, old, still warm from the oven. Take the curious case of spaghetti alla carbonara; now it's a juggernaut of the Roman kitchen, but it didn't surface on restaurant menus or in cookbook recipes until after World War II. And even though it's so young, no one can say with any certainty where it comes from. Some believe it to have been a creation of the coal miners of nearby Abruzzo, the *carbonari*, who emerged ravenous from the mines to eat this spare but satisfying pasta. Others believe it was born out of American GIs' nostalgia for bacon and eggs during the post–World War II reconstruction. And though the ingredients are few, the arguments abound: pancetta or *guanciale*, made from the pork jowl instead of the belly? Cubed or thinly sliced? Pecorino or Parmesan? Garlic or no? And then there's the matter of the egg: a whole egg or just the yolk? Five or six ingredients but hundreds of possible permutations. The dish is young, enigmatic, and malleable—not qualities we typically associate with Italian cuisine.

I haven't been around long enough to know new from old, so the first thing I do after the train pulls into Roma Termini is

seek out the smartest cooks and eaters in the country and bombard them with questions: Is *la cucina della nonna* alive and well? How has the Roman kitchen evolved? Is Italian food getting better? I do nothing my first week but chew and listen.

The results of the informal survey, to say the least, are mixed. Some can't even agree if Rome is a great eating city or not. "You know Rome's food culture is the worst in Italy, right?" says Elisia Menduni, a journalist and author of various tomes on Italian cooking. Says who? I ask, smelling hyperbole on her breath. "Everyone." According to Elisia, Roman cuisine is hampered by a lack of written history, a lack of a central thesis, by the scourges of tourism.

"People have been complaining about Roman food for twenty-five hundred years," says Katie Parla, an American expat who fell in love with Rome in 2003 and has been writing passionately about its food ever since. (Her 2015 cookbook, *Tasting Rome*, is a gorgeous love letter to her adopted city.) "Rome has been a tourist destination for eating for over five hundred years. In the past fifteen years the way people eat, where they eat, how much they eat has been radically transformed by the economic crisis. People are drawn by quantity and the perception of value."

Looking for the perspective of someone behind the line, I turn to Massimo Bottura, Italy's most renowned chef, whose Modena-based Osteria Francescana was named the world's best restaurant in 2016 by *Restaurant* magazine, the default arbiter on these matters. If anyone knows about the tension between the past and future of Italian cuisine, it's Massimo. For years, Italians branded him a heretic for his subversive tipping of Italy's sacred cows: tortellini in brodo, lasagne, Parmigiano-Reggiano. When I ask him if Italian food is getting better, he's unequivocal: "This is the most amazing time to be a chef in Italy. The shackles have been thrown off! The country is creating incredible culinary talent."

But opinions on food are like fingerprints in Italy. "I love Massimo and everything he does, but he is the capo of modern Italian cuisine. Of course he would say that."

The food writer Alessandro Bocchetti tells me this over lunch at Litro, a lovely osteria in the hilltop neighborhood of Monteverde, perched above Trastevere. We are eating warm bread slathered in cold butter and topped with salty anchovies, one of those three-ingredient Italian constructions—a shopping list more than a recipe—that can stop a conversation in its tracks. A cold bottle of malvasia gets the engine roaring once again. "Now is a difficult time for Italian cuisine. Young chefs are concerned with what's in fashion, with flash and trends. But the Italian family still suffers from Italy's deep recession." His concerns aren't with the restaurants at the top of the food chain but with those in the middle. "There are twenty restaurants today where you can eat as you never have before in Italy, but those are just twenty restaurants. The bigger picture isn't quite so rosy."

Ristoranti, the most formal class of dining in Italy, have the prices and the worldly clientele to experiment, but the heart of Italian food culture, especially Roman food culture, is the trattoria, an

The one-and-only carbonara, a dish of endless debate.

institution historically built on an infallible formula: good product, unfussy technique, reasonable prices. According to Alessandro, there are only a few true trattorie left in Rome, and he dispatches me to one with a friend, Andrea Sponzilli, another intrepid food writer. "He'll know what to order."

Among the pillars of Italian cuisine, pasta is the most sacred—the one that has inspired thousands of books, millions of journeys, and infinite debates about the way to do it right.

The rest of the world openly wonders what makes Italian pasta so good and theirs so mediocre, but the answer is right in front of their faces: the pasta itself. The bond between flour and water (and in some cases egg) is sacrosanct, and it must not be broken unnecessarily, compromised by sloppy cooking or aggressive saucing or tableware transgressions. That means cooking it properly, ignoring package or recipe instructions and instead relying on a system of vigilant testing until only the barest thread of raw pasta remains in the center of the noodle. That means saucing it spar-

ingly, in the same way a French chef might dress a salad, carefully calibrating the heft and the intensity of the sauce to the noodle itself. That means refraining from unholy acts of aggression: throwing it against the wall, adding oil to the boiling water, spinning the pasta against your spoon, or for God's sake cutting the noodles with a knife and a fork. Above all, that means thinking not addition but subtraction, not *what else can I add, but what can I take away?*

Italian cuisine, at its very best, is a math problem that doesn't add up. A tangle of noodles, a few scraps of pork, a grating of cheese are transformed into something magical. $1 + 1 = 3$: more alchemy than cooking.

No strain of regional Italian cooking expresses that more clearly than the iconic pastas of Rome: *gricia*, *carbonara*, *amatriciana*, and *cacio e pepe*. "They are the four kings," says Andrea as we peruse the menu of Cesare al Casaletto, a trattoria in Monteverde. It's ten minutes from the center of Rome, but for tourists who rarely cross the Tiber except to dip a toe in Trastevere, it might as well be in Florence. Our table of four decides to divide the royalty among us, and when the four dishes of arrive, a silence falls over us. There's a near-spiritual significance to having these four pastas on the table at once—each revered enough to have achieved canonical status among carb lovers the world over, but none containing more than a handful of ingredients.

Carbonara: The union of al dente noodles (traditionally spaghetti, but in this case rigatoni), crispy pork, and a cloak of lightly cooked egg and cheese is arguably the second most famous pasta in Italy, after Bologna's *tagliatelle al ragù*. The key to an excellent carbonara lies in the strategic incorporation of the egg, which is added raw to the hot pasta just before serving: add it when the pasta is too hot, and it will scramble and clump around the noodles; add it too late, and you'll have a viscous tide of raw egg dragging down your pasta.

Cacio e pepe: Said to have originated as a means of sustenance for shepherds on the road, who could bear to carry dried pasta, a hunk of cheese, and black pepper but little else. *Cacio e pepe* is the most magical

and befuddling of all Italian dishes, something that reads like arithmetic on paper but plays out like calculus in the pan. With nothing more than these three ingredients (and perhaps a bit of oil or butter, depending on who's cooking), plus a splash of pasta cooking water and a lot of movement in the pan to emulsify the fat from the cheese with the H_2O, you end up with a sauce that clings to the noodles and to your taste memories in equal measure.

Amatriciana: The only red pasta of the bunch. It doesn't come from Rome at all but from the town of Amatrice on the border of Lazio and Abruzzo (the influence of neighboring Abruzzo on Roman cuisine, especially in the pasta department, cannot be overstated). It's made predominantly with *bucatini*—thick, tubular spaghetti—dressed in tomato sauce revved up with crispy *guanciale* and a touch of chili. It's funky and sweet, with a mild bite—a rare study of opposing flavors in a cuisine that doesn't typically go for contrasts.

Gricia: The least known of the four kings, especially outside Rome, but according to Andrea, gricia is the bridge between them all: the rendered pork fat that gooses a carbonara or *amatriciana*, the funky cheese and pepper punch at the heart of *cacio e pepe*. "It all starts with gricia."

And that's where I start, lifting the pasta from the big-bellied bowl and marveling at its humility: nearly naked, with only the faintest suggestion of human interference. To truly enjoy a pasta of this austere simplicity is to surrender yourself entirely to the scope of its achievement: How to extract so much from so little? How many ingredients in any other cuisine around the world would it take to create a dish as satisfying as this one? Why doesn't my pasta taste like this?

You could argue that the two central ingredients at the heart of Rome's pasta culture aren't really ingredients at all: the first is water. Not just any water, but the water used to cook all those batches of pasta throughout service, each successive batch of noodles leaving behind a layer of starch that steadily transforms the water into an exquisite binding agent, perfect for adding

to a pasta sauce to adjust the consistency and clinginess.

The other vital ingredient in the Roman pasta canon is a simple but vital technique: a flick of the wrist, the aggressive movement needed to emulsify the cooking water with the fat in a pan of pasta sauce. By swirling the pan with one hand and using a set of tongs with the other to keep the starch in constant motion, like a Cantonese chef taming the breath of the wok with a hand that never stops moving—what Italians call *la mantecatura*—a thirty-second mating ritual of intense amorous energy wherein pasta and condiment become one. Without water and without the wrist motion, *cacio e pepe* would be nothing more than pasta dressed with cheese and pepper, gricia would be noodles in a mess of rendered pork fat. (Of course, most non-Italian cooks don't even attempt this delicate dance, opting instead to go the route of poor Nigella, adding cream to their carbonara and *cacio e pepe*.)

The Cesare specimens are among the finest I've tasted. Using rigatoni instead of spaghetti for carbonara would evoke an avalanche of angry Facebook posts from pasta purists, but there's no doubt that the hollow shape makes a more generous home for the silky sauce. The *gricia* is deserving of its fame across the city, the toothsome strands of housemade *tonnarelli* robed in a soft blanket of warm pig fat and pecorino. And the *cacio e pepe*, well, let's just say the *cacio e pepe* will follow me everywhere across this country in the months to come, a three-ingredient measuring stick for the greatness of Italy's regional cuisine. Albert Einstein said he saw the possibility of a higher power in the harmony of the natural world; some find it in the magnificent complexity of the human body. I see it in the miracle of *cacio e pepe*.

Before the hushed reverence of our pasta moment threatens to turn lunch awkward, the sound of happy eaters snaps us out of our silence. "The story of Roman cuisine is the story of the neighborhood restaurant," says Andrea. "Any real *romano* will always believe the best osteria is next door. Their loyalty is always to the neigh-

borhood." You can feel that loyalty in the room today: parents linger over dessert as their kids play under the table, old couples hold hands as they finish off the last few sips of wine. Maybe some have made the trip from other parts of Rome—it's certainly worth it—but chances are that most live within strolling distance.

After a lineup of stellar *secondi*—braised tripe, fried lamb chops, veal *braciola* simmered in tomato sauce—Andrea and I wander into the kitchen to talk with Leonardo Vignoli, the man behind the near-perfect meal. Cesare al Casaletto had been a neighborhood anchor since the 1950s, but when Leonardo and his wife, Maria Pia Cicconi, bought it in 2009, they began implementing small changes to modernize the food. Eleven years working in Michelin-starred restaurants in France gave Leonardo a perspective and a set of skills to bring back to Rome. "I wanted to bring my technical base to the flavors and aromas I grew up on." From the look of the menu, Cesare could be any other trattoria in Rome; it's not until you twirl that otherworldly *cacio e pepe* (which Leonardo makes using ice in the pan to form a thicker, more stable emulsion) and attack his antipasti—*polpette di bollito*, crunchy croquettes made from luscious strands of long-simmered veal; a paper cone filled with fried squid, sweet and supple, light and greaseless—that you understand what makes this place special.

Ask a *nonna* why she does something in the kitchen—why she cuts the vegetables a certain size or why she uses red wine instead of white in the ragù—and you're likely to get a shrug. *That's the way I was taught, and that's the way I've always done it.* Leonardo, on the other hand, does everything with an intense sense of purpose. He shows me the embers gently hissing in the brick oven for the roasted meat, the big-bellied, wide-rimmed bowls that keep the pasta warmer longer, the shimmering olive oil in the fryer, already changed out in anticipation of the dinner service.

"We are still a trattoria," says Leonardo. "We still serve the same dishes most others do. We still charge the same prices. We just put a little more thought into the details."

Few people put more thought into the tiny details than the team behind the ever-expanding Roscioli empire, one of the nerve centers of the *cucina romana moderna*, found just a few steps from the Campo de' Fiori. Sitting at a small table inside the Ristorante Salumeria Roscioli, a hybrid space that functions as a deli counter in the front and a full-service restaurant in the back, general manager Valerio Capriotti tells me with conviction that Italian food is flourishing—advancing in ways it hasn't in years, if ever, thanks in large part to the efforts of small producers who put their lives into raising rare breeds of pig, growing heirloom varietals of wheat, and milking pampered dairy cows and sheep to create the types of ingredients that drive restaurants like Roscioli forward. "Modern Italian cuisine isn't about technique," he tells me, "it's about ingredients. We know more now than we ever did about how things are made and what they do when we cook and eat them."

Exhibit A: the Roscioli carbonara. The pasta comes from a small artisanal maker in Abruzzo, the *guanciale* from pampered local pigs, the eggs from the rock-star farmer Paolo Parisi in Pisa, and the black pepper from Malaysia. Every single ingredient is the best in its class, but in the end, it's still a carbonara: no seasonal vegetables, no innovative garnish, no games played with temperature or texture—a beautiful reminder that restraint may be the most important ingredient in the Italian larder.

Exhibit B: the Roscioli burrata. In a world oversaturated with half-hearted burrata dishes, Roscioli serves up a category killer. Again, the brilliance comes down to the sourcing—in this case, from a small cheese maker in Andria, the heart of Puglia's burrata culture. Try it with semidried cherry tomatoes, an explosively sweet-and-sour counterpoint, and squares of Roscioli's habit-forming *pizza bianca*, and you'll realize you've probably never tasted real burrata before.

Ristorante Salumeria Roscioli is not a traditional trattoria. The menu is full of eccentricities, some successful (rigatoni with *bottarga* and yuzu butter), some less so (Camembert consommé with fried

fish), but the philosophy behind its best dishes (the cheese, charcuterie, and classic pastas) is what matters: subtle, persistent advancements in the few areas where improvement is still possible. "The evolution of cooking is about accumulating wisdom and using it when needed," says Valerio. "We take lessons from *nonna*, but we adapt them for a more contemporary perspective."

But the ethos that made Roscioli into one of the most influential institutions in Rome, if not all of Italy, doesn't end with carbonara and charcuterie. It doesn't even start there. Antico Forno Roscioli isn't exactly new—it opened in 1824, almost four decades before Italy became a country. But the work of its latest leader, Pierluigi Roscioli, and his team have turned the bakery into a brilliant bridge between past and future. He makes Rome's finest *pizza bianca* (which should be eaten early and often during a Rome stay) with organic, heirloom wheat and bakes heroic breads with ancient grains long out of favor in the country's bakeries: kamut, spelt, and rye from Trentino. "Bread is a pure

PANE
AZZIMO
€ ...

MINI
PANETTONE
al cioccolato
€ 1,50 l'uno

PANE
al OLIVE
€ 9,00 ...

PANE
con NOCI
€ 8,00 ...

CROCC...
...

PANBRIOCHE
di INCIRAZIONE
... al Kg

SFOGLIATELLE
NAPOLETANE
€ ... l'una

FROLLA
RICOTTA
e VISCIOLA
€ 2,50 l'una

PANE
... al Kg

PANE
con FARINA
di GRANO KHORASAN
€ 10,00 al Kg

PITA
ARABA
€ 0,80 l'una

INTEGRALE
Semi di CUMINO
€ 6,00 al Kg

€ 8,00 al Kg

221TTI
FARINA ...
... NO NERO e
... A SALE
... LIEVITO
... RALE

Antico Forno Roscioli, redefining
Roman baking for generations.

expression of raw ingredients," says Pierluigi. "It's not about technical advancement."

Not content with rethinking bread, cheese, and pasta, in 2016 the Roscioli crew brought its philosophy to one of the most immutable pillars of the Italian culinary forum: coffee. Roscioli Caffè, a few doors down from their other ventures, does a lot of special things, from its next-generation pastry display to the modern cocktails and antipasti they serve in the evenings, but the real innovation is in the *caffè* they serve every day to hundreds of busy Romans.

Italy didn't invent coffee, of course (that distinction belongs to the Ethiopians, who began boiling coffee cherries a millennium ago), but they did invent café culture and with it a set of unspoken rules as rigid as the ones that govern the food world: no milk after 11 A.M., no takeout, no tongue-twisting requests for skinny this or caramel that.

In the same way that Italian cuisine has been largely resistant to the whims of modern fads in the kitchen, Italian coffee culture has scarcely changed since 1884, when Angelo Moriondo presented his blueprint for the espresso machine at the General Exposition of Turin. While the rest of the world cycles through "waves" of coffee (FYI, we're currently on the Third Wave, marked by an increase in bean quality, technical brewing advancements, and overall snobbery), Italy remains happy to do *caffè* (*espresso* is rarely used in Italian coffee parlance) the way it's always done it.

Popular belief has it that you can't find bad coffee in Italy; sidle up to a bar anywhere in this country, from a tiny southern village to a gilded urban institution to a highway gas station, and you'll be treated to an espresso or cappuccino of extraordinary quality. Though it's true that the average coffee you drink in Italy is better than what you find elsewhere in the world due in large part to the ubiquity of gorgeous, expensive espresso machines—and the presence of talented baristas everywhere who know how to play those machines like orchestral instruments—the quality of what comes dribbling out of those machines has been steadily declining over the years. Italy's espresso economy is dominated by giant coffee producers (Lavazza, Illy, Segafredo), which maintain a stranglehold on the market by providing everything from branded machines and signage to napkins and coffee cups in exchange for long-term contracts guaranteeing the use of their espresso beans. Though Segafredo is leagues better than, say, Folgers or Bonka, it's still an industrial coffee product that can't compete with the quality of small-production, single-origin beans that form the heart of modern coffee culture in Tokyo, Stockholm, and San Francisco.

Turin (the home of Lavazza) and Trieste (the home of Illy) host Italy's highest concentration of coffee institutions, old-school bars hermetically sealed off from outside trends. But Rome isn't far behind. Places such as Antico Caffè Greco, La Campana, and Caffè Eulalia make good *caffè*, and are perfect pit stops for refueling during a long day wandering across the city, but all serve the same species of dark, hard-roasted, bitter espresso with little to no variation.

Beyond a generally high standard of quality, two characteristics define Italy's coffee culture: speed and low price. Italians might drink five espressos a day, and they want them to be both fast and affordable. The latter is so critical that the government regulates the price of espressos and cappuccinos.

So no, don't expect to find an Italian paying $5 for a pour-over coffee that takes ten minutes to make and twenty to drink. But at Roscioli Caffè, Salvatore Cerasuolo and his team of well-dressed baristas have been quietly incorporating the best of modern coffee principles and folding them into the rhythms of a traditional Italian *caffè*. "Italian coffee culture is five hundred years old," he says. "Over the years, there's been an explosion of commercialization and automation across the industry. Part of that means the raw materials aren't always great." In a world defined by speed and ease, Salvo obsesses over the finer details: the age of the coffee bean, the height at which it was grown, the subtle differences of the temperature and length of its extraction. "All of these elements are slowly getting better in Italy," he says. Salvo sources his coffee from Laboratorio di Tor-refazione Giamaica Caffè, Italy's premier small roaster, a Verona-based operation that eschews the dark, oily roasts that are standard across the country in favor of a lighter, more subtle coffee bean. You won't detect notes of strawberry and passion fruit in your cappuccino; this is still assertive Italian coffee, but with more nuance than you'll find at the corner spot.

If Salvo looks like the moody barista at your neighborhood coffee shop in Brooklyn (crisp white button-up, black suspenders, black handlebar mustache), that's because Italy invented the dapper, dedicated barista. But don't expect a lecture on water temperature or a grimace when you ask for sugar. Salvo and his crew will happily make you a V60 pour-over or a batch of coffee brewed in the glass curves of a siphon, but in a dozen mornings of sipping cappuccinos at Roscioli's gorgeous bar, I saw not a single filtered coffee ordered. No siphon swirls, no long, slow savoring of a Chemex coffee. Instead, it's *caffè* and *cornetto*, cappuccino and *brioche con panna*, the customers coming

and going so quickly that they barely break stride as they mainline the caffeine. The clients at Roscioli probably don't know the difference between shade-grown and sun-grown coffee, between Panama Geisha and Guatemalan Bourbon, but they come here because the combination of old and new makes for the best *caffè* in Rome. And that's what counts.

Not every change is so subtle. There are chefs in Rome taking the same types of risks other young cooks around the world are using to bend the boundaries of the dining world. At Metamorfosi, among the gilded streets of Parioli, the Colum-bian-born chef Roy Caceres and his crew turn ink-stained squid bodies into ravioli skins and sous-vide egg and cheese foam into new-age carbonara and apply the tools of the modernist kitchen to a create a broad and abstract interpretation of Italian cui-sine. Alba Esteve Ruiz trained at El Celler de Can Roca in Spain, one of the world's most inventive restaurants, before, in 2013, opening Marzapane Roma, where frisky diners line up for a taste of prawn tartare with smoked eggplant cream and linguine cooked in chamomile tea spotted with microdrops of lemon gelée.

At Retrobottega, not far from the constant churn of Piazza Navona, a crew of young chefs have taken their years of staging at the temples of high Italian cuisine and unleashed their accumulated skills in a decidedly downscale environment. Diners sit at the bar or a series of high tables, pull out their own silverware from drawers, fetch and open their own wine, and collect plates from the pass as the chefs call them out from the open kitchen. Regardless of how you feel about chatting with line cooks or playing server to yourself, the payoff comes on the plate: zucchini and anchovies in a tart *scapece* with pureed mushrooms; fried chicken hearts, scattered across the plate like popcorn and cut with little curls of pickled vegetables; and a plate of *linguine aglio e olio*, one of Italy's staple pastas, tricked out with a pool of *grana* fondue below the tight nest of noodles.

To taste some of the more radical transformations, you'll need to travel farther afield, beyond the swaths of mediocre restaurants that clog up the city's central arteries. On an unsuspecting residential block in Centocelle, a working-class neighborhood on the outskirts of Rome, a tiny restaurant with a single communal table and a chalkboard menu on the wall is pushing the classic notion of a casual neighborhood eatery. Every night, it fills up with locals and foreigners, pasta freaks, and gastro geeks all partaking of a rare and exceptional take on modern Roman cuisine.

The husband-and-wife team Marco Baccanelli and Francesca Barreca are known as "the Fooders" among Rome's culinary cognoscenti, a nickname they earned during years of catering and pop-ups in the run-up to opening Mazzo. "It gave us time to tweak, to play with new ideas," Francesca tells me late one afternoon before dinner service. A group of young Italians crowds the front patio, sipping Spritzes. Down the table from us, a beautiful blonde takes alternating drags off a book of poetry and a glass of pinot grigio. "We love food, but we love music, design, art, and we want to find ways to bring it all to our restaurant."

The result has made the duo into one of Rome's culinary power couples. It takes but a few minutes to spot the synergy between Francesca and Marco—they crack jokes, debate new ideas, and finish each other's sentences. "He's the grandma in our kitchen," Francesca says, gently elbowing her husband. "He's here making pasta by hand every day, like a good *nonna*, but we're always thinking of new ways to cook it."

Beyond being the foundation of so much of Italy's cooking, the grandma plays a central role in the Italian culinary psyche. "*Nonna* cuisine has a definite cultural value, both for Italians and for foreigners," says Marco. All else being equal, would you rather see an eighty-year-old woman in a worn apron or a thirty-five-year-old man with a long beard and a tilted Yankees cap rolling out your *tortelli*? For his part, Marco relishes the chance to challenge stereotypes. "Every batch is different," he says with a mix of enthusiasm and consterna-

tion, "but I'm especially excited about how it came out today."

Dinner starts with a ceviche of beef, the love child of northern Italy's raw beef culture and the couple's interest in assertive flavors from around the world. Depending on the day, you may find lemongrass, cilantro, and miso—perfect strangers across Italy—canoodling with cured anchovies and handmade pastas. "It's not fusion," says Francesca. "We don't ever think 'How can we work a bit of Asia into this plate?' If it makes sense on the fork, then we go for it."

From there Francesca takes me through the entire menu: from the esoteric and unexpected—fried snails over a dashi-spiked potato puree, glazed pork belly with *cavolo nero* kimchi—to gentle riffs on the soul food you'd find in a traditional trattoria—fried artichokes dipped into an anise-spiked mayonnaise, tender pork sweetbreads with tiny candy-sweet asparagus and a slick of Mazzo's exceptional olive oil. "Roman cuisine isn't frozen in time," says Francesca in one of our midmeal exchanges. "We don't have any set way we come up with dishes—

Francesca and Marco, aka the
Fooders, stand tall at Mazzo.

sometimes they grow out of tradition or a dish we ate while traveling. Other times, a single ingredient."

Marco's rigatoni finally emerges, wearing a meaty, fatty, unapologetically aggressive ragù. The pasta it clings to, cooked to the outer edge of al dente, would make the most battle-tested *nonna* proud.

To my right are three middle-aged Italians deep in conversation about Roman politics. To the left are a religion writer from Washington, D.C., and her husband, decked out in a button-up Hawaiian shirt, who found their way out here on the recommendation of a journalist friend. Both seem amused by their presence at a communal table in Centocelle, as if they're not quite sure how they keep ending up at these hip restaurants. Francesca comes out of the kitchen to talk to all the diners, introducing herself in Italian and English and asking everybody about the food. When she makes it to the couple, the pescatarian wife looks up with cabernet eyes and a Parmesan smile. "That was an interesting ceviche dish. What kind of fish was that?" Francesca looks nervously at me, and I tell the woman gently that it wasn't fish at all. She takes it with a smile, and Francesca relaxes.

"Well, it was a lovely meal," the writer says, swirling the last of the wine in her glass. "But it didn't feel very Italian."

Ancient Rome was one of the world's first street food cultures. With one million residents packed into a space now occupied by a tenth of that number, the cramped quarters left little room for personal kitchen space. To cook at home meant building a fire, a dangerous proposition with so many souls packed in so tightly. Instead, an economy of casual food cooked on street corners and sold to the masses took shape: flatbreads, grilled sausage, fried fish.

Over the centuries, Rome shed its sardine-can concentration of inhabitants, but the presence of handheld snacks persisted. Panini, *tramezzini*, fried mozzarella, the crunchy rice snacks known as *supplì*: the Roman love of carbs, cheese, and meat arranged in various expressions knows no bounds.

The king of these expressions, here and everywhere in Italy, is pizza. Not the round, blistered, knife-and-fork pizzas of Naples, but pizza of a different shape and stature: thin, light, crispy, portable. Glistening gold rectangles of *pizza bianca* have long been a street snack powering Rome: crunchy and tender, bitter from a slick of olive oil and sweet from the slow browning of grains, with shards of coarse salt that explode in your mouth at random intervals. Some eat it hot out of the oven; others slice it and fill it—with mortadella, prosciutto and figs, anything you might find on an antipasto plate.

But even the simplest, most sacred foods need updating. One of the chief catalysts of pizza's recent evolution is Gabriele Bonci, virtuoso bread man, who set off a small revolution in the Italian baking and pizza world years ago when he opened Bonci, a small outpost on the far side of the Vatican where you'll find a dozen varieties of pizza, sold by weight and changing daily, if not hourly. It's easy to be taken in by Bonci's ambitious flavor combinations—mortadella with a chickpea puree, grilled octopus and bitter greens—but the real innovation, the one that stirred a lot of soul-searching in a pizza world resistant to change, comes down to the dough itself. Bonci works with small producers growing ancient varietals of grains, which form the base of his high-hydration, long-fermented dough—crispy, tender, and gently sour, a masterpiece of complex flavors and contrasting textures. Leave the raw porcini, grilled beef, and smoked salmon to the Instagrammers; the best stuff at Bonci are the slices that show off Bonci's grain work, simple, sober displays of craftsmanship: *pizza rossa* with a thin blanket of crushed tomatoes and floral drifts of oregano; *pizza Margherita* made with half a dozen different combinations of mozzarella and tomato; and the *pizza con le patate*, a carb-on-carb affair possessed of an impossible lightness of being.

If Bonci is the "Michelangelo of pizza," as some have dubbed him, Stefano Callegari is the pizza world's Willy Wonka, delivering waves of shock and delight to people who have spent their entire lives eating the same slices. Callegari grew up in Rome's Testaccio neighborhood, working at a bakery, making *pizza bianca* for the local clientele. After a fifteen-year stint as a flight attendant for Alitalia, he finally grounded himself and set about constructing a new world of dough and cheese. At Sforno, the pizzeria he opened in Cinecittà in 2005, he mastered the basics but also began to explore new frontiers. Combinations such as headcheese and Campari or Stilton with a port reduction caused a stir in the Roman pizzarazzi, but the big breakthrough came with his *pizza cacio e pepe*, a feat of technical wizardry that involves baking the dough with chipped ice on its surface, creating enough residual moisture to hold the pecorino and pepper in place.

But here, in his restaurant Trapizzino on his home turf in Testaccio, he took the genre bending a step further. Using a newspaper, sugar packets, and animated hand motions, Callegari reenacts the creation of the Trapizzino, a pocket of crispy dough that eats like the love child of pizza and *tramezzino*, Italy's triangular sandwich. Skeptics might see in the Trapizzino the sad pizza cone found on food trucks in the United States and beyond, but this is no half-hearted gimmick: crispy and tender, light but resilient, it is an architectural marvel of pizza ingenuity. Not content with traditional pizza toppings, Callegari instead ladles slow-cooked stews of meat and vegetables—tongue in salsa verde, *pollo alla cacciatora*, artichokes and favas with mint and chili—that perform magnificently against the crunch and comfort of this warm pizza pocket. "The best of old Roman cooking is like great ethnic food—slow-cooked, humble ingredients with big flavor."

"Yes, it's about the ingredients, but it's a cook's job to transform those ingredients into something special." Callegari has since expanded his Trapizzino vision to the United States (New York) and Japan (Tokyo and Kyoto) and plans to open more, but the Testaccio shop, the one flooded by a constant flow of the young and hungry, is the nerve center of his pizza genius.

Testaccio makes a fitting home for a shape-shifting pizzeria; on the banks of the Tiber, just southeast of the city center, it's the neighborhood that best represents the modernizing face of Roman culture. Once home to the municipal slaughterhouse, one of the largest in Europe, and the blue-collar citizens who kept it running, the neighborhood has undergone the type of transformation that replaces the old and the static with the young and the restless. Testaccio still clings to a piece of its humble former self, but when Eataly, the massive high-end Italian market, took over an old train station at the edge of the neighborhood, it was only so long before the fixed bikes showed up to do battle against the cobblestones.

The Testaccio Market anchors the neighborhood, an esoteric collection of commercial merchants, ambitious food and wine purveyors, and casual food shops. You can eat a slice of pizza, shop for shoes, pick up a dozen long-stem artichokes, have a straight-razor shave, and wash it all down with a bottle of biody-namic pinot grigio. Market dining may be standard fare in cities around the world, even in other parts of Italy, but when Testaccio Market reopened in 2012, it was a new style of eating for the *romani*. (In the years since, the concept has caught on and spread across the city.) There are a dozen places to eat, from crispy, four-bite *pizzette* to soup and sandwiches from Michelin-starred chef Cristina Bowerman, but you're really here for Mordi e Vai. Sergio Esposito worked as a butcher in the neighborhood, where he had been a promoter of *quinto quarto*, Rome's legendary offal culture—named for the idea that the viscera is "the fifth quarter" of the animal. Esposito's earlier career gave him an idea: What if we took the intense, rib-sticking offal stews and braises of the neighborhood and turned them from knife-and-fork fare into sandwiches?

Thus the *quinto quarto* panino was born. Today you'll find Esposito and his crew stuffing soft rolls with slow-cooked honeycomb tripe, *coratella* (braised lamb innards) and artichokes, and *fegato alla macelleria*,

A Trapizzino trio in
Testaccio.

butcher-style liver with tomatoes and caramelized onions. The best of the bunch,
allesso di scottona, is an old-school braise
of beef brisket, best when topped with a
thicket of sautéed chicory and an extra
ladle of the cooking juices. They're edible
monuments—to Testaccio before its transformation, to the Jewish ghetto, the source
of so many of Rome's greatest dishes—
many slowly finding their way off the en-
dangered species list thanks to people like
Esposito and Callegari.

Beyond being superlative street food,
Esposito's sandwiches solve two persistent
challenges: they give a new life to classic
Roman dishes that had fallen out of favor
and turn the normally prosaic panino—a
sandwich housing a lonely slice of prosciutto or a lifeless wad of mozzarella—into
something worth standing in line for.

In an extra layer of innovation, Esposito
turned to the classic pasta sauces of Rome
for inspiration, stuffing panini with his riffs
on *amatriciana* and *cacio e pepe* and a pepper-bombed carbonara spiked with chunks
of veal. Imagine *la scarpetta*, the Italian

31

ritual of scraping the bottom of a pasta bowl with hunks of bread, in sandwich form, and you get an idea of Esposito's genius.

Of course, more than pizza cones and tripe sandwiches, the most ubiquitous street food in Rome is gelato. It's also one of the Italian pillars most in need of reinforcing. Despite the museum-worthy beauty of so many of Rome's central gelato spots, the trend for decades has been moving away from natural ingredients and toward prefab concoctions and chemical-laden mixes riddled with emulsifiers, stabilizers, and food coloring. Artfully displayed garnishes— clusters of hazelnuts, swooshes of Nutella, rainbows of fresh fruit—are a red herring, a cheap and easy way to pull in clientele with the appearance of handmade quality.

But a countermovement has been taking shape for years, prompted by those looking to keep gelato from losing its soul entirely. Claudio Torcè is one of the godfathers of Rome's gelato resurgence, whose opening of Il Gelato di Claudio Torcè in 2003 helped establish a set of new standards: local, seasonal ingredients, refined tech-niques inspired by high cuisine, and the embrace of esoteric, overlooked, and counterintuitive flavors. At his mother ship in EUR, on the southern edge of the city, he offers one hundred flavors daily, many only vaguely suggestive of dessert (Parmesan, habanero, mortadella), but all defined by a minimum number of ingredients and a maximum expression of flavor. Anyone can fashion ice cream out of a funky ingredient and wait for the world to react; only masters like Torcè can make it delicious.

In the end, the good ones are more gelato chefs than gelato makers, dedicated to doing whatever it takes to concentrate as much flavor as possible into a single cold bite. Few embody this idea more thoroughly than Marco Radicioni at Otaleg in Colli Portuensi. From the street, a glass-walled laboratory packed with gadgets announces Radicioni's ambition to passersby: this isn't an old man in the back hand-churning gelato from today's batch of vanilla; this is a man driven by the idea that there's always a way to make something a little bit better.

True to its name (gelato spelled backward), Otaleg is swimming against the tide of cost-cutting convenience that dominates Italy's ice cream industry. Sixty flavors at a given time, rotating daily—most rigorously tied to the season, many inspired by a pantry of savory ingredients: mustard, Gorgonzola with white chocolate and hazelnuts, pecorino with bitter orange. He seeks out local flavors, but never at the expense of a better product: pistachios from Turkey, hazelnuts from Piedmont, and (gasp!) French-born Valrhona chocolate. Extractions, infusions, experiments—whatever it takes to get more out of the handful of ingredients he puts into each creation. In the end, what matters is what ends up in the scoop, and the stuff at Otaleg will make your toes curl—creams and chocolates so pure and intense they must be genetically manipulated, fruit-based creations so expressive of the season that they actually taste different from one day to the next. And a licorice gelato that will change you—if not for life, at least for a few weeks.

Radicioni and Torcè are far from alone in their quest to lift the gelato genre. Fior di Luna has been doing it right—serious ingredients ethically sourced and minimally processed—since 1993. At Gelateria dei Gracchi, just across the Regina Margherita bridge, Alberto Monassei obsesses over every last detail, from the size of the whole hazelnuts in his decadent *gianduia* to the provenance of the pears that he combines with ribbons of caramel. And Maria Agnese Spagnuolo, one of Torcè's many disciples, continues to push the limits of gelato at her ever-expanding Fatamorgana empire, where a lineup of more than fifty choices—from basil-honey-walnut to dark chocolate–wasabi—attracts a steady crush of locals and savvy tourists.

But don't expect the rest of Rome to suddenly follow suit, especially if you like to get your gelato fix within melting distance of a gladiator or a famous fountain. There are hundreds of gelaterie in Rome today, and very few dispense the real stuff. Why pay the money and spend the time to do it right when your onetime customer, never to be

—

seen again, doesn't know the difference? It's a cynical equation, but it's the same math that has converted Times Square, Las Ramblas, and other tourist-dense pockets the world over into culinary black holes.

They'll continue to open packages and dispense prefab gelato dressed to impress. And the people will continue to eat it up. Because, like sex and pizza, even when gelato is bad, it's still pretty good.

But life's too short for average ice cream. In the end, there are a dozen ways to explain why the gelato at Otaleg or Torcè or Fatamorgana is better—the ingredients! the laboratories! the creativity!—but there is an even simpler explanation, the same one at the heart of all great food: because its creators care more than everyone else does.

🌱 🍇 🍷

Over the weeks in Rome, the old and the new begin to bleed together, and I struggle to pull them apart. Maybe it's the impossible history, the one that paints every street corner with a mix of tragedy and promise. Maybe it's the rivers of olive oil, the puddles of pork fat, the snowdrifts of grated *cacio* that gather in my blood. Maybe it's the bottle of Dr. Schulze's THC drops that my friend Alessandro gifts me upon my arrival in Italy ("Add a few to your pasta, and you'll see Italy in an entirely different way!"). The world begins to wobble.

I am supposed to be going to Italian class to sharpen my skills before the long march across the country, but I can't bring myself to sit down. Distracted by the morning market in Campo de' Fiori, where the colors of the countryside—purple crowns of asparagus, orange-lipped squash blossoms—shine with hallucinogenic intensity; by the sounds of Italy caffeinating itself, the low drone of the espresso machine, the clank of the cappuccino cup as it lands between glass plate and metal spoon; by the promise of another meal, good or bad or indifferent, around every corner, another glimpse under the veil. What classroom could compare to the city at large?

Instead, I wander. Past the bones of

an empire scattered across the cityscape, peeking through parks, crowding the street corners, rubbing up against shiny buildings that reflect the sunlight. Through the hills of Monteverde, where Rome opens up like an artichoke past its prime. Along the streets of Trastevere, where every cliché of Italian life unfolds so vividly you wonder if Disney isn't holding the strings: old woman in her window observatory, sharing secrets with the neighborhood; mustachioed man perched on a stool, peeling porcini in the shadows. Art and life become indistinguishable, an imitation game that goes around in stunning circles.

SPQR: Sono Pazzi Questi Romani. These Romans Are Crazy.

I start to dream of *cacio*. Not daydream, not wonder lustily when my next bite of salty sheep's-milk cheese will come, but deep REM visions of *cacio* in every texture imaginable: resting delicately above a plate of pasta, browning into a crispy shell on a flat-top griddle, turned into a tea with kernels of black pepper bobbing on the surface. *Cacio e pepe*: black and white like a Fellini film,

this speckled union follows me everywhere across Rome—into the crunchy *supplì* at La Gatta Mangiona; onto the pizza at Tonda; smothering a burger at Luppolo Station, a dive bar on the outer edge of Trastevere—a burger so impossibly good that I return the next night to eat it again, to make sure I wasn't dreaming. (I wasn't.)

I keep going back to the same places, to Roscioli for a morning *cappuccio* and an afternoon burrata; for slices of *pizza bianca* from Bonci, which I fold like a letter home I keep forgetting to send and devour; to Mordi e Vai and Trapizzino, where they send me out to the streets with handheld poems to Rome's past.

I follow a bread-crumb trail to other tastes of a Roman future: to Open Baladin to drink in Italy's staggering craft brew scene, a freewheeling counterpoint to the country's well-established wine world; to Emma, where I eat pizza so thin and crunchy it nearly vanishes before I have a chance to chew. Every time I stray from the path and choose a place for its beauty, the city extracts a price: a bad bowl of pasta,

▬

a sad scoop of gelato, a lifeless puddle of espresso, precious space wasted.

Consistency was never a strong suit in Rome. The city is at turns austere and extravagant, luxurious and shabby, regal and bohemian, deadly serious and surprisingly playful. Eternal and fleeting. When you've lived as many lives as Rome has, you're allowed to be malleable.

Armando al Pantheon is located just a few steps from the namesake monument, in what might qualify as the least likely place in Rome to find an exceptional restaurant. I stumble into the kitchen one morning and ask for the owner, Claudio Gargioli. One of his daughters is whipping eggs for tiramisù. His other daughter, recently graduated from culinary school, works the burners with a handful of pans that form the base of the restaurant's pasta game. Artichokes are in various stages of undress across the kitchen. An older man peels the thistles down to their core before dropping them into a bath of boiling olive oil; they emerge in golden brown bloom minutes later. A younger man works his own batch,

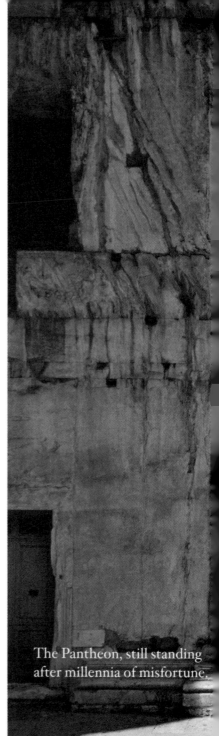

The Pantheon, still standing after millennia of misfortune.

stuffs them with a single garlic clove and a bay leaf, adds a few inches of water to the bottom of the pan, covers it, and sets it on a burner before going on to the next prep item. It's hard to imagine a more honest kitchen than the one buzzing before me.

Claudio looks up when he sees me at the kitchen threshold. "You mind if I finish this pan of *guanciale* before we talk?"

Claudio's father, Armando, opened the restaurant in 1961, and throughout the 1970s and '80s, Claudio cooked alongside his family, taking an ever stronger role in the food. "I wanted to do pure Roman food *e basta*. That meant focusing on a few things: seasonal ingredients, a few great pastas, *quinto quarto*." The only point that everyone I spoke with in Rome agrees upon is that Armando al Pantheon is one of the city's last true trattorie.

Given the location, Claudio and his family could have gone the way of the rest of the neighborhood a long time ago and mailed it in with a handful of passable pastas and a stash of fresh mozzarella and prosciutto. But he's chosen the opposite path, an unwavering dedication to the details—the extra steps that make the oxtail more succulent, the pasta more perfectly toothsome, the artichokes and favas and squash blossoms more poetic in their expression of the Roman seasons.

"I experiment in my own small ways. I want to make something new, but I also want my guests to think of their mothers and grandmothers. I want them to taste their infancy, to taste their memories. Like that great scene in *Ratatouille*."

I didn't grow up on *amatriciana* and offal, but when I eat them here, they taste like a memory I never knew I had. I keep coming back. For the *cacio e pepe*, which sings that salty-spicy duet with unrivaled clarity, thanks to the depth charge of toasted Malaysian peppercorns Claudio employs. For his *coda alla vaccinara*, as Roman as the Colosseum, a masterpiece of *quinto quarto* cookery: the oxtail cooked to the point of collapse, bathed in a tomato sauce with a gentle green undertow of celery, one of Rome's unsung heroes. For the vegetables: one day a crostino of stewed favas and pork cheek, the next a tumble of bitter *punta-relle* greens bound in a bracing anchovy vinaigrette. And always the artichokes. If Roman artichokes are drugs, Claudio's are pure poppy, a vegetable so deeply addictive that I find myself thinking about it at the most inappropriate times. Whether fried into a crisp, juicy flower or braised into tender, melting submission, it makes you wonder what the rest of the world is doing with their thistles.

At the end of service on my last night in Rome, Claudio comes out of the kitchen beaming, a man who lives to feed people. We talk about pasta, about the little moves that make his so memorable. We talk about the wrist action that a good Roman cook needs to do a proper carbonara or *gricia*. We talk about the importance of pasta water, the unsung hero of the Roman kitchen, how it gets better as service wears on, the starchy ghosts of noodles past turning the boiling water into a murky spa of magical powers.

More than a deeply talented cook and convivial host, Claudio's a scholar of Roman cuisine. He can speak eloquently about the dual roles of the Jews and the pope in influencing Roman cuisine, about the slow evolution of the city's pasta culture, about the future. If anyone knows where food is going around here, it's Claudio. "Innovation is a beautiful thing, as long as we never forget our roots."

I leave Claudio and step out into the Roman night. The broad shoulders of the Pantheon wait for me just around the corner. It looks eternal in the golden night glow, a temple built to honor the gods back when the Romans believed in more than one. But it fell twice since then—burned first in A.D. 80, in a great fire that engulfed much of the city. Thirty years later, it was struck by lightning, brought to its knees by a bolt from the sky. War and weather, time and temperament: all have taken their toll. Yet here it is, standing strong, just a block from the kitchen where Claudio makes his *cacio e pepe* with peppercorns from a far-off land.

That's the beautiful part of the story of Rome, the story of Italy: You don't erase the history. You build on top of it.

KNOW BEFORE YOU GO

(01) Italy is a very young country.

The Risorgimiento, the movement that turned a collection of states into a unified country, took sixty-six painstaking years, ending in 1871, making Italy an infant in the global order of nations. More than a homogeneous body of sixty million people, Italy is a loosely connected collection of twenty regions, each with its own distinctive DNA. People will nearly always identify themselves as Romans or Sicilians or Tuscans before Italians. Keep that in mind before making or accepting broad generalizations about the nature of Italians. Well-worn clichés—that people are warmer in the south, more serious in the north, for example—don't always hold up to scrutiny. You'll need to dig deeper to understand the many faces of Italy.

(02) Go (hyper) local.

Italy is no monolith, and neither is its cuisine. In a world of hyper-local food traditions, recipes don't just change from region to region, but from one house to the next. Dialects, customs, spices, pasta shapes—all are subject to dramatic change as you travel across very small distances. Your mission is to immerse yourself in the full panoply of regional cultures, often determined as much by geographical challenges as political realities. Spend time in a coastal town, a mountain village, a far-flung city. Buy local salumi and wine at the markets, order dishes you've never heard of before at the trattoria, and be prepared to trade the comfort of the familiar for the excitement of the unknown.

(03) Surrender yourself.

Italy is not a country that organizes life down to the minute like its Swiss neighbor to the north. Even the best-laid plans can be demolished by train delays (despite what Mussolini said, the trains decidedly do not run on time), unexpected restaurant closings, or any of a dozen unforeseeable factors. Oftentimes, said factor is a proud Italian host wanting you to taste just one more local specialty or inviting you to one last glass of wine. More than seeing monuments and checking off boxes on the tourist trail, this is why you're here. Surrender your meticulously constructed schedule and be ready to improvise and adjust—not just because you will need to but because you'll want to.

(04) Venture into parts unknown.

Italy is the fifth most-visited country in the world, with 53 million foreign tourists making the journey in 2017. But the distribution of tourism skews especially heavily on the star spots: Rome, Tuscany, Venice, Naples. All are lovely places, but in years of travel, I've yet to find a corner of Italy not to love. This book celebrates a few of the paths less traveled—magical places like Sardinia and Puglia—but I could have just as easily dedicated chapters to the enchanting villages of Abruzzo, the surf-and-turf culture of Liguria, the spice and solitude of Calabria. Strike a balance when planning your trip: Spend half the time in the famous places with the selfie-stick legions and the other half making your own discoveries in parts unknown by most visitors.

KNOW BEFORE YOU GO

05 Know the hierarchy.

06 Make friends.

Italian establishments for eating and drinking operate on a clearly delineated hierarchy of price and formality. At the top of the heap is the ristorante, a relatively formal institution with tablecloths, well-dressed servers, and excellent if fussy food. The trattoria is a less-formal, (usually) family-run affair where the food is rustic, local, and seasonal, if not exactly fancy. The osteria was once a place for drinking wine with a bit of food on the side, but these days *osterie* serve full menus of rustic, daily-changing dishes. For more concentrated drinking, slake your thirst at an enoteca, a dedicated wine bar. Those warm visions of long, lazy meals? Most of those take place at the trattoria and osteria, so that's where most of your eating efforts should be focused.

Few people are more open and inviting than the Italians. Much of this stems from pride to share a slice of their world with anyone who shows true interest. Armed with a generous smile and a few words of Italian (preferably about how great X town or region is), you'll make friends everywhere you go, especially as you work your way toward more rural areas of the country. (No joke: I make more friends in a day in an Italian village than I do in a year in Barcelona.) Look alive! It's these moments that really count—to break bread with locals who can clue you in to a given area's DNA, to see a bit of Italy through the eyes of those who live it every day, and maybe, if you're lucky, to score an invite home for dinner.

07 Refine your rhythms.

This is southern Europe, where life moves at a different pace than it does elsewhere on the continent. That means adjusting the rhythms of your day to the Italian clock. Days start early—you'll always find a bar serving *caffé* and *cornetti* before the sun comes up. Italy is magical at this hour, before the big churn begins, so push yourself. As for the rest of the day, think Spain Light: lunch goes down from 1 to 3 p.m. and dinner typically falls between 8 to 10 p.m. Italy's version of a siesta may not be as well known as Spain's, but it still keeps many shops across the country closed for a few hours in the afternoon. Shake off the post–pasta slumber with an *aperitivo*, a late-afternoon drink and a light bite—a cherished bridge between afternoon and evening.

08 Act like an Italian.

You'll never be Italian, but you can do your best to act like one while you're here. Bring the best of your wardrobe: the Italians are among the world's best dressed and will appreciate the extra effort. Learn a few key words in Italian. Offer a spirited *buongiorno* during the daytime when you walk in and out of cafés and restaurants, a robust *buonasera* as evening sets in. When greeting a friend or meeting a friend of a friend, offer *due baci*, two kisses, starting with the right cheek. At the bar and the table, tap into your most extroverted self: solicit opinions from locals, lay down your own beliefs, and defend them with lighthearted vigor. As for eating like an Italian, that takes a special skill set—turn the page to start developing your own.

Life Skills

EAT LIKE AN ITALIAN

Italians eat better than anyone.
Here are eight ways you can share in their brilliance.

 01

MAKE EVERY MEAL COUNT

A meal is not just a chance to fill up, but an opportunity to gather, share, debate, and disconnect from the distractions of the outside world. Make every meal into an event: Pack your tables with people, order with gusto, linger a little longer—lunch or dinner can (and should) last two or three hours in Italy.

 02

BUILD YOUR OWN FEAST

Break free from the restaurant routine and dive deeper into Italy's pantry. Buy 100 grams (*un etto*) of three or four kinds of *salumi* (see page 226), add a wedge of cheese, olives, roasted peppers, artichokes, a hunk of focaccia, and a bottle of wine. Find a piazza or a park and enjoy a picnic par excellence.

START SWEET

Breakfast in Italy looks a lot like dessert in other parts of the world: cream-stuffed pastries, pistachio-crusted cannoli, chocolate-laced croissants. Sicilians are kings of the sweet breakfast: gelato-stuffed brioche is a perfectly acceptable start to the day. Life's short; start with dessert.

GET IN WITH GRANDMA

The *nonna* has long been the progenitor of Italian food culture—the expert on ingredients, the developer of recipes, the protector of food's place at the center of life in Italy. If you're not lucky enough to have (or befriend) an Italian *nonna*, try RentaMamma.com for a chance to spend an evening feasting in a real Italian home.

OWN THE MARKET

More than genius cooks, Italians are genius shoppers driven by a belief that it's their God-given duty to return from the market with the best meat, fish, and produce possible. Whether buying a single tomato or a pound of sardines, be selective, demanding, relentless in your search for perfection.

SHOW SOME RESTRAINT

Restraint is the common bond between all great Italian regional cooking—a culture where Parmesan on many pastas (especially seafood-based pastas) is a sacrilege, and even a wedge of lemon can be seen as an assault on pristine seafood. Savor the simplicity and the chance to be in a world where less is almost always more.

07

MANAGE THE MENU

Five categories dominate the Italian menu: *antipasti* (appetizers), *primi* (pasta, rice, and soup), *secondi* (mains), *contorni* (vegetables), and *dolci* (dessert). At best, you'll have room for three, so choose wisely. My personal strategy rarely wavers: antipasto, pasta, split *dolce*, and a bottle of wine.

08

MANGIA! MANGIA!

The only thing more perilous than a lack of patience in Italy is a lack of appetite. Everywhere you turn, expect to be implored to eat—by new friends, garrulous servers, wild-eyed cooks. Enthusiastic eating is an easy way to both show and gain respect, so loosen your belt and dig deep.

Chapter Two

PUGLIA

—

Vito Dicecca has made mozzarella in thirty-three countries. He made it in Australia, two weeks after arriving, just eighteen years old and looking to devour the world. He took a job in a kebab shop, grew restless with the towers of spinning meat, and instead sought out his people: cheese makers. He found them not far away on a dairy farm making French-style cheeses with goat's and sheep's milk, but he couldn't find anything that looked or tasted like home. So he showed them home: fist-size balls of mozzarella, taut and shiny and fresh as a newborn. He made mozzarella in Thailand, on Ko Pha Ngan island, out in the middle of the Gulf of Thailand. It was the night before the island's infamous Full Moon Party, and with time on his hands, he befriended a local, who introduced him to a buffalo farmer, who provided him with the milk to weave brilliant braids of the cheese of his homeland, and just as the sun set and the full moon rose and boatloads of drug-addled travelers descended on Haad Rin beach for their taste of the apocalypse, Vito and his new friend sat on the sands, enjoying warm slices of Thai buffalo mozzarella with leaves of purple basil. He made mozzarella outside Phnom Penh, Cambodia, with a farmer who had always dreamed of making cheese with the milk of his herd of water buffaloes. Vito traveled to his farm on the back of a motorbike, and the two made mozzarella, burrata, and fresh yogurt. Later they took their creations down to a local children's hospital and gave samples to the young patients, and the kids and the farmer and the cheese maker from Italy shared a taste of authentic Cambodian buffalo mozzarella.

Paolo Dicecca has made mozzarella in twenty-one countries. He first made mozzarella in Phuket, Thailand, where the abundance of island buffaloes provided the milk for a perfectly respectable version of burrata, a combination of shredded mozzarella and fresh cream wrapped in a thin skin of mozzarella, which Paolo sold to the tourist-crushed island's smattering of Italian restaurants. He made mozzarella in Michoacán with a Mexican farmer who had everything he needed to make cheese—expensive machinery, milk—except the knowledge. Today, Michoacán has a source of first-rate Mexican mozzarella. In 2015, Paolo traveled to Ivory Coast to make cheese. He saw an industrial brand of mozzarella on sale in a supermarket for an astronomical price, and he wanted to show the people of Africa that real mozzarella can be made for very little. In a village he found cows with perfectly good milk, and though he had to pasteurize it due to the heat and the hygiene, Paolo made cheese he remembers as being some of his best. Pictures from the trip show the young cheese maker on a dirt road in a village, smiling widely, surrounded by young children all reaching for a taste of Italy.

Angelo Dicecca has made mozzarella in twenty-five countries—from Argentina to the South Pacific to the iron heart of Manhattan. The most improbable mozzarella Angelo ever made didn't happen on a tropical island or in an African village but in Santa Marca, Colombia, at his ex-girlfriend's house at one in the morning. They had been drinking, partying, enjoying the kind of slow-burning night that seems to stretch on for days in South America. She wanted to dance; he wanted to make cheese. "Let's just say that it came out . . ." he trails off, his mind taking little nibbles of that early-morning mozzarella, ". . . artisanal."

—MANTECA— —BURRATA—

CREMA
DI
RICOTTA —TRECCIONE—
GRANNATURE

The Brothers Dicecca:
Angelo, Paolo, and Vito.

Vito, Paolo, Angelo: the brothers Dicecca. They roam the earth like bounty hunters, possessed by one simple idea: where there's milk, there's mozzarella. It has driven them everywhere—from countryside to cityscape, from the far Far East to the tip of South America, more than sixty different countries in total—in an unwitting effort to show the world that good mozzarella is more about craft than country.

But for all their itinerant cheese adventures, Vito, Paolo, and Angelo, along with their sisters, Maristella and Vittoria, make and sell mozzarella primarily in one place: Altamura, Italy, a hilltop town on the western edge of Puglia.

Altamura isn't the most beautiful town in Puglia—that distinction would go to Lecce, home of the famous limestone used to construct an endless labyrinth of piazzas and churches and impossibly perfect wine bars, or Otranto, the same ancient limestone architecture spread out dramatically on a shelf above the crystalline convergence of the Ionian and Adriatic seas. Both bear the mark of Magna Graecia, the

Greek settlement that dominated southern Italy from the time of the Trojan War through the dawn of the Roman Empire and that still echoes throughout Puglia today—in the stone pillars, local dialects, and humble coastal cooking that define the region.

It's not even the most beautiful town in the near vicinity. Matera, twenty-three kilometers west on the edge of Basilicata, is a Roman town with deep scars from bygone eras of poverty and starvation. But now it is best known for its neighborhoods of ancient caves built directly into the side of a ravine, one of the most majestic destinations in this most majestic of countries.

In most regards, Altamura is a perfectly normal midsize town perched on a hill fifty kilometers southwest of Bari, Puglia's capital—safely removed from the brilliant beaches that attract throngs of well-oiled domestic sunhounds to the region every summer. There are a hulking, thirteenth-century cathedral, a clearly demarcated old town and new town, an open-air market for produce and protein, and a thirsty population of young college students who flood the streets on the weekends.

There are two things that almost everyone in Italy knows about Altamura: First and foremost, *il pane di Altamura*, a thick-crusted, swollen-domed semolina loaf, bronzed and built to last, one of the most revered breads in Europe and the first in Italy to be designated with Denominazione di Origine Protetta (DOP) status, one of the highest designations for food products in Europe. At all hours of the day, the town smells of campfires and toasted grain.

The second piece of Altamura lore that made this town a known quantity across Italy is the short, unhappy life of McDonald's. When the Golden Arches arrived here in 2001, it had its detractors, but Altamura largely accepted its presence as the cost of upward mobility in a modernizing world. It opened right on the edge of Altamura's old city, where some locals found jobs and many more found a spot for the occasional hamburger. But as the months wore on, the tide turned against Ronald and his clown posse. Locals began to view the Arches as

an attack on their culture—one defined by time and tradition, not speed and convenience. When the chain erected a giant neon *M* that cast its sinister yellow glow in the shadow of the giant cathedral, the citizens of Altamura mobilized.

They fought back the only way they knew how: with food. Community leaders organized events to highlight local foods—the cured meats, breads, and cheeses of Altamura. Businesses ran counterattacks by offering anti-McDonald's specials on their edible goods. In the most aggressive offensive, Di Gesù, the town's most famous bakery, opened an outpost directly adjacent to McDonald's, serving warm, freshly baked focaccia for less than the plain hamburgers sold next door.

"What took place was a small war between us and McDonald's," Onofrio Pepe, a retired journalist, told the *New York Times* in 2006. "Our bullets were focaccia. And sausage. And bread."

Those weapons, including no small amount of hand-stretched mozzarella, ultimately vanquished the burger-slinging Goliath. Two years after it opened its doors, the fast-food juggernaut quietly packed up its things and got the hell out of town—a victory for the artisans, traditionalists, and serious eaters of Altamura.

But Altamura has something else that no other town in Puglia or the whole of Italy has: *la famiglia* Dicecca. Vito, Paolo, and Angelo, the mozzarella masters, who along with Maristella and Vittoria, run Caseificio Dicecca, one of the greatest cheese shops in a region built on the back of great cheese shops.

The tip of Italy's boot is one sprawling lactic fantasy, a sparsely populated landscape filled with cows and buffaloes, sheep and goats, where the average citizen consumes 23 kilos of cheese a year—more than any other region in Italy. Not just salty, funky pecorinos and firm cow's milk cheeses such as caciocavallo but a different class of cheese entirely: fresh cheese made every morning in any of the 318 *caseifici* (producers and vendors of cheese) that dot this flat coastal landscape—cheese still warm from production, sold from glass dis-

play cases a few paces from where it's made, so fresh and fragile it travels home in the same water it was born in.

Cheese in most parts of the world is either a luxury or an afterthought—an indulgence that we allow ourselves to eat in small portions at specific moments or a condiment added as a postscript to a sandwich, an omelet, a salad. In Puglia, cheese is neither a treat nor a topping; it's a fundamental part of the region's DNA, right down to the double-helix braid of the mozzarella. In fact, they don't even call the types of cheese consumed here cheese—they call them *latticini*, products made with milk and eaten fresh. Some of the fiercest food fights I've seen have been between southern Italians and unsuspecting eaters insisting that mozzarella is *formaggio*.

Whatever you call it, the closest relation to the *latticini* of Puglia is bread, something that you buy daily, that you consume quickly and constantly, that finds its way effortlessly to the table at nearly every meal. Fittingly, the production of the fresh cheeses of Puglia closely mirrors the making of bread—

elemental in its base, endlessly complex in its execution—a culture that employs thousands of people across the region that spend each day making and selling cheese that will be gone by tomorrow.

And like bread, the cheese of Puglia is born before most of the world has begun to stir.

🌿 🐄 🍷

6:05 A.M.
Be there at 6 man. My brother waits for no one.

The text message came in from Vito overnight. But the only person to be found on the streets of Altamura at this hour is an older, heavyset man dressed in a white apron seated on the stone steps beside the cheese shop.

When he sees me coming, he shrugs his shoulders. "I don't know. They should be here. But they're kids, you know?" Then he pauses, looks down at his hands, reconsiders. "They're not that young. I mean, they're adults now. They should be here."

Michele Saliano has been making cheese

in Altamura since 1980. For many years, he had his own shop down the street, but competition in this town is stiff, and making and selling cheese are two different skill sets. Still, years later, Michele can't speak about his failed business without a wistful glaze in his eyes. "It was a beautiful store. All the equipment was new. *Bellissimo.*"

It's 6:15. Still no sign of the *fratelli* Dicecca. Michele and I talk about cheese, the one love I know we share. "It's not easy. You watch people make it, and it might look easy. But it's not." The hardest part? "*Il latte.* Learning to control the milk. In a *caseificio* like this one, a real *caseificio*, the milk is different every day."

A BMW pulls up, and out spill three young men in various states of slumber. They say nothing, walk dead-eyed directly into the bar across the street, and mainline espresso.

Properly caffeinated, Vito, Paolo, and Michele open the work area in the back of the shop and begin to prepare for the day's production. Angelo and I have a different mission: We load into the Dicecca milk

PUGLIA IS THE LAND OF BREAD AND CHEESE, A LANDSCAPE FILLED WITH ROAMING MAMMALS AND GOLDEN HILLS OF GRAIN.

truck—mounted with a long, silver tank with a 1,500-liter capacity—and drive into the countryside. Normally, Salvatore Dicecca—*papà* Dicecca—drives the truck out of Altamura at dawn to collect the milk for the day, but just weeks earlier, he had an accident on the job and he's been sidelined—temporarily or permanently, no one can say.

Angelo is filling in as milkman today. By the time the spires of the cathedral of Altamura vanish, the caffeine puts an end to Angelo's prolonged silence. "Everything starts with the milk. I've been working with milk since I was ten years old. It takes a lot of passion and a lot of patience to build your life around milk."

Angelo, thirty-seven, is the oldest of the five siblings, and the first to venture beyond Altamura. With his thick, shoulder-length locks, wraparound sunglasses, and white Dicecca polo with the constantly popped collar, he looks like a yacht deckhand who may or may not be sleeping with the owner's trophy wife. He takes selfies constantly, even while driving, especially with a reporter and his notebook riding

shotgun. I smile nervously, eyeing the trees and gullies flashing by inches from the window.

"I left home when I was twenty. Went straight to Phuket. My parents thought I'd be scared and lonely and that I'd be back in four days. But I kept traveling." Nearly two decades later, and he's helped establish a global network of cheeseheads, some of whom he revisits, all of whom he keeps up with through social media while planted back in Puglia. "The point isn't just about cheese; it's about exporting our culture."

I tell Angelo that I have three older brothers and that despite my fondness for them I can't imagine spending twelve hours a day together in confined spaces. He shrugs his shoulders. "It's what we do. It's what we've always done—work as a team. As the oldest, I try to set a good example, but there's no boss. We're all equal partners in this business."

Thirty minutes outside Altamura, in the heart of the Alta Murgia National Park, down a long tree-lined dirt road, we come upon the Didonato Farm, ground zero of Dicecca cheese. The Diceccas have been buying milk from the Didonato family for more than sixty years. Vito Didonato, the newest in the line of family dairy farmers, keeps a small herd that feeds off the dense flora surrounding the farm. "That's the difference between our milk and everyone else's."

The tank half filled, we climb back into the truck and head to a second farm—smaller, tucked right into the edge of a small village—for a top-off. "These are the two best farms in the region. We go to both because we want the right balance of fat and acidity in the milk. In the end, it gives us a more interesting product."

Latticini like those produced by the Diceccas aren't static creations; they are expressions of the Pugliese *terreno* from one day to the next. In the late spring, when the fields grow thick with flowers and herbs, the milk takes on hints of thyme and wild oregano. Come winter, when the rains soak the surrounding area and the herd feeds off a blend of dried cereals, the milk is fattier, less aromatic. It's those subtleties Angelo

or his dad or whoever else gets behind the wheel of the Dicecca milk truck chases each morning.

"Most cheese makers in Italy don't have their own trucks. They make a phone call, and the milk suddenly appears. But I'm not in the office, making calls from a desk, relaxed. I'm up early in the truck, taking risks."

One could argue that in a modernized food system, the milk wrangling is superfluous—that the cheese will still be the cheese regardless of how the milk travels, that the customers don't care if the *latte* came from a massive truck making the daily rounds or a family-owned vehicle driven by Angelo just as the first espresso is setting in.

As we ride from one distant farm to the next, I crunch the numbers. It starts innocently enough—the corner cutting. Too expensive and time-consuming to fetch the milk yourself? Pay the farm to deliver it, and if the one that grows its own grass and herbs can't do it, find one that will. Margins on that local sheep's-milk specialty too thin to justify? Strike it from the board, along with that aged goat cheese that takes too much time and space to make. Suddenly, who needs the hands of a human to shape mozzarella when a machine can do it twice as fast at half the cost? In the world of craftsmanship, compromise is always a slippery slope.

"I love it, but it's hard work," says Angelo. "I'm tired. We're all tired. My fantasy is that one day a Chinese businessman will make his way to Altamura and offer us ten million euros for the *caseificio*. It needs to be ten because there are five of us and we each need two million to survive." He grows quiet afterward, eyes fixed on the road, as if he's spending all that cash already. "With two million, I'd buy a farm outside Belo Horizonte in Brazil. Two cows, two goats. I'd make cheese two or three times a week—never to sell, just for me and my friends."

7:36 A.M.

By the time we pull the truck up to the side door of Caseificio Dicecca and run a hose from the gleaming milk tank to the massive stainless steel vat inside, Vito, Paolo, and Michele, the old cheese maker I met on the steps this morning, are deep into the day's production.

Across the five-hundred-square foot working space, in industrial mixers and plastic tubs, in shiny steel baths and hard-plastic buckets, the journey from liquid to solid is well under way. Milk is manipulated into every possible texture and temperature: salted and scalding hot, cool and au naturel; thin and transparent, partially coagulated, in mountains of dense and crumbly curds, in thick ivory ropes ready to be stretched and shaped. To the outside observer, it's almost impossible to follow the various permutations of protein and fat, curds and coagulants, liquids and solids and squishy, weepy in-betweens.

Milk is a miracle. By its very nature, it's a complete nutritional package, a ready-built diet with a pitch-perfect balance of fat, protein, and carbohydrates that can sustain mammalian life indefinitely. This same package of macronutrients makes it ripe for manipulating—butter, yogurt, cream. And, of course, milk's most magnificent expression: cheese.

Cheese making is one of human's earliest acts of culinary manipulation, stretching back some four millennia to the times of Chinese warlords and Egyptian pharaohs. It started as a rudimentary product, more an accident than a conscious creation. Civilizations as diverse as the Sumerians and the ancient Chinese used animal stomachs to transport food, including milk, only to discover that the rennet in the stomachs acted as a natural coagulant—spontaneously creating something close to cottage cheese. The ancient Romans were the ones to elevate cheese making to a fine art. Pliny the Elder, one of history's most voracious and astute gourmands, chronicled the variety of cheeses produced across the expanse of the empire—from the cow's-milk cheeses of the Alps to the sheep cheeses of Liguria. (By Pliny's estimation, a smoked goat cheese made in Rome itself was the finest cheese of its day.)

The great cheeses of Europe were born during the Middle Ages—Cheddar in southern England in the twelfth century, Gouda in the Netherlands not long after; Parmigiano-Reggiano, the king of Italian cheeses, emerged as a staple of the cuisine of Emilia in the thirteenth and fourteenth centuries. From there, cheese began its inexorable march toward diversification, from sharp, funky blue cheeses aged in caves to unpasteurized triple creams to tangy pucks of goat cheese rolled in lavender and fennel pollen. By some estimates, more than four thousand varieties of cheeses are produced today—a thousand in France alone—made from a dozen different kinds of milk: cow, sheep, yak, reindeer, even human.

Italy's cheese culture is as diverse and hyperregionalized as the rest of its food culture. In the far north, in Val d'Aosta, cheeses such as fontina and toma more closely mirror the high-mountain cheeses of Switzerland and France. In Sardinia, where sheep outnumber humans, pecorino predominates—found in dozens of expressions, including the infamous *casu marzu*, the maggot-covered sheep's-milk cheese still considered a delicacy in certain parts of the island. But these are very different cheeses from the ones that dominate the *caseifici* of southern Italy. The Diceccas work in the cheese family known as *pasta filata*—stretched or pulled cheeses, a reference to the technique used to form this class of soft, fresh cheeses. *Pasta filata* is the dominant form of cheese making across Puglia, where before refrigeration the warmer climate reduced cheese's shelf life from months to a matter of days.

Behind the daily transformation of milk into cheese is a science that could fill a grad school syllabus. For the sake of sanity, yours and mine, I'll give you the short, simplified version: Milk becomes cheese through a process of coagulation, splitting milk into two core ingredients: liquid whey and solid curd. To coagulate milk, producers add a souring agent (mostly yeast, but sometimes vinegar or even other cheese) and rennet, an enzyme that helps form stronger curds. The curd is the base of which all cheese is formed: you can serve it straightaway

as fresh, light cheeses such as ricotta and *formaggio fresco* or extract more liquid and compress the curds to make harder, more assertive cheeses that can stand up to aging.

To make stretched cheeses such as mozzarella, cheese makers submerge the curds in near-boiling water, then use large wooden paddles to stir, mix, and eventually stretch the amorphous mass, working the long protein strands the same way a baker does when she kneads a ball of dough. This action gives mozzarella both its elastic texture and its exceptional meltability.

No matter how big or small the cheese operation, production begins with the curd (called *cagliata* in Italian), the only difference being the quality of the curd. The brothers use a fresh *cagliata*, made with the day's milk delivery activated with natural yeast and rennet. It sits in the center of the room, piled high on a stainless-steel table, a living, breathing bridge between raw ingredients and an artisanal product. The brothers hack away at the mountain throughout the morning, cutting custardy slabs off to initiate each new batch of cheese. But these days handmade *cagliata* is becoming more and more scarce in cheese making. "It's too easy to buy a German curd that they'll deliver to your doorstep for pennies," says Angelo. "But you can taste the difference immediately."

The Diceccas typically start each day with around 1,500 liters of cow's milk, which will be transformed into mozzarella in at least five different shapes and sizes, from *nodini*, small one-bite knots, to *treccine* and *nodi d'amore*, bulky braids of mozzarella weighing up to a kilo. Beyond that, they'll make burrata, ricotta, and straciatella. A separate supply of goat's milk and sheep's milk is used on odd days to create a handful of the Diceccas' specialty products—including Don Vito, a pecorino modeled after the recipe first developed by the boys' grandfather, plus a few of the cheeses that set them apart from other regional *caseifici*.

Today is Tuesday, which means they make pecorino from 800 liters of sheep's milk on top of the normal production schedule. By the end of the morning, the three brothers plus Michele will have made

ten different types of cheese—more than 200 kilograms, the majority of which will sell before the sun sets tonight.

8:05 A.M.
The day's first customer waddles through the front door, an older woman with a small cart ready to be filled with the morning's grocery haul. From now until 8:30 P.M., minus an extended break in the middle of the day, as in any upstanding Italian business, not a minute will pass without the arrival of a new customer. In the back, the four cheese makers continue their delicate dance of scalding and stretching while the sisters attend to the steady drip of locals.

The Caseificio Dicecca is a fourth-generation operation, started by the brothers' great-great-grandfather in 1908. In 1930, the shop opened in its current location, a small storefront on Via Bari, a few blocks from the stone archway that leads into Altamura's historic center. For most of the life of the *caseificio*, the Dicecca family has lived in the apartment above the shop.

At first glance, the main display case at

THE DELICATE DANCE OF SCALDING AND STRETCHING.

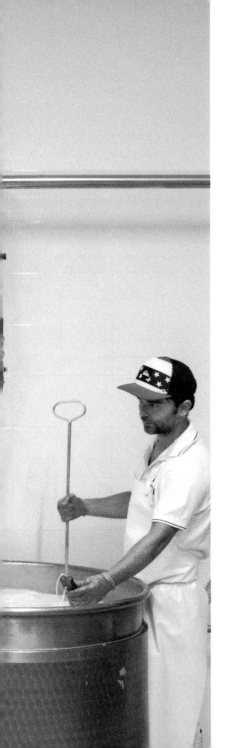

Dicecca today looks like a selection you'll find in any cheese shop in Puglia: tubs of milky water covering hunks of mozzarella in its many guises; strings of swollen *scamorze* dangling from the ceiling, bronzed by their stopover in the cold smoker; small plastic containers of creamy ricotta ready to be stuffed or spread or eaten straight with a spoon. But look closer and you'll see some unfamiliar faces staring back at you through the glass: a large bucket brimming with ricotta spiked with ribbons of blue cheese and toasted almonds, served by the scoop; a wooden serving board paved with melting slabs of goat cheese weaponized with a cloak of bright red chili flakes; a hulking wheel of pecorino, stained shamrock green by a puree of basil and spinach. These are the signs of a *caseificio* in the grips of an evolution, one that started more than a decade ago as the brothers took the reins from their parents and began to expand the definition of a small, family-run cheese shop.

For three generations, that family-run shop produced the same selection of cheeses you find in shops across Puglia:

mozzarella in various shapes and sizes, burrata, ricotta, pecorino, caciocavallo. Today, Caseificio Dicecca is home to dozens of ingredients that previous generations of Diceccas wouldn't have recognized: chocolate from Venezuela, whiskey from Japan, smoked paprika from Spain. But the cheeses that Vito, Paolo, and Angelo create aren't errant experiments by a pack of wild-eyed youths; they are edible tales from their travels, of the people they met and the tastes they discovered along the way. This is the other side of the Dicecca brothers' vision: to bring mozzarella to the world and bring the world to mozzarella.

Vito emerges from the back with a new stack of cheeses that he arranges in the case like a kid setting up for a science fair. Bushy beard, backward hat covering an aggressive shock of strawberry blond hair, arms wallpapered in tattoos documenting his travels, Vito could double as a roadie for Metallica. He first started making cheese when he was six years old, when he would wander down from the family's apartment to help his grandfather shred the cheese to make strac-

ciatella. "It's like a language or any other skill—it's best to learn to make cheese when you're young." None of the Dicecca boys took to the classroom—Vito least of all. He dropped out at twelve years of age, told his parents he was done with formal education, spent his teenage years making mozzarella and mistakes in equal measure, and at eighteen left Altamura with nothing but a backpack and a one-way ticket to Australia.

As the ancient adage goes: If you know how to tend bar, cut hair, or make cheese, you can find work anywhere. Vito spent the next five years wandering the world, from the sparkling beaches of the Gold Coast to the mountains of New Zealand and up through Asia, to the islands of Thailand and the pulsing urban centers of Japan. The cheese and the travels worked in tandem, one informing the other—he wanted to see more of the world, and mozzarella became the vessel through which he experienced it. Eventually he turned west, trekking through California before crossing the border into Mexico. He made mozzarella in southern Mexico, on the Yucatán

Peninsula, on the gringo-packed shores of Playa del Carmen, where he grew tired of lying on the sand and soaking up the scenery and decided, as he always did, to find a way to make mozzarella. It was there, somewhere between the lapping waves of the Gulf of Mexico and the mozzarella-devouring guests at the hotel he worked at, that Vito had a revelation: "I saw that teaching people to make mozzarella meant I was doing something good for the world. But I wanted to do something good for my family and for me." It was time to go home.

He wasn't going back alone, though. He had in his head a scrapbook of the tastes that had impacted him the most during his travels: goat cheese and olive oil in California, the tropical fruits and chilies of South America, everything that had touched his lips in Japan. When Angelo and Paolo talk about their travels, they turn to the memories—the parties, the people, the crazy times had, always with the metronome of mozzarella beating in the background. But what followed Vito were the flavors—the

dishes, ingredients, and techniques unknown to most of Italy.

"When I came back from Japan, there were six kilos of matcha, two kilos of coconut powder, and twelve bottles of Nikka whiskey in my bag. In Rome they stopped me and they opened the bag. They thought they had caught me with cocaine. I told the guy to open up the bag and taste."

Vito didn't drink that Nikka (he and his brothers rarely drink alcohol); instead, he emptied all twelve bottles into a wooden bucket, where he now soaks blue cheese made from sheep's milk to make what he calls *formaggio clandestino*. He stirs a spoon of high-grade matcha powder into Dicecca's fresh goat yogurt and sells it in clear plastic tubs, anxious for anyone—a loyal client, a stranger, a disheveled writer—to taste something new.

Vito uses these flavors as a way to both hold on to the past and share it with others. When he proposed to his girlfriend, a German woman he met through the travel service Couchsurfing (he's the chief host in Altamura), he didn't do it with champagne and strawberries; instead, he soaked a heart-shaped blue cheese in red wine, covered it in cranberries, and paid a server to deliver it to his dinner table.

In the side refrigerators, where Vito so carefully arranges the morning's new attractions, you'll find even more examples of a traditional *caseificio* gone rogue: a wheel of aged goat cheese coated in a rough armor of wild herbs; a thick, blue-veined goat cheese soaked red with purple with Primitivo wine; goat yogurt in half a dozen international flavors.

You won't be surprised to find that the early efforts of the Dicecca boys were met with opposition—both from the family and the regular clientele. Each brother has a story about the resistance he has encountered along the way—the parental eye rolling at the cacao-coated goat cheese, the sisterly skepticism about mango-stuffed burrata, the customers' confusion at the latest experiment to emerge from the lactic laboratory in back. Every story ends the same way: with one or all of the family members doubting the viability of another

esoteric cheese, followed by the long, slow acceptance by enough customers to justify its real estate space in the display case.

"When I started making cheese with the Nikka barrel, they made fun of me, said I was destroying the taste of the cheese. Now they're copying me. That's the pattern we always see: at first they make fun, then they start to copy."

If the making of the cheese is handled by the Dicecca brothers, the selling is captained almost exclusively by Maristella and Vittoria, the Dicecca sisters. They know nearly every customer by name, have their orders committed to memory, so that the conversations they have during this brief little window of the day are more personal than transactional. *You seen Leo's new car? Madonna! How's your brother recovering from his hip surgery? When are you going to invite us over for dinner?*

Vittoria cuts a strong presence behind the counter, both sweet and accommodating but unwilling to take bullshit from anyone, especially her brothers. As the face of the business, the sisters walk a careful balance between supplying their loyal clientele with the cheese they know and love and finding the moments to push their siblings' more far-flung lactic adventures. If a client takes a small step toward the unconventional—say, the chili-spiked goat cheese—Maristella might offer a taste of the wild side, say a spoon of whiskey-soaked blue cheese.

Their own stance on the extreme cheeses is something closer to tolerance than encouragement, but even that has its limits. "Vito, stop playing with the cheese! Get back there and make ricotta!" Vito, now taking photos of the creations on his phone, appears unmoved by the protestations. It's hard to tell how much of the back-and-forth represents true tension or is just playful ribbing—the *pugliesi*, like the *napoletani*, are masters at straddling the line between genuine consternation and playful provocation. Unthinkable in Milan or Bologna, where appearances are maintained and decorum endures, most of this takes place in plain view of the gathered clientele, who not only are unfazed but from time to time participate in the back-and-forth. This, after all, is southern Italy, where lives are led publicly, where a ball of burrata can be a window into someone's world.

When sales slow, Maristella makes a run at her hourly whip cracking on the brothers. When she makes it back, I squeeze in a question before the next customer—if all this sibling exposure wears on her. "Yes, my brothers can be a pain in the ass," she says, turning to a customer. "But I love this job. What else could I ask for?"'

9:04 A.M.

When everything is firing, when the milk becomes curd and the team hits a groove and the morning melts away, the rhythm of mozzarella making takes on a musical quality: the light splash of hands breaching the hot water, the muted thump of wooden paddle against stretched curd, the baritone kerplunk of knots and braids of flying mozzarella landing in a salt bath across the room. The hiss of hot water rushing out of the hose. Close your eyes, and you can imagine the long, methodical buildup of an experimental jazz joint that never takes full form.

The men work in silence, save for when one of the brothers calls me over to show me something: the twist of the wrist needed to make perfect one-bite *nodini*; a piece of mozzarella fashioned into an elephant. Paolo is especially proud of his lactic sculptures, and he wants to make sure I'm capturing every inch of his oeuvre with both camera and pen. "Matteo! Come over here! You see this!" He poses with dairy braids and mozzarella animals, turning toward the street until both he and the cheese sparkle in the morning light pouring through the open door.

Paolo, the middle brother, used to spend the summers as a kid in the back of the shop with his father and grandfather stretching cheese. "They had me doing *nodini*—my little hands were perfect for tying the small knots." He dropped out of school at thirteen and went to work at the *caseificio*—the first of the siblings to officially take up cheese making in a formal capacity. "There were a lot of different cheese makers who passed through the shop, and I learned something new from all of them."

But a cheese shop in Altamura can start to look tiny to a twenty-year-old with a curious mind, so Paolo stuffed all the lessons he'd learned into the bottom of a backpack and hit the road. He spent a lot of time in South America and found himself falling for a bit of everything: Colombian chocolate, Brazilian beaches, Venezuelan women. If he came to a town or a city with a reliable source of milk and a decent Italian restaurant, he had all the ingredients for a pop-up mozzarella business. "It's a lie when people tell you you can only find good mozzarella in Italy. Bullshit. If you find good milk—with good fat and good acidity—and you work it well by hand, it can be every bit as good anywhere in the world."

Paolo loved the adventures as much as his brothers did, but he was anxious to get his hands back into the scalding waters of the *caseificio*. He views his role at the *caseificio* as an unspoken contract, a promise to repay the lessons taught by his father and grandfather by writing the next chapter of the Dicecca cheese story. "My parents are exhausted. They made a lot of sacrifices to make this shop work. We do well now, but it wasn't always like that. My father used to ride his bike to get the milk, a ten-year-old with two containers of milk. Now what does a ten-year-old do? Not a damn thing."

While his brothers handle ricotta, caciocavallo, pecorino, and the bulk of the cheese experiments, Paolo works almost exclusively on mozzarella, which makes up the lion's share of production at Dicecca. The large spheres we're used to seeing are only one expression of mozzarella—you'll find at least six others at Dicecca, all made from the same base, all slightly different in size and shape and therefore use in the everyday lives of the *pugliesi*. *Bocconcini* might find their way into a salad, *nodini* be plucked straight from the fridge for a midafternoon refuel, and the more dramatic and substantial braids be saved for

SO FRESH IT TRAVELS HOME IN THE SAME WATER IT WAS BORN IN.

platters put out when guests arrive.

Those summers tying mozzarella knots as a boy paid off for Paolo; his shaping skills are unrivaled in the family. His braids are tighter, his spheres both plumper and lighter. Whereas Angelo and Vito can look lost in a daydream at certain points during the morning's production, Paolo's attention never turns from the hot water and *cagliata* before him. On the Dicecca's Facebook page, you'll find videos of Paolo turning long ivory ropes of stretched curd into massive meters-long braids. "Every maker leaves his mark," he says, running his finger across the cheese's seam. "Look at the difference between Michele's and mine. When you buy mozzarella, you want to see the mark of human hands on the cheese.

"You need to treat mozzarella like a girlfriend—gently, but with confidence. See this," he says, motioning to a dozen little white spheres bobbing in the water, "see how light and delicate it is? It doesn't sink in the water, it floats on the surface." When Paolo talks about the importance of working water into the cheese, it's because

he's not after a dense, fatty mozzarella; he wants a light product, easy to eat and easy to digest—not an occasional indulgence but an integral part of the daily diet.

The most vaunted mozzarella in Italy is Mozzarella di Bufala Campana—mozzarella made from the water buffaloes that roam the countryside outside Naples, a cheese with DOP status and international fame. It closely mirrors the earliest iterations of mozzarella, the ones that first surfaced nearly a thousand years ago in the hills of Basilicata and central Campania. Water buffaloes produce milk high in fat, and for many, the cheese made from their milk is the highest expression of the *pasta filata* discipline—with a concentrated creaminess and a lactic tang that teases your taste receptors and propels you to eat more.

Not all mozzarella can be so brilliant. With the ascendance of pizza into a global icon in the second half of the twentieth century, mozzarella transformed from a regional staple into one of the most consumed cheeses on the planet. Pizza made mozzarella popular, but it also made it mediocre. Somewhere along the way, to keep up with the growing appetite for pizza and the making of pizza in places farther and farther from its birthplace, mozzarella was murdered and reincarnated as an entirely different product—an industrialized cheese meant to travel and built to last. Durable, semiversatile, inoffensive—the Hugh Grant of cheeses. A massive industry has developed, complete with food scientists, marketing execs, and assembly lines, to turn mozzarella into the most amorphous and unobjectionable cheese possible. That product, the one that melts like a dream but tastes like a missed opportunity, has more in common with Velveeta than it does with the mozzarella being made before me.

Forget about the stuff you buy in your supermarket—the cheeselike substance that comes in a single solid block that lasts for months or preshredded in a resealable plastic bag that lives on ominously and indefinitely in the belly of your refrigerator. The Dicecca brothers take personal offense at the existence of such cheeselike substances and the fact that they share the

same name as the product they stretch and shape every morning. They might taste good, because even bad cheese tastes good, but it doesn't taste like this: delicate but robust, intense but ethereal, with a whisper—grass? herbs? pixie dust?—that fades just before you can hear it.

So why such a yawning gap between the mozzarella of southern Italy and that of the rest of the world? If the boys can show up in an African village or on a Kiwi farm and make cheese of remarkable quality, if they can turn pebbly curds into long ivory ropes of mozzarella in the drug-addled din of a Full Moon Party on an island in Thailand, then why is it so damn hard to find great mozzarella outside Italy?

To start with, it's a physical and technical challenge few can pull off on a daily basis. Periodically during my time in Altamura, I try my hand at mozzarella. Everything that can go wrong does: I fumble the curds, I tear holes through those gorgeous sheets of suspended dairy, I find it's impossible to duplicate the precise knots that the Dicecca team make so effortlessly. Above all, I scald my hands in the near-boiling water holding the *cagliata*, even with gloves on. After I let the burns retreat and the confidence return, I try again and again, only to have the cheese remind me just how little I know.

Technical challenges can be overcome with books and YouTube tutorials and apprenticeships, and any argument about the quality of the milk outside Italy the brothers rebuke every time they pack their bags. There's also a sort of cultural inertia at play here, one wherein the rest of the world, despite the ravenous rate with which it consumes mediocre mozzarella, doesn't have the motivation and the wherewithal to pull off the good stuff. Sure, you'll find pockets of excellence here and there, but almost always it's an Italian, a southern Italian to be pre-

THEY CONTINUE THEIR RELENTLESS QUEST FOR NEW FLAVORS.

cise, making the effort to do it right. In some cases, those little lighthouses of quality were lit by the Dicecca brothers themselves.

10:14 A.M.
One of the last cheeses of the morning production is the one that originally brought me to Puglia: burrata.

More than mozzarella, which is largely associated with Campania, where the bulk of Italy's mozzarella production takes place, burrata is Puglia's most renowned creation. Like everything else worth eating in Italy, burrata comes from humble origins. A farming family in Andria, now the burrata capital of Puglia, first started making the cheese in the 1920s as a way to use up yesterday's mozzarella. It migrated slowly, gaining popularity in the north of Italy only in the 1960s and '70s. It first started showing up beyond Italy sometime at the dawn of the twenty-first century, when a few enterprising Italian distributors in places such as New York and London established a direct pipeline to Puglia's cheese world.

For many years, burrata remained elusive, a cheese so rare and fragile that chefs planned their weeks around its arrival. Demand surged as savvy cooks and smart restaurateurs realized that all they had to do was drop a weeping ball of burrata on a plate, dressed with a few tomatoes and a thatch of greenery, and they could charge $20 and still look like geniuses. These days, you can't drop a fork in a pizzeria in Osaka, a café in Vancouver, or a trattoria in Hanoi without it landing on a mass of burrata.

Throughout the morning, Paolo and Vito take turns doing the job their father first taught them back when they were barely tall enough to reach the cheese: shredding yesterday's unsold mozzarella by hand to make stracciatella—"little rags." Mixed with a healthy measure of fresh cream, this forms *il cuore*, the heart, of burrata, to be deposited directly into a thin outer skin of mozzarella. The entire package is a little miracle, but it's the oozing, addictive filling that drives the world's serious eaters so fucking crazy.

Michele grabs a golf ball chunk of curd from the warm bath and uses his palm to work it flat, like a *pizzaiolo* shaping dough. When the cheese is thin and round, he holds it up by the edges as Paolo deposits a ladle's worth of the cream-soaked stracciatella directly into the shell, like an edible knapsack. Michele squeezes the edges closed, works it around in his palm, then rips off the excess cheese and seals the package with a pinch and a twist.

Real burrata is a creation of arresting beauty—white and unblemished on the surface, with a swollen belly and a pleated top. The outer skin should be taut and resistant, while the center should give ever so slightly with gentle prodding. Look at the seam on top: As with mozzarella, it should be rough, imperfect, the sign of human hands at work. Cut into the bulge, and the deposit of fresh cream and mozzarella morsels seems to exhale across the plate. The richness of the cream—*burrata* comes from *burro*, the Italian word for "butter"—coats the mouth, the morsels of mozzarella detonate one by one like little depth charges, and the entire package pulses with a gentle current of acidity.

The brothers, of course, like to put their own spin on burrata. Sometimes that means mixing cubes of fresh mango into its heart. Or Spanish anchovies. Even caviar. Today, Paolo sends me next door to a vegetable stand to buy wild arugula, which he chops and combines with olives and chunks of tuna and stirs into the liquid heart of the burrata, so that each bite registers in waves: sharp, salty, fishy, creamy. It doesn't move me the same way the pure stuff does, but if I lived on a daily diet of burrata, as so many Dicecca customers do, I'd probably welcome a little surprise in the package from time to time.

While the Diceccas experiment with what they can put *into* burrata, the rest of the world rushes to find the next food to put it *onto*. Don't believe me? According to Yelp, 1,800 restaurants in New York currently serve burrata. In Barcelona, more than 500 businesses have added it to the menu. Burrata burgers, burrata pizza, burrata mac and cheese. Burrata avocado toasts. Burrata kale salads. It's the perfect food for the globalized palate: neutral enough to fit into anything, delicious enough to improve everything.

In burrata's rocket-ship rise to stardom you can trace the anatomy of a global food craze: Find an ingredient either unknown or overlooked by the rest of the world. Build a signature dish around the ingredient that filters well on Instagram. Strip it of all culinary context until it fits comfortably into a million different manifestations. Wait for people to tire of it. Move on to the Next Big Food.

Only the last step remains for burrata. Who knows, maybe the world's appetite for Puglia's humble invention will never wane. In the meantime, the big question is: Where the hell is all this cheese coming from? Sure, a handful of larger, ambitious producers in Puglia export burrata (pro tip: most goes out on Monday, so get yours at the top of the week), but demand outstripped supply long ago. Chances are, if you're slicing into a ball of creamy cheese in a posh café in Mexico City or an Italian restaurant in Copenhagen, it may be perfectly delicious, but it ain't burrata from Puglia.

No country in the world faces more threat of counterfeit food than Italy. The value of Brand Italy, and the country's cornucopia of world-class artisanal products, makes it vulnerable to imitators both inside the country and out. Years ago, the 'Ndrangheta, the Calabrian mafia, infiltrated the world of high-end olive oil and has been selling tens of millions of dollars' worth of fraudulent bottles to global buyers (mostly Americans) ever since. In Emilia-Romagna, home to some of Italy's most famous ingredients, task forces have been established to root out counterfeit Parmesan, prosciutto, and balsamic vinegar. So widespread is the epidemic that a new class of food detectives, trained to identify fakes, has emerged over the past decade.

In the face of global demand, the cheese makers of Andria have taken a cue from their counterparts in the north and formed a coalition aimed to protect their coveted creation. Along with help from the Puglian government, they have codified everything from working conditions to chemical makeup to the proper shape and size of true burrata. They also secured the coveted Indicazione Geografica Protetta (IGP) status for the cheese, which means that complying producers can add a special label to their cheese. But no rules or regulations can compete with the ferocious appetite of a fickle food world and the forces ready to capitalize on Brand Italy. If someone, whether a hardened criminal or just a savvy marketer, wants to take advantage of burrata's good name, he'll find a way.

Up until this point, I had been dreaming of returning to Barcelona with a suitcase swollen with burrata, but Vito looks reticent. Rarely does Dicecca burrata travel outside Altamura, let alone the Italian peninsula. "Real burrata needs to be eaten the same day, two days at the most. It begins to die slowly the second after it's made."

10:47 A.M.

The front of the shop has its first line of the day as the streets of Altamura buzz with midmorning traffic. Vittoria and Maristella deftly handle the waves of customers, doling out hunks of *scamorza*, pack-ages of burrata, the occasional wedge of blue or round of goat cheese.

"Angelo! Caciocavallo! We need it now!"

In the back, the brothers make the last push of the morning. Michele and Paolo initiate the daily deep clean—hot water coursing through the battery of stainless steel—while Angelo ferries cheese to the front of the store. Vito works the last vat of milk while thumbing through his Facebook feed. Ricotta, literally "recooked" in Italian, is always the last fresh cheese produced, a final surge of heat used to get just a little bit more out of the day's milk supply. He uses a six-foot metal whisk to stir and cut through the hot mixture, separating the liquid from the curds that settle below the surface. Later, he works through a stack of plastic baskets, filling each with a generous deposit of the soft curds that he fishes out of the murky depths with a giant slotted ladle.

Experiments are generally left toward the end of the morning, when the rest of production is winding down. With the ricotta lined up in baskets on the countertop, the last of the watery whey draining through holes of the basket containers, Vito goes through the cheese lockers tucked in the corner and begins to pull out and test a few of his ongoing projects.

In between his trips up front, Angelo rolls wheels of fresh goat cheese in a bed of dried herbs—*centodieci erbe*, 110 herbs. "I was on my mountain bike riding through the natural park, smelling the wild arugula, the herbs. I said, 'Fuck, why don't I do a cheese with the herbs?'" If herb-crusted goat cheese doesn't sound radical to you, keep in mind this is Italy, where neither fresh goat cheese nor adding 110 herbs to simple fare is standard practice. "Everyone at first was like 'Why would you ruin the cheese with herbs?'" An eighty-year-old man, a friend of Angelo's who lives in the park, collects herbs for him in exchange for free cheese.

The modern food world is flush with technical and cross-cultural experimentation. Usually it comes from the younger generations, who want to unleash the soaring guitar solos without first learning the chords. All over the world, you'll meet chefs who can turn hazelnut oil into tiny, edible spheres and parsley stems into bubbling, ethereal foams but can't cook a steak or scramble an egg.

By those measures, the boundary pushing pursued by the Diceccas is relatively tame. More important, it comes after fifteen years of learning and refining the core techniques of *pasta-filata*. There's a reason why every day starts with the fundamentals: a battery of cheeses made with nothing more than milk, water, and four generations of repetition. Simple, unadulterated mozzarella and burrata will always be the engine that drives Puglia's cheese culture, and the Diceccas will never abandon tradition. But that doesn't mean there isn't time and space to innovate.

"Our dad thought we were crazy, and continued to think that until the cheese sold," says Angelo. "In the last ten years, I've sacrificed ten kilos of cheese a day giving out samples, educating our customers. These aren't cheeses they've seen before."

Remember: This is the town that beat

McDonald's, that chose ciabatta over cheeseburgers, focaccia over French fries. Matters of the stomach are not taken lightly here. Food isn't calories; it's history, heritage, life. To budge an inch means to give up a foot. To make a compromise is to stop believing. Most of the world doesn't have this ethos simmering beneath the surface, ready to boil over whenever threatened, which may hinder advancement but keeps the bread and the cheese tasting as they always have.

But it also means that the Diceccas' innovations in the *caseificio* are up against a tough audience—one that doesn't take well to mango in the burrata and cranberries on the blue cheese. Yet they continue to push forward in the quest for new flavors. Maybe it's the outsiders buying up their funky cheeses? you ask. There are no outsiders— the cheese doesn't travel well, nor do they want it to travel when it doesn't need to. Ninety-five percent of the Diceccas' sales come directly from the storefront.

Vito brings an armful up to the front, where the scene teeters on the edge of chaos. Angelo cuts a caciocavallo the size of a watermelon with a long cheese knife while Maristella yells at him from the other side of the counter. "That's not how you cut caciocavallo!"

A man rolls by in a BMW and honks his horn from the street corner. Angelo grabs a plate of cheese scraps and offers him a taste through the window. "He'll be back to buy more later," he says with a satisfied smile.

An older woman steps up to the counter and Vittoria passes a small bag over without more than a "Ciao" exchanged between the two of them. "*A domani!*" she says before shuffling out. *See you tomorrow.*

Vittoria fills a portable cooler with a full selection of Dicecca *formaggio*: a few balls of burrata, a massive braid of mozzarella, a round of chili-covered goat cheese. A businessman from Altamura, now living in Poland, oversees the construction of the care package, his face jostling between grin and grimace. "It's been hard to adjust to eating outside of Altamura," he says. "I miss it all, especially the cheese. This is always my last stop on the way to the airport."

A *nonna* in a black dress and shawl is staring at the cheeses in the side cooler, home to the Diceccas' most aggressive experiments. She looks perplexed. Vito spots her and comes from behind the counter to assist.

"*Buongiorno, Anna! Come stai?*"

"*Bene, bene.*"

"Would you like to try something today?"

"Why not? What is this, pistachio?"

"No. That's matcha."

"What's matcha?"

She takes a taste of the tea-spiked goat yogurt; her eyes open wide at first, then drift to the corner of the room, avoiding direct contact with any of us looking on. "Very interesting."

In the end, she buys two balls of burrata and a scoop of *nodini* and moves on.

9:47 P.M.

"*Vaffanculo! Che cazzo! Pezzo de merda!*"

The five Dicecca siblings are gathered around the television at their parents' house, watching the European Cup quarterfinal between Italy and Germany. After two scoreless extra periods, the game comes

down to a final shoot-out, and nobody is happy with the way things are going. When Darmian misses the second penalty kick in a row for Italy, a chorus of curse words rains down on the television screen.

On the table are the fruits of the *caseificio* cornucopia: balls of mozzarella, one-bite *nodini*, wedges of *scamorza*, and a single swollen sphere of burrata, waiting to be breached. Plus *pane di Altamura*. That's it: bread and cheese. What we ate for breakfast and for lunch. If you think working in a *caseificio* all day, every day, might curb your appetite for cheese in the off hours, you'd be wrong. Vito, Angelo, and Paolo eat each cheese as if it might be their last.

"I don't eat a lot of meat or fish," says Vito. "I mostly just eat cheese." On cue, Paolo scoots by and air-drops a few *nodini* directly into his mouth.

The match ends in victory for the Germans, and a collective groan echoes across the country. Mom comes in. She's been at the hospital, caring for her husband, who's recovering slowly from his accident. It's clear that his days at the *caseificio* are

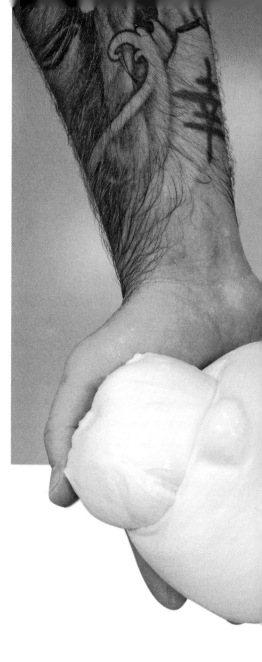

behind him. She makes her way around the room, kissing her children one by one. She turns to me. "Have you eaten?"

With the match over, they return to the table one by one. Angelo grabs a slice of Altamura bread and caps it with half a ball of mozzarella. Vito works a fork through the soft folds of a burrata. Paolo pops *nodini* into his mouth like popcorn kernels.

Their relationship as brothers takes on the same rhythms as their relationship as partners in the store: a near-wordless synchronicity, wherein they orbit constantly around one another but rarely come into direct contact. There are moments of subtle tenderness—a midmorning espresso delivery by Angelo, a cigarette shared during a quick break from production—but for the most part, they go about their business and their lives in silent symbiosis.

Each speaks almost exclusively in the first person—"my trip," "my cheese," "my experiment." At first it's disarming, as if the small space of the *caseificio* hasn't left enough room for "we," but the more time I spend with the brothers, the more I realize

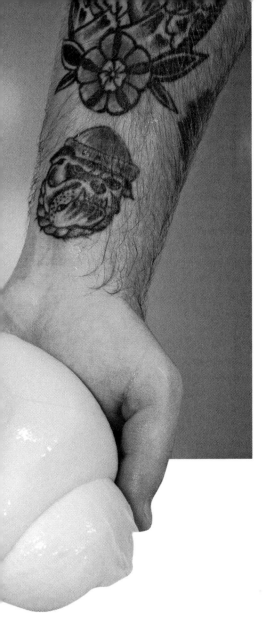

that it's a way of maintaining a footprint of independence in a world where everything—jobs, meals, cigarettes—is shared.

"That's the beauty of it," says Vito. "I can leave tomorrow, and I know my family will be just fine. Same goes for Paolo or Angelo." Fine for a time, sure. Paolo will take up the ricotta duties, Angelo will watch over Don Vito and the *formaggio clandestino* and whatever experiment his brother has brewing. They'll all share cheeses through a constant stream of messages and find a way to get by, but something will be missing.

"I have so many places I want to go," says Vito. "My brothers, too." He rattles off a list of the latest outposts in need of mozzarella aid: a trattoria in Hong Kong; a farm outside Vancouver; an island waiting to be discovered, where the milk is dense and aromatic and the moon never sets.

"It would be beautiful if we could travel together," says Paolo. "But we need to be careful. Maybe the day we all leave together is the day we never come back."

FOOD
FIGHTERS

Preserving the traditions of Italian cuisine

Pane di Altamura; Altamura, Puglia

THE BREAD BROTHERS

Once upon a time in Puglia, dense-crusted, tender-crumbed semolina loaves were the lifeblood of roaming shepherds, who could count on the bread to stay good for a week of wandering with their flocks. Today, the shepherds have cars and smartphones, but *pane di Altamura* is no less vital to life in these parts. It is the only bread in Italy to receive DOP (Denominazione di Origine Protetta) status, a loaf that Italians hold sacred. Panificio di Gesù is a keeper of the flame, an institution in Altamura that still makes the bread way it did in 1838: kneaded by hand, slow-proofed with wild yeast, cooked in an ancient wood-fired oven. Run by brothers Giuseppe and Giuseppe, the fourth generation of Di Gesù bakers, who famously chased McDonald's out of town with a bread offensive years back. Go for the famous namesake bread, but stay for the earth-shattering tomato focaccia pocked with cloves of roasted garlic.

MAMMA LEA

NAME: Lea Pallotta

CITY: Colledara

REGION: Abruzzo

SPECIALTY: I love to make *timballo*—similar to lasagne, but with small meatballs and skinnier pasta layers called *crespelle*. I also love cooking rabbit, but only if we raise our own.

KITCHEN HERO: My daughter. She's my inspiration.

FAVORITE FOOD MEMORY: My surprise fifty-year wedding anniversary. We spent the entire weekend cooking with our closest friends.

REGIONAL STYLE: It's complex, very elaborate, and pretty heavy, but it's good like that because here in Abruzzo it gets really cold.

RISOTTO

HISTORICAL GRAINS

The Arabs brought rice to Italy in the thirteenth century, first growing it in Sicily, then in the wet flatlands of the Po Valley. Today the Po is one of the largest rice-producing regions in Europe, specializing in short-grain varietals like arborio and vialone nano, perfect for risotto.

THE RISE OF RICE

Risotto first appears in recipes around 1809 in Milan, the closest urban center to the rice fields of the Po. By 1891, the great Pellegrino Artusi published the recipe that still stands today: butter, onion, white wine, saffron, nutmeg, and chunks of melting bone marrow.

MILANESE

THE GOLDEN TOUCH

Like Spanish paella, risotto Milanese combines two huge Arabic contributions to the Italian kitchen: rice and saffron. Popularized in the Middle Ages as a symbol of wealth, Italian saffron comes from the Abruzzo region, and you'll find it used in dishes both savory and sweet.

THE MOVE THAT MATTERS

What makes risotto special in the pantheon of rice dishes is the slow addition of broth and the near-constant stirring—teasing out the starch in the rice, giving the dish its lovely sheen and creaminess. Italians like their rice like their pasta—al dente—so expect a gentle chew to the grain.

📍 BROS

One of Italy's most exciting and ambitious restaurants, where young Floriano Pellegrino and his partner, Isabella Poti, apply skills acquired at some of the best restaurants in the world to the remarkable pantry of Puglia.

📍 TRATTORIA LE ZIE

If Bros is a glimpse of the future, Zie is a window to the past, where the simple, rib-sticking food (handmade pastas, crispy meatballs, stewed vegetables) and warm environment makes it feel like having dinner at a friend's house.

LECCE

The Florence of the south, they say, but Lecce
needs no guidebook moniker to be fully appreciated;
it's beauty and charm will hit you the second you
slide a sole across the famous limestone blocks that
form the bones of the city. Ambitious restaurants
and lazy wine bars pepper a cityscape of ancient
ampitheaters and skyscraping cathedrals, a natural
convergence of past and future unlike any you'll
find elsewhere in Italy.

QUANTO BASTA

Lecce was never a cocktail town,
but that didn't stop Diego Melorio
and Andrea Carlucci from opening
one of the best cocktail bars in all of
Italy, a major milestone in the city's
culinary transformation. These guys
take their drinking very seriously.

BALDO GELATO

A gelateria worth traveling for, one
where the country's best ingredients
(Calabrian licorice, Sicilian almonds,
Sorrento lemons) are deployed like
depth charges of outrageous flavor.
And their composed desserts are
works of delicious ingenuity.

Chapter Three

BOLOGNA

—

La Grassa. The fat one. Bologna has earned its nickname like no other place on Earth. The old city is awash in excess calories, a medieval fortress town fortified with golden mountains of starch and red cannons of animal fat, where pastas gleam a brilliant yellow from the lavish amount of egg yolks they contain and menus moan under the weight of their meat- and cheese-burdened offerings.

I had long dreamed of nuzzling up to Bologna's ample waistline. As a high school kid with a burgeoning romance with the kitchen, I was hungry to consummate my love with what I regarded as the world's finest cuisine. The intermediary was a young, heavyset Italian American named Mario Batali. Every morning at 10:30 during summer break, I sank into our Chianti red couch and watched the chef with orange clogs and a matching ponytail motormouth his way across Italy, breaking down the regional cooking of the country in exquisite three-plate daily tasting menus. I wanted to taste the swollen breads of Puglia, the neon green pestos of Liguria, the simmering fish stews of Le Marche, the pepper-bombed pastas of Lazio. But, above all, I wanted to feast on the Italy of Molto Mario's most spirited episodes, the Italy of Parmigiano ("the undisputed king of cheeses!"), of mortadella and *culatello*, and, of course, the Italy of *ragù alla bolognese*, the most lavish and revered of all pasta creations.

It took a broken heart to bring me to Bologna's bulging belly. I fell in love with a girl in Barcelona who didn't share my lofty feelings, so I escaped to Bologna to drown my rejection in a bottomless bowl of meat sauce. For three weeks I sought out ragù in any form possible: caught in the tangles of fresh *tagliatelle*, plugging the tiny holes of cheesy tortellini, draped over forest green handkerchiefs of spinach lasagne.

Since the dawn of Christianity, Emilia-Romagna—birthplace of ragù, home of the city of Bologna—has been one of Europe's wealthiest regions, a center of trade with a heavy agricultural presence. Few things say wealth as loudly as a sauce made up of three or four cuts of meat, two kinds of fat, wine, milk, and a flurry of one of the world's most treasured cheeses—all served on a pasta so dense with egg yolk it looks like a sunset run through a paper shredder.

Slow-simmered meat-based stews were common throughout Italy in the fifteenth and sixteenth centuries, but pasta, a luxury enjoyed by the upper class until the Industrial Revolution made wheat more accessible, didn't enter the equation until the early nineteenth century, when the aristocrats of Emilia-Romagna found it in their hearts and wallets to combine the two. Pellegrino Artusi, a successful businessman and noted gastronome, is often credited with the first published recipe for *ragù alla bolognese*, dating back to 1891 in the self-published *Science in the Kitchen and the Art of Eating Well*. Not satisfied with the panoply of meats and cooking fats, Artusi recommended goosing the dish with porcini, chicken livers, sliced truffles, and a glass of heavy cream.

Just as Artusi's version reflected his privileged times as a wealthy merchant carousing about Emilia-Romagna in the mid–nineteenth century, ragù has always been a barometer of sorts, a dish that closely mirrors the conditions of its makers. Substantial meat-heavy ragùs took hold in the relatively fat times of the early twentieth century, but in the hardscrabble years after World War II, pasta found itself nearly naked, slicked with lard and vegetable scraps and little else. Only as Italy climbed out of the postwar depression in the 1950s and '60s did meat rejoin the recipe as the central constituent.

Over the years, other parts of Italy developed their own take on the bubbling meat sauce. (And let it be said now that *sauce* is a misnomer—sauce implies a level of liquidity that you'll never find in a true ragù. Instead, the Italians would call it a *condimento*, a condiment meant to accompany the pasta, not smother it relentlessly.) *Ragù alla barese*, from the heart of Puglia, is made from thin slices of meat—pork, beef, lamb, even horse—with the sauce served over *orecchiette*, ear-shaped pasta, and the protein eaten separately. Italy's second most famous ragù after Bologna's belongs to Naples, where a giant vat of tomato sauce is used to render huge chunks of meat fork tender (the inspiration for Italian America's Sunday gravy). But the scope of ragù goes well beyond these famous offshoots: travel Italy today, and you'll find ragù made from fish, duck, and wild boar, laced with everything from cumin to dried chili to chocolate.

Through all those years and all those iterations, Emilia-Romagna has remained ground zero of Italy's ragù culture, but even here the differences between one village's ragù and the next's can be a catalyst for controversy and recrimination.

Of course, uniformity was never part of the equation: from the start, *ragù alla bolognese* has been a reflection of subtle differences in terrain, weather, and wealth that defined one town from the next throughout the region.

Today, the list of variables runs longer than the list of ingredients. Is ragù pure pork? Pure beef? A mixture? Is the meat ground, chopped by hand, or braised and then shredded? Does pancetta or another type of cured pork product belong in the mix? How about liquid: stock or water, red wine or white? In some parts of the region, where dairy cows are aplenty, milk makes it into the sauce; in other parts, it's considered a sacrilege. Spices: salt, maybe pepper, usually bay leaf; sometimes, in rare cases, nutmeg.

The biggest source of dispute, undoubtedly, is the tomato: How much, if any? Fresh, canned, or tomato paste?

So is there one true ragù? One best way to make it? One expression of this meaty amalgam that best represents the DNA of this region? That's what I've come back to Emilia-Romagna to find out.

🌿 🍖 🍷

Twenty miles outside of Bologna, at a roadside restaurant, I meet Alessandro Martini, short and thick and boiling over with life. He runs Italian Days Food Experience, a full-day binge on Emilia-Romagna's most famous ingredients: cured meats, Parmigiano-Reggiano, aceto balsamico di Modena ("twelve years aging minimum!" as he likes to say). His Facebook page is dominated by pictures of tourists feeding each other pasta, hoisting massive hunks of cheese, slurping hundred-year-old balsamic vinegar from plastic spoons. On any given day, depending on the whims of TripAdvisor's algorithms, Alessandro's tour is the most popular activity in all of Europe.

For a short period in 2010, Alessandro was my truffle dealer, sending freshly dug specimens across the Mediterranean to Barcelona, where I was then living, one kilo at a time. I would keep them under my pillow for a few days until my dreams smelled of tubers before selling them off to Michelin-starred chefs around Barcelona. I remember waking up to messages from Alessandro during those heady days after an early-morning truffle hunt: "I have the white gold!"

Alessandro hails from the heart of ragù country and lives for these types of belt-loosening food adventures. This is a man who celebrated the birth of both his son and daughter by gifting them with batteries of aceto balsamico—a series of wooden barrels that hold balsamic vinegar as it ages over the course of a lifetime. When I emailed him two weeks before the trip and asked him to be my guide, his answer was short and definitive: "*Sì! Sì!* We go to see the best Italian grandmas and the ragù kings. Don't worry!"

We start at Ristorante Bonfiglioli in the hilltop town of Zocca. An hour before

Beef or pork: the eternal ragù debate.

lunch service, the kitchen looks like what I imagine when I close my eyes at night and see Italy. All women, mostly grandmas, all performing backbreaking acts of an intensely nurturing and homemade nature. One rolls out long sheets of emerald green spinach pasta for *lasagne verde*. Another fries little rectangles of dough for *gnocchi fritti*. A pair of older women in bonnets stuff hundreds of pasta squares with a mix of ground pork, mortadella, and Parmesan before pinching them into tortellini. In the corner, over a lone burner, a younger woman stirs a pot that, judging by the savory perfume, can contain only one thing.

When Alessandro announces that we've come to talk ragù, the flurry of activity comes to a sudden halt and the women gather around the mountain of tortellini.

"Well, what do you want to know?" the young sauce stirrer asks. "Everything," I say.

And that's pretty much all it takes. The women launch into their personal recipes, exchanging barbs about protein choices and seasoning philosophies. Finally, Zia Maria Lanzarini, the oldest cook in the kitchen, quiets the crowd and offers some well-earned wisdom: "The meat can change based on the circumstances. The liquid can, too. But the one thing a ragù never has in it is garlic."

The only other point of agreement among the group: ragù should be made with pignoletto, an acidic, lightly fruity wine that you can see growing by looking out of the restaurant's windows. "It's a Bolognese sauce, it should be made with a Bolognese wine."

The official version at Bonfiglioli, what Alessandro calls "the noble ragù," would be a source of controversy for most in the area—including, apparently, a few of the cooks in this kitchen. It is made from 100 percent beef, a rarity in the region but an act of recycling in a restaurant with mountains of beef scraps leftover from the strip steaks it is famous for. Those scraps are combined with onion, carrot, and celery, a few glugs of pignoletto, plus peeled and seeded fresh tomatoes, and simmered for four hours, the cook adding water at her discretion if the ragù starts to dry out.

"The cooking is the most important part. It must be slow," says Signora Elena, Maria's tortellini accomplice. "It's the slow cooking that gives the sauce its flavor."

She passes me a spoon, and the ragù, a gentle orange color from the emulsion of tomato and fat, sits up like a well-trained dog. It tastes of the mineral intensity of good Italian beef corrupted by nothing more than a light tomato acidity, the sweetness of the vegetables, and a whisper of wine in the background. The women try to ply us with other delights of the Emilian kitchen, and I start to give in, but Alessandro intercedes and ushers me to the door. The day is young.

Three hilltops over, at Trattoria Lina in Savigno, we sit down to a light lunch of spinach *gramigne*, hollow fish hooks of pasta, with sausage ragù; *polpette*, massive, dense meatballs made from pork, beef, chicken, mortadella, and an absurd amount of Parmesan; thick shanks of *osso buco*;

tomato-braised rabbit *alla cacciatora*; and tortellini in brodo.

We are surrounded by cyclists, runners, large, spirited families—people in need of sustenance. Alessandro loves this restaurant, and for good reason: the food is intensely satisfying, especially the chewy pile of *gramigne*, hiding nubs of sausage in their knots, and the tortellini, another regional specialty, which are belly buttons of ground pork, mortadella, and Parmesan afloat in a clear, soul-soothing chicken broth.

But after a few bites of the ragù, he flashes me a look of disappointment: "I'm sorry, my friend. The ragù is good, it is fine, but there is too much *doppio concentrato*. Tomato paste has no place in ragù!" To hear Alessandro say these words about a restaurant he himself selected, one in which the owners greeted him with hugs and asked about his children, underscores just how hard it is to please an Italian—especially with ragù.

As we waddle our way back toward his van, he tells me: "These are great examples for a beginner, but later, I will show you the true ragù."

🌱 🍖 🍷

The rest of the week in Emilia-Romagna is a blur of ground pork and durum wheat. I spend days in Bologna, plodding from one restaurant to the next, faithfully ordering *tagliatelle al ragù* even when my stomach cries out for clear liquids or a few green leaves of vegetation.

Bologna is my kind of town: ancient in its cobbled avenues but youthful in its constituency, big enough to capture a certain urban energy but small enough for you to never need anything other than your two feet to take it all in. Above all, it's a civilization seemingly constructed for the sole purpose of eating.

Everywhere you turn you see signs of its place at the top of the Italian food chain: fresh-pasta shops vending every possible iteration of egg and flour; buzzing bars pairing Spritz and Lambrusco with generous spreads of free meat, cheese, and vegetable snacks; and, above all, osteria after osteria, cozy wine-soaked eating establishments from whose ancient kitchens emanates a moist fragrance of simmered pork and local grapes.

Osteria al 15 is a beloved dinner den just inside the *centro storico* known for its sprawling plates of charcuterie, its crispy flatbreads puffed up in hot lard, and its classic beef-heavy ragù tossed with corkscrew pasta or spooned on top of béchamel and layered between sheets of lasagne. It's far from refined, but the bargain prices and the boisterous staff make it all go down easily.

Trattoria Gianni, down a hairpin alleyway a few blocks from Piazza Maggiore, was once my lunch haunt in Bologna, by virtue of its position next to my Italian-language school. I dream regularly of its *bollito misto*, a heroic mix of braised brisket, capon, and tongue served with salsa verde, but the dish I'm looking for this time, a thick beef-and-pork joint with plenty of jammy tomato, is a solid middle-of-the-road ragù.

Bologna's finest casual restaurant, All'Osteria Bottega, is the kind of place you would do unholy things to have transplanted into your neighborhood. Everything—from the tortellini in brodo to the *lasagne al forno* to the heroic plates of thinly sliced mortadella and *culatello*—is a master class in Emilia-Romagna's special brand of soulful sophistication. The ragù—chunky and rich, with only a whisper of tomato—finds a perfect delivery vessel in the eggy, toothsome *tagliatelle*.

The best ragù I taste in Bologna is a white ragù of rabbit folded between a dozen thin layers of lasagna, served at Pappagallo, a polished restaurant in the shadow of the two towers that climb from Bologna's center. It is a paradigm of sophistication and refinement next to the hefty classic versions, but with bunny as its base, it is not a ragù that could bear the name of this city.

Any of these dishes would qualify as the best plate of pasta in your town or my town or any town outside of Italy, but there's nothing that makes me want to change my return flight. Eventually, the Bologna ragù all begin to bleed together in a delicious but indiscernible pool of animal fat.

Alessandro has a simple explanation for my conundrum: "Bologna is not where you will find the best ragù. Too many tourists, too many students, not enough *nonne*. You must come with me to my town."

Savigno is a lovely little village of two thousand people nestled in a valley framed by rivers and oak trees and the gentle humpbacks of humble vineyards—the kind of place you start mentally retiring to the second you lay eyes on it. Beyond being the capital of the region's white truffle industry, Savigno is a major pillar in Emilia-Romagna's ragù culture.

At Amerigo dal 1934, a restaurant famous throughout the region for its slow-simmered sauces and truffle-driven cuisine, Alberto Bettini and his family before him have spent the past eighty years refining the region's most famous dish.

"There are thousands of recipes for ragù," he says. "I can't tell you one is right and the other is wrong. This is Italy: if you go five kilometers from here, you'll find a completely different ragù."

Nevertheless, a few axioms hold true across the spectrum of possibilities. Above all, Alberto espouses what could be the bedrock ethos of Italian cuisine. "The *materia prima* is the most important part. You can't make good ragù with bad ingredients."

His ragù begins the same way all ragù begin: with finely diced onion, carrot, and celery sautéed in olive oil, the sacred *soffritto*. "It's important to really caramelize the vegetables. That's where the flavor comes from."

Later come two pounds of coarsely ground beef ("from the neck or shoulder—something with fat and flavor") and a pound of ground pork butt, browned separately from the vegetables and deglazed with a cup of white wine (pignoletto, of course). Peeled tomatoes, tomato paste, bay leaves, and three hours of simmering over a low flame. Seasoning? "Salt. Never pepper."

In the dining room, after an array of truffle-showered starters, Alberto serves us three ragù—a blind tasting of today's and yesterday's sauces, along with a jarred version he sells in upscale markets, so we can judge the effects of time and temperature on the final product. He doesn't serve the ragù on *tagliatelle*, though, but on little rounds of toasted bread—the better for us to appreciate the subtleties of the sauce, he says.

Alessandro and I both immediately choose the day-old ragù. It's not dramatically different, but the flavors are deeper, rounder, more harmonious. In all of them you taste the quality of the meat, the silken texture from the long simmer, the ghost of bay leaf. They are lovely creations, but there is perhaps too much tomato sweetness for the taste of a purist like Alessandro. He's happy, but not euphoric—which is a state he hits a few times a day when he's eating and drinking well.

For Alessandro, we seem to be perpetually one or two steps away from the one true thing, constantly circling the simmering pot, as if the dozen ragù we eat together around Savigno are all preludes to a more perfectly realized vision. "Come, my friend. I will show you how we do it at home."

As we walk through Savigno, the copper light of dusk settling over the town's narrow streets, we stop anyone we can find to ask for his or her ragù recipe. A retired policeman says he likes an all-pork sauce with a heavy hit of pancetta, the better for coating the pasta. A gelato maker explains that a touch of milk defuses the acidity of the tomato and ties the whole sauce together. Overhearing our kitchen talk below, an old woman in a navy cardigan pokes her head out of a second-story window to offer her take on the matter: "I only use tomatoes from my garden—fresh when they're in season, preserved when it gets cold."

Inspired by the Savigno citizenry, we buy meat from the butcher, vegetables and wine from a small stand in the town's piazza, and head to Alessandro's house to simmer up his version of ragù: two parts chopped skirt steak, one part ground pancetta, the sautéed vegetable trio, a splash of dry white wine, and a few canned San Marzano tomatoes.

"People talk about *materia prima, ma-teria prima*, then they dump in a bunch of *doppio concentrato. Vaffanculo!*"

We leave the ragù to simmer and race off into the hills above Savigno to meet with Alessandro's truffle dealers ("the truffle season doesn't start until Tuesday, so don't tell them you're a journalist"). The sauce we return to, one that took all of fifteen minutes of active preparation to create, is straightforward and beautifully balanced, an honest expression of the handful of ingredients we put into the pot.

It's clear that after years of dedicated pasta consumption across all corners of this region, Alessandro has learned a few things about ragù.

"We're getting closer," he tells me.

🍴 🥕 🍷

The *tagliatelle al ragù* at Osteria Francescana in Modena stands six inches tall and costs $55. It also takes a battery of chefs and nearly seventy-two hours to make. Its height, price, and layers of manipulation, at the very least, are befitting a restaurant of

—

Francescana's stature: it has three Michelin stars and is currently ranked number one in *Restaurant* magazine's list of the World's 50 Best Restaurants.

Massimo Bottura, Francescana's wild-eyed Captain Nemo, is no stranger to controversy when it comes to his treatment of the sacred pillars of Italian cuisine. When he first opened Osteria Francescana in 1995, Modenese grandmas were lining up to bash him with their rolling pins. One of his first enduring creations, a dish that morphed five different Parmesan cheeses into five different textures (a twenty-four-month pudding, a fifty-month "air"), prompted the type of rabid public reactions you'd expect for a politician selling state secrets to the enemy.

In Italy, where dishes pass from one generation to the next without as much as a grain of salt out of place, evolution doesn't come easily. Massimo's great contribution to Italy's modern food culture is his willingness to challenge the notion that Italian cuisine is already a fully realized vision, a museumworthy collection of perfectly con-ceived dishes that can only be weakened by modern intervention. That's not untrue: few people on this planet can do as much with five ingredients as the Italians. *Cacio e pepe*, pasta alla carbonara, *pizza Margherita*: in their most honest iterations, they are near-perfect foods, deeply revered as expressions of the richness of Italian culture, and most God-fearing countrymen will be damned to watch a half-mad chef fuck with their formulations in search of his own stardom.

But Massimo—a man who finds culinary inspiration in Walt Whitman and Miles Davis—never saw it like that. Like the other heavyweights of the postmodern cooking world—Ferran Adrià in northern Spain, England's Heston Blumenthal—he sees food as a medium for man's greatest ambitions: experimentation, transformation, accelerated evolution. "We don't want to lose our history, but we don't want to lose ourselves in it, either. That's why we are always asking ourselves questions about the best way to do things."

The best way, according to Massimo,

A pan of *tagliatelle al ragù*
from Amerigo dal 1934.

isn't always the traditional way, and that didn't sit well with certain people in this country, especially in conservative Modena. It wasn't until Massimo won over international critics and achieved global fame that he managed to convince locals. "Suddenly they started to defend me." (And for anybody who continued to doubt him, he won the gold medal for the best balsamic vinegar in Modena, the most revered craft in one of the most tradition-driven cities in Italy—a barrel-aged middle finger to those who think he knows only how to manipulate.)

He's in the middle of recounting his vinegar triumph when an old man with a bike at his side pokes his head into the door to ask Massimo a question. "*Mi scusi, maestro! Maestro!*" The chef stands up from his desk and greets the man like a great don of the neighborhood. When he returns, he flashes a grin and raised eyebrows: "See that? Now they call me maestro!"

The master has strong opinions about everything, especially ragù. While the differences from restaurant to restau-

rant and grandma to grandma tend to be minimal, especially to the outside eater, Massimo's two main pillars of ragù are nothing short of controversial in this highly charged world. First he insists that the meat shouldn't be ground before cooking but rather cooked in large pieces, then shredded by hand. "Ninety-nine percent of ragù starts with machine-ground meat. But why?" He insists that big pieces of braised meat give deeper flavor and better texture to the final dish.

Massimo's Second Law of Ragù is even more explosive: no tomato. "We never had tomatoes in Emilia-Romagna, so how did they end up in the sauce? Tomato is used to cover up bad ingredients."

In some dusty corner of the Emilian culinary history Massimo's version may have its antecedent, but the ragù he fabricates is a severe departure from everything else I've tasted so far. Though the individual components of the dish constitute a showcase of the avant-garde technique and fuck-the-rules philosophy that characterizes so many of the world's most lauded restaurants today, the final result tastes deeply, gloriously of ragù.

"Vision is the crossroads between the rational and the emotional," says Massimo in one of his frequent moments of existential reflection in the dining room. The rational mind says that hand-torn meat rich in gelatin will make a lusty, powerful sauce with no need for excess ingredients. The emotional one tells him that it must still look and taste like home.

Later in the meal, the full extent of Massimo's whimsy-driven modernist vision will be on display—in a handheld head of baby lettuce whose tender leaves hide the concentrated tastes of a Caesar salad, a glazed rectangle of eel made to look as if it were swimming up the Po River, a handful of classics with ridiculous names such as "Oops! I dropped the lemon tart"—but it's the ragù that moves me the most. The noodles have a brilliant, enduring chew, and the sauce, rich with gelatin from the tougher cuts of meat, clings to them as if its life were at stake.

Most Italians would laugh at the price tag and blush at the modernist art–strewn room in which it is consumed—a poor replacement for their *nonna*'s kitchen, they'd say—but with a twirl of a fork, the sculptures and canvases and credit card payments would disappear and all that would remain is a taste of childhood.

Time and nostalgia add intensity to the flavors of our earliest memories, and in many ways the mission of modernist kitchens playing with sacred staples of home cooking is to find ways to make the reality live up to the impossibility of the memory. In the case of Massimo's ragù, that means making the noodles with a thousand egg yolks, then cooking them in a concentrated Parmesan broth. That means braising nothing but the richest cuts of meat at very low temperatures for a very long time, then pulling them apart by hand to make a sauce of extraordinary depth and intensity. That means twisting the noodles into a tight spiral so that the pasta towers above the plate, the same way it does in the memories of those who eat it.

While I work my way down the tower

Nonna Anna filling the well for a
batch of *tagliatelle*.

to the bottom of the bowl, all I can think about is that this is why so many of us fantasize about being Italian, because to be Italian means to have memories that taste of this plate of pasta.

🌿 🍇 🍸

At 5:30 P.M. in the village rec room of Savigno, a cabal of ragù-making grandmas has assembled at a long wooden table. Alessandro has convened an emergency council, calling on the time-tested *nonne* of this scenic town to—hopefully—bring a final bit of clarity to the murky issue of Emilia-Romagna's slow-cooked sauce. He seems concerned that I still haven't fully understood ragù—that perhaps my mind has been clouded by the tourist-friendly osterie of Bologna and the Michelin-friendly pageantry of Modena. "Don't you worry, *amico*. If anyone knows something about making ragù, it is this group of *nonne*."

It is a comic-book cast of grandmother shapes and sizes: There's Lisetta, tall with a thick wave of black hair. Maria Pia, mid-sized, modest, and crowned with a dark half-fro. Anna no. 1, short, plump, square-faced, and generously jowled. And Anna no. 2, smallest in size, largest in stature among the old ladies, a woman who not only directed the famous pasta program at Amerigo dal 1934 but twice traveled to Tokyo to take ragù to the people of Japan. "I walked into the subway, and there I was, larger than life, making pasta on a Japanese billboard. Madonna!"

Anna's far-flung adventures notwithstanding, these are women born and raised in this fertile valley of golden grapes and hidden tubers. They have ragù in their soul.

I have a long list of questions that have been vibrating in my head over the past week—about the deployment of dairy, the browning of proteins, the ever-controversial issue of tomato. But ultimately I manage only one feeble query—"How does everyone here make their ragù?"—before the council takes over and I'm rendered a silent spectator.

"*Piano piano*," says Lisetta; slowly, step by step. "You cannot rush a good ragù."

"The 1950s were full of misery," says Anna no. 2. "Back then ragù was just a bit of tomato and onion and lard. It changed slowly over the years, when people had more money to buy meat. A little pork, a little pancetta."

"A proper ragù should be made with half pork, half beef," says Anna no. 1.

"No, no! One-quarter pork and the rest beef."

"More pork than beef—it has better flavor. I use one kilo of beef and one and a half of pork."

"Pancetta. Always."

"No! Not if you already have pork. That's too much pork."

"Can we all agree that skirt steak is the best?"

"No, no, no. In *ragù alla bolognese* there's no place for skirt steak."

"*Piano piano.*"

"Fresh tomato is better in the summer. If not, *concentrato* works."

"Canned DOP tomatoes are more consistent."

"When do you add milk?"

"I don't use milk. Only with the *ragù di prosciutto*. It helps mellow the saltiness."

"You know there are people who serve their ragù with spaghetti."

"Spaghetti! Oh, please, no. *Tagliatelle. Sempre tagliatelle!*"

"Good ragù comes from someone's house, not a restaurant."

"*Piano piano.*"

As the debate rages across the table, I feel a sudden and overwhelming need to be one of their grandsons. Whatever food argument you've ever had with a friend or family member feels trivial by comparison; the differences at the heart of the discussion may sound minuscule, but it's clear that they matter deeply to everyone in this room. I have zero doubt that the best ragù for me would be whichever one of their homes I happened to be eating in at the moment.

Despite the raised voices and the wild gesticulations, nobody here is wrong. The beauty of ragù is that it's an idea as much as it is a recipe, a slow-simmered distillation of what means and circumstances have gifted you: If Zia Peppe's ragù is made with nothing but pork scraps, that's because her neighbor raises pigs. When Maria cooks her vegetables in a mix of oil and butter, it's because her family comes from a long line of dairy farmers. When Nonna Anna slips a few laurel leaves into the pot, she plucks them from the tree outside her back door. There is no need for a decree from the Chamber of Commerce to tell these women what qualifies as the authentic ragù; what's authentic is whatever is simmering under the lid.

Eventually the women agree to disagree and the rolling boil of the debate calms to a gentle simmer. Alessandro opens a few bottles of pignoletto he's brought to make the peace. We drink and take photos and make small talk about tangential ragù issues such as the proper age of Parmesan and the troubled state of the prosciutto industry in the region.

On my way out, Anna no. 1 grabs me by the arm. She pulls me close and looks up into my eyes with an earnestness that drowns out the rest of the chatter in the room. "Forget about these arguments. Forget about the small details. Just remember that the most important ingredient for making ragù, the one thing you can never forget, is love."

Lisetta overhears from across the room and quickly adds, "And pancetta!"

THE PASTA MATRIX

Pasta is an ever-evolving expression of regional history, tastes, and traditions—from the fresh egg-based pastas of the affluent north to the dry flour-and-water shapes of the south. Here is but a small taste of the hundreds of pasta styles you'll encounter across Italy.

GNOCCHI
Lombardy

AGNOLOTTI
Piedmont

TONNARELLI
Lazio

TAGLIATELLE
Emilia-Romagna

MALLORREDDUS
Sardinia

PACCHERI
Campania

TROFIE
Liguria

ORRECHIETTE
Puglia

BIGOLI
Veneto

ORECHIETTE ALLE CIME DI RAPA

One of the finest examples of Italy's *cucina povera* comes from one of its poorest regions: Puglia, where cooks transform flour and water and dark leafy greens into a triumphant dish.

Where to Eat:

Antichi Sappori, Montegrosso

CACIO E PEPE

Rome's iconic two-ingredient pasta, a simple but skillful union of aged cheese and coarse black pepper that demonstrates the best of Italian culinary alchemy.

Where to Eat:
Felice a Testaccio, Rome

PASTA CON LE SARDE

The briny-sweet-funky pride of Palermo. Sardines, fennel, saffron, raisins, and pine nuts form an edible distillation of the island's Arabic-inflected cuisine.

Where to Eat:
Ferro di Cavallo, Palermo

TORTELLINI EN BRODO

Another triumph of Emilia-Romagnan cuisine, these labor-intensive parcels of pork and Parmesan float like life preservers in a shimmering meat consommé.

Where to Eat:
Broccaindosso, Bologna

SPAGHETTI ALLE VONGOLE

From Capri to Cagliari, Positano to Palermo, wherever there is coastline, you will find pasta with clams. It varies by region, but expect garlic, white wine, and parsley (and never cheese!).
Where to Eat:
As close to the sea as possible

TROFIE AL PESTO

Italy's emblematic sauce of basil and pine nuts comes from the coastal region of Liguria, where they use it to dress tight coils of pasta, often mixed with boiled green beans and potatoes.

Where to Eat:
Osteria Baccicin Du Caru, Melu

FOOD FIGHTERS

Preserving the traditions of Italian cuisine

Romagnola Pigs, Montetortore, Emilia-Romagna

THE PIG PROTECTOR

Stop me if you've heard this story before: Mora romagnola pigs once dominated the hills of Ravenna in central Italy, twenty-two thousand fiesty, black-haired beasts known for their abundance of sweet fat. But the menace of modernity reduced that number dramatically until just fifteen remained at the dawn of the twenty-first century. Cue the food fighters: a small handful of farmers set about reviving the romagnola, determined not to let the quick-fattening white pig favored by industrial farms crowd out an important native species. Beppe and Emanuel Ferri of Ca Lumaco are father-and-son pig farmers dedicated to raising the wily heritage breed exclusively. Three hundred and fifty pigs roam freely through their forests, fattening on a diet of acorns and chestnuts and mountain grasses. A good life and a noble afterlife: these prized pigs make some of the finest prosciutto, coppa, and lardo in Italy.

CASTELUCCIO

Let the tour buses have Tuscany; you'll find the same magical convergence of rolling landscapes, postcard villages, and incredible country cooking just south in Umbria. At the foot of the Apennine Mountains, bobbing in a vast sea (of wildflowers in the spring, snow in the winter), Casteluccio stands as an island of old-world wonder, of cobblestone corners and slow-simmered culture. Make your base in nearby Norcia, where porchetta and truffles and some of Italy's finest *salumi* can sustain you for a week (or a lifetime).

⦿ LOCANDA DE' SENARI

If driving up a narrow, winding road to a gorgeous mountain village just to eat a bowl of lentil stew seems like a bad idea to you, you probably shouldn't be traveling through Italy

⦿ AGRITURISMO ANTICA CASCINA BRINDAMARTE

The kind of place you come for a day and stay for a week: a refurbished farmhouse with generous mountain views and a gift for feeding people

MANTICA NORCINERIA FRATELLI ANSUINI

A treasure trove of Umbria's finest products, from golden-green tides of peppery olive oil to local black truffles to a dozen works of porcine art,

PALAZZO SENECA

For when you need to splash out. Beautiful rooms in an ancient palace, a world-class restaurant, and a breakfast spread that will make you want to wake up twice each morning.

Chapter Four

SICILY

Palermo is not one of the grand cities of the world. It doesn't have the history of Rome, the beauty of Paris, or the energy of New York. It doesn't even have the population of El Paso. But greatness is often defined by what's missing, and what Palermo doesn't have could fill a book: rainy weather, long lines, exorbitant prices, an inflated sense of self. It is gloriously free from the jungles of selfie sticks, the markets of mass seduction, the burdens of breathless magazine profiles. And don't expect that to change anytime soon: with three thousand years of history behind it, Palermo isn't the type of place that tolerates abrupt pivots.

That's not to say the Sicilian capital is static. Locals will tell you that change is afoot, not just in the faces you see around town but in everything else you see around town. Suddenly a handful of boutique hotels have materialized, decaying *palazzi* have been restored, a few restaurants have started cooking food that isn't Italian. People whisper about a rising tide of tourism—of cruise ships and package tours and the specter of international interest that could further fuel a citywide transformation.

But you don't come to Palermo to stay in minimalist hotels and eat avocado toast; you come to Palermo to be in Palermo, to drink espressos as dark and thick as crude oil, to eat tangles of toothsome spaghetti bathed in buttery sea urchins, to wander the streets at night, feeling perfectly charmed on one block, slightly concerned on the next. To get lost. After a few days, you learn to turn down one street because it smells like jasmine and honeysuckle in the morning; you learn to avoid another street because in the heat of the afternoon the air is thick with the suggestion of swordfish three days past its prime.

You come here because everyone wants to pretend, for a few days at least, that they are Italian, and there is no easier city in which to do that than Palermo. You can walk the markets without bumping shoulders with other tourists; eat ice cream, like a Sicilian, at any hour of the day; have a late dinner down an alley cast in an orange summer glow; rent an apartment on a narrow street in the old city and hang your wet clothes from the balcony. Before you pack your bags and catch that flight back to Cork or Colorado or Copenhagen, you can have one last lemon granita at the sidewalk café that has quickly become your second home in the city and think to yourself, *So this is what it would be like.*

🌿 🍃 🍷

Of course, life in Palermo is more complex than a few espressos and a plate of pasta might suggest. Over the past three thousand years, Palermo has been passed around like a giant doobie among history's most fiendish conquerors: from the Phoenicians to the Greeks, from the Greeks to the Carthaginians, from Hannibal's men to the legions of the Roman Empire. Everyone took a toke: the Muslims, who laid siege to Sicily in the ninth century and made Palermo the capital on a scale with Córdoba and Cairo; the Normans, who spent great sums of money ushering in an era of ostentation and hedonism before abandoning the island four hundred years later; the Spaniards, rulers of the island for nearly three hundred years during the height of their empire, administered by viceroys who struggled to balance the demands of the monarchy with the will of the Sicilians.

Eventually the great general Giuseppe Garibaldi, sailing down from Genoa with just a thousand men, liberated Sicily from the Bourbons and set it on the path to become a part of the new Kingdom of Italy, as the country of Italy as we know it now unified in 1861.

But Palermo's history as a receptacle of tragedy and invader angst didn't end there. Even in unified Italy, it was something of a neglected stepchild. For a country whose history and culture owe so much to the bottom half of the boot, it's shocking how easy it is for the north to write off the south in a few flippant pronouncements. "It's a mess down there," they say in the cafés of Milan and Turin. "The south is corrupt. Confused. Stuck in time." They are the same people who would draw a line south of Rome and divide the country once again.

The twentieth century wasn't kind to the south of Italy, and it wasn't kind to Palermo. Crushing poverty ensured a mass exodus in the early 1900s, as hundreds of thousands of Sicilians fled to Australia and the United States in search of a future beyond their desolate island.

In 1943, the Allies, led by US warplanes, brought war to the city, bombing its port and old quarter back into the sixteenth century. In the wake of the war, with the country in ruins, the Mafia found ways to exploit the island's gripping poverty and torpid reconstruction, transforming the Cosa Nostra from a countryside collective into a powerful urban organism. (The fact that the Mafia and the Allies had, by some reports, a working relationship during the war only further solidified its holdings across Sicily.)

For the last half of the twentieth century, Palermo served as a nerve center for organized crime across Italy as the city descended into a bubbling cauldron of assassinations, citizen shakedowns, and crippling government corruption. La Cosa Nostra: this thing of ours became a thing of theirs, spreading like a virus through all facets of Sicilian life (and to the lives of Sicilians abroad). *Il Sacco di Palermo*, the Sack of Palermo, saw the orange groves, greenways, and rustic villas on the outskirts of the city replaced with shoddy apartment blocks controlled by the Mafia and its friends in government. Combined with the devastated old city, Palermo lost much of its soul, and those who could afford to move began their exodus off the island.

You don't need another recitation of mob brutality—Hollywood and history books have done too much of it already—but what you need to know is that Sicily fought back: brave judges and emboldened politicians, angry citizens and activist organizations spent the 1980s and '90s countering the Cosa Nostra, chipping away at that great granite albatross of Sicilian society until it was nothing but pebbles and dust. Law officials estimate that up to 70 percent of local businesses still pay "protection" fees to the Mafia, but the collective efforts have crippled the Cosa Nostra in ways it is unlikely to ever recover from.

Today, Palermo wears the marks of its many rulers over the past three millennia: Greek columns and Roman arches, couscous and currants, bombed-out buildings and corner-store kickbacks. Though the events that shaped the looks and smells

and tastes of this city may have been harsh, even by history's cruel standards, the result is something to behold, a multicultural milieu that greets you on every street corner, market stand, dinner table.

Palermo's position as a bellwether of the whims of geopolitics shows no sign of waning. In fact, there is a new force stirring in the south that once again will test the resolve of the entire island.

The latest group of invaders doesn't come to conquer; it comes to survive. Beginning in the early 2000s, as the perils of life in Africa grew too great to tolerate, huge swaths of immigrants in search of a new life set off for European soil. At first it was a trickle—one boat of families embarking from Libya, another of young men looking for work. Most took the land route through Turkey and into Greece, when the border was porous enough to let thousands enter each week. But in early 2016, the European Union signed a controversial deal with Turkey that effectively closed off the route, forcing the tens of thousands of migrants leaving northern

An afternoon ride through Piazza Pretoria.

and eastern Africa to seek out a new route across the sea.

Not only is the trek up through northern Africa harrowing, it exposes migrants to two extraordinary dangers: first, the sinister network of human traffickers in Libya set up to take advantage of the wave of desperation. And second, the perils of the sea itself—a 160-mile stretch between Libya and the island of Lampedusa whose calm appearance belies its ability to capsize and crush those who seek to cross it. The two coexist in a vicious calculus: desperation equals demand, and as the ticket prices grow, space on the shabby sea vessels shrinks and, with it, the possibility of survival.

In 2016, more than five thousand migrants died on the sea voyage to Europe, turning the Mediterranean into a watery graveyard. But the economy of people moving shows no signs of slowing, as Italy's ports of entry buckle under the weight of the African exodus. Those who do make it into European waters are rescued by the Italian navy, interned on Lampedusa

or in one of the other main way stations, then typically granted access to the rest of Europe. Many dream of opportunity in northern Europe, but for an increasing number of migrants, Sicily is the first and final stop. From 2015 to 2017, 400,000 African refugees arrived in Sicily, many of them adopting Palermo as their new home.

Africa has always been a vital thread in the Sicilian tapestry; of all the invaders who left their mark on this island, none had a deeper impact on Sicilian culture than the Arabs. "Norman minds dissolved in the vapors of Muslim culture," wrote John McPhee in *The New Yorker* in 1966, claiming that the Catholics "went Muslim with such remarkable style that even Muslim poets were soon praising the new Norman Xanadus." That meant clothing, architecture, and dialect; but above all, the most enduring impact has been on the cuisine of Sicily—in the sprawling economy of citrus, so ubiquitous that even your dreams are suffused with its sunshine fragrance; in Sicily's superlative pastry culture, fueled by almonds and pistachios, crushed, puffed, and pureed into countless forms; in the stamens of saffron, the kernels of couscous, the sweet-and-sour soul of so many of Sicily's most emblematic dishes. The rapid return of the same peoples who helped shape this island feels like Sicilian culture coming full circle.

To witness the demographic transformation at its most potent, head to the Ballarò district in Palermo, long ground zero of Sicily's immigrant population. This is the birthplace of Mario Balotelli, an international soccer star and one of Palermo's most famous sons, the child of two Ghanaian immigrants who came here for the same reason that tens of thousands of Africans risk their lives every month to make the crossing.

Located in the dead center of the city, Ballarò is also home to Palermo's largest market, a meandering outdoor pantry that feeds much of the city. Over the years, the market has evolved to reflect the changing population of Palermo—both the constituents and the ingredients have grown more colorful since I was last here in 2012.

At no time does Ballarò flex its multicultural muscle harder than on the weekend. "Go on Sunday morning," a journalist friend from the island tells me over drinks. "That's when Palermo becomes Africa."

By first light, immigrants haul crates of melons and buckets of ice over the narrow cobblestone streets. Old men sell salted capers and branches of wild oregano while the young ones build their fish stands, one silvery torqued body at a time, like an edible art installation. It's a startling scene: gruff young *palermitani*, foul-mouthed and wreathed in cigarette smoke, lovingly laying out each fish at just the right angle, burrowing its belly into the ice as if to mimic its swimming position in the ocean. Sicilian sun and soil and ingenuity have long produced some of Italy's most prized raw ingredients, and the colors of the market serve as a map of the island's agricultural prowess: the forest green pistachios of Bronte; the Crayola-bright lemons and oranges of Paternò; the famous *pomodorini* of Pachino, fiery orbs of magical tomato intensity.

The enigmatic, ever-evolving
Ballarò market.

The only thing brighter than the Sicilian produce is the African apparel: kente cloth and head wraps, tribal dress and hand-carved accessories. Women in hijabs peel and chunk yucca beside vats of simmering beef spleen and wheels of pecorino. On the fringes of the market, men push televisions in baby strollers as Nubian queens hold down the park benches like curbside thrones. On balconies above, families break bread in village vernacular. Below, young Sicilian couples haggle over the price of faux Nikes and pleather purses in the Palermo dialect.

By 10 A.M. on Sunday, a line forms outside the Kubis barbershop as young men await their date with the clippers. A collage of famous faces outside serves as the menu: the Will Smith, the Terrence Howard, the Drake, and, of course, the always-evolving Balotelli, who changes hairstyles like most of us change our minds.

Across from the blankets and the boys at the barbershop, looking out from his halal butcher store Bismillah, Anwar Bhuiyan remembers his early days in Palermo. "That was me eighteen years ago," he says, stroking the end of his foot-long white beard as if it were a cat curled up on his chest. He arrived from Bangladesh, an educated English teacher with little prospects for survival back home. "I started selling just like them—small stuff directly off the street." Eventually he earned enough to trade the blanket for a table, a semiofficial post in the Ballarò market. From a table to a stand to a storefront, eighteen years of sweating it out under the Sicilian sun, waiting for returns on his life's investment. Now he sells cuts of lamb and beef and spices to Muslims and Christians alike.

In Anwar's story you find a blueprint for integration, but he isn't hopeful for the latest wave of immigrants. "There are too many of us and too few jobs. The system is broken. We are hungry."

Palermo has long been one of Italy's poorest cities. Unemployment hovers near 25 percent—hardly an inviting number for newcomers. I ask Anwar if he ever thinks about pushing farther north, as so many do in search of better prospects. "I can't leave now. My son was born here. He doesn't speak my language. He's Italian."

✦ ❧ 🍷

Leoluca Orlando has lived a thousand lives. Award-winning actor in Germany. Respected Jesuit scholar. Close friend of Hillary Clinton and Al Gore. *Consigliere* to Pope Francis. Anti-Mafia crusader. Political firebrand. Mayor of Palermo three times over.

No doubt he's busy living one of those lives right now. I've been waiting in the mayor's palace for more than an hour. When I received the directions from his assistant, I figured that "mayor's palace" might be a euphemism for a corner office in an old building, but by every working definition—the velvet tapestries, the chiaroscuro art hanging from the walls, the embarrassment of marble—Mayor Orlando runs Palermo from a *palazzo*. I spend the better part of thirty minutes admiring the marble busts of mayors past of Palermo: Salesio Balsano with his cue-ball dome and

bushy mustache; Giovanni Raffaele, he of tiny eyes and aggressive chin strap; and Pietro Ugo delle Favare, three-time mayor during the late nineteenth century, with a mop of a mustache and muttonchops that tickle his neck.

Orlando, bucking the trend of his prodigiously bearded predecessors, is clean-shaven, with a dark drift of the midlength hair that Italian men wear so well. He's built like Diego Maradona: short, thick, and athletic, with a lounge singer's martini-soaked good looks. He explains that he's late because he's spent all day on Lampedusa, the first port of call for the migrant boats that make it to Europe. He played pickup soccer with the refugees, and you can still see the residual sweat above his brow. (He moves and thinks with such frenetic energy, it seems unlikely that the sweat ever dries.)

"English is okay, right? It's my third language. Sicilian's my first. German's my second." After a long pause, he adds with a mischievous smile, "Italian's my fourth."

Orlando first arrived on the political

scene in the late 1970s. Back then, as a rising star in Sicily's Christian Democratic Party, he joined the ranks of a young contingent of crusaders bringing the fight directly to the Mafia. One by one, the judges and politicians on the frontlines of the battle were killed in an increasingly brazen series of assassinations. When the president of Sicily, Piersanti Mattarella, Orlando's close friend and partner in those efforts, was shot in the streets of Palermo in January 1980, he left behind a dying wish to have Orlando inherit his political legacy. In 1985, still in the grips of the Mafia battle, Orlando was elected mayor of Palermo. Since then, more than four thousand mafiosi have been jailed as the Cosa Nostra has lost its stranglehold on Sicilian society. "I haven't gone anywhere in thirty years without five bodyguards," he tells me.

But the life I'm most interested in is his current one as third-term mayor of Palermo. Twelve years and thirteen lives after his first two terms running this city, Orlando decided to run once again for mayor in 2012, against protégé-turned-rival Fabrizio Ferran-

delli. He won with 74 percent of the vote. His latest tenure has coincided with a substantial transformation of the city's infrastructure: the reshaping of the old part of Palermo into a burgeoning commercial and tourism district, the naming of Palermo's Arabic-influenced churches as a UNESCO World Heritage Site.

But what matters most to Orlando, what he sees as his most pressing and consequential charge, is managing the stream of migrants pouring across the Mediterranean, with only his island between them and a new life in prosperous Europe. He doesn't see Sicily as a stepping-stone for those in search of more prosperous territory but as a final destination.

"Palermo isn't a Sicilian city in Italy. It's a Middle Eastern city in the middle of the Mediterranean." To the conservative contingent, that might sound like an insult, but to Orlando, it's a source of pride. He motions to the Chiesa di San Cataldo, seen through the window of his office: Norman facade, bulging red domes, Arabic merlons; once a mosque, now a Catholic church. He knows Palermo's past and who and what built this city, and he sees the immigration crisis as the next chapter in the city's impossible history.

I ask him at what point the migrants can consider themselves *palermitani*. "From the second they arrive in this city. The resident card is the new form of slavery, the migrant boats the new slave ships. We need to accept that globalization isn't just an economic reality but a human one, too." Unlike many critics of mass immigration, Orlando sees no need to distinguish refugees from economic immigrants: both are in desperate need of a new life.

His political style turns around a mixture of bluster, blunt-force determination, and a sense of boundless optimism. He's been known to dismiss the very real criticisms of his opponents with platitudes. When I voice the concerns I've picked up from cabdrivers, food stand owners, and citizens like Anwar, he brushes them aside: "I won the mayoral race with seventy-four percent of the vote. The people are with me. It's the politicians who don't understand."

In the short time I spend with Sindaco Orlando, I find myself persuaded by his vision for the new world—one in which borders slowly dissolve, in which cultures blend into tapestries, in which mayors have more power than presidents and prime ministers. But I am an outsider, free to bask in the sunny glow of Orlando's vision without suffering through the grinding reality of daily life in Palermo. Who to believe: the immigrant cook? the world-weary taxi driver with an unemployed son and a family to feed? the overzealous mayor?

For every enthusiastic politician who views Palermo as a grand and thriving experiment, there's a cabdriver struggling to make sense of a city he no longer recognizes. For every immigrant who finds a home in the bustle of Ballarò, a refugee family struggles to survive in Sicily. But this isn't a zero-sum game: Orlando wants to believe that Palermo, a city that throughout history has survived and adapted, can once again bend and stretch to fit the demands of its shifting citizenry.

🍃 🐌 🍷

Before I leave the mayor's palace, he reaches into his desk and pulls out a folder thick with printouts. He's done his homework. Though we've spent an hour discussing immigration efforts and local politics, he knows I'm here to eat. "Palermo is ranked the fifth greatest city in the world for street food. Don't forget that most of it came from Africa. Go taste for yourself."

Little does he know that I've been tasting for myself on nearly every block since I first touched down. Keep in mind, this isn't the street food of Southeast Asia, where fresh herbs and citrus and chilies conspire to pack huge flavor into small packages. The street food of Palermo isn't meant to stretch your taste buds into acrobatic positions; it's meant to obliterate appetites.

In fact, much of what you do in Palermo will involve eating more than you probably should. "A person eating must make crumbs" goes one of the great Palermo proverbs, and this city makes its crumbs in all shapes and sizes.

Palermo is dotted everywhere with *frittura* shacks—street carts and storefronts specializing in fried foods of all shapes and cardiac impacts. On the fringes of the Ballarò market are bars serving *pane e panelle*, fried wedges of mashed chickpeas combined with potato fritters and stuffed into a roll the size of a catcher's mitt. This is how the vendors start their days; this is how you should start yours, too. If fried chickpea sandwiches don't register as breakfast food, consider an early evening at Friggitoria Chiluzzo, posted on a plastic stool with a pack of locals, knocking back beers with plates of fried artichokes and *arancini*, glorious balls of saffron-stained rice stuffed with ragù and fried golden—another delicious ode to Africa.

Indeed, frying food is one of the favorite pastimes of the *palermitani*, and they do it—as all great frying should be done—with a mix of skill and reckless abandon. Ganci is among the city's most beloved oil baths, a sliver of a store offering more calories per square foot than anywhere I've ever eaten. You can smell the mischief a block before you hit the front door: pizza topped with french fries and fried eggplant, fried rice balls stuffed with ham and cubes of mozzarella, and a ghastly concoction called *spiedino* that involves a brick of béchamel and meat sauce coated in bread crumbs and fried until you could break someone's window with it. A hundred meters down the road you'll find a handful of fruit stands with artful produce arrangements and spinning cylinders of fresh juice to wash away your sins.

This type of blunt street food is a source of passion and pride in Palermo. Take another local favorite: *pane con la milza*, or *pani ca' meusa* in Sicilian: beef spleen stewed in lard, then stuffed into a roll slathered with more lard and topped with grated caciocavallo cheese. Antica Focacceria S. Francesco, a nineteenth-century institution down one of Palermo's loveliest streets, serves up the oldest version in the city, along with other great Sicilian classics, but most prefer the sandwich from Pani Ca' Meusa near the port. Regardless of where you buy it, eat it fast; as it cools, it becomes

more and more apparent that you are eating a spleen burger.

Even the nonfried, nonorgan offerings pack a punch. *Babbaluci*, thumb-size snails, are a star of the Ballarò market scene. Eat them like a Sicilian, sucking the little coil of meat directly from the shell and with it the bath of olive oil, garlic, and parsley they're cooked in. *Sfincione*, Palermo-style pizza, takes the basic staple and adds heft: thicker crust, stronger cheese, bread crumbs, anchovies. Look for the thick, spongy, addictive squares peddled from the backs of the three-wheeled trucks that announce their slices through a loudspeaker.

Gelato serves as the city's collective palate cleanser, and a scoop is never more than a few blocks away. For the greatest illustration of Sicily's I-don't-give-a-fuck-what-time-it-is attitude about ice cream, head to Ideal Caffè Stagnitta, a shoebox-sixed bar of impeccable beauty in the shadow of the Martorana, the wondrous church of Arab and Norman stock built in 1143. The baristas here pull one of the city's finest shots of espresso and a textbook

Gelato: Breakfast of *campioni*.

ristretto, but you're here for a cold caffeine fix. The coffee granita belongs in a museum: bracing in its bittersweet intensity, alarming in the purity of its flavor and power of its caffeine kick. Try it in a glass with a scoop of thickened cream, or go for glory and have it tucked into a pillow of brioche, made dark with currents of espresso folded into the dough. Be sure to savor this morning moment for everything it's worth; it will be the high point of your day.

You could live a happy life (or a long vacation) in this city subsisting on fried chickpeas and loaded pizza, simmered guts and espresso ice cream, but you would be missing a cornerstone of Palermo cuisine: the trattorie, those bastions of satisfying, inexpensive cooking strewn throughout the city. There's no place better to start your hunt for a trattoria than at Piazza Vigliena, Palermo's central crossroads since the viceroys built the intersection in the 1600s—a model of European urbanization for centuries to come. It's also known as the Quattro Canti—Four Corners; nearly identical at first glance, each corner is marked with a different Spanish king of Sicily, a different season, and a different patroness of Palermo. Each marks the entrance to a different barrio: Albergheria; Seralcadio; Castellammare or Loggia; and Kalsa: the heart of the city.

Positioned on the western corner of the Quattro Canti, Bisso Bistrot is a Palermo institution made new again. For twenty-one years, the restaurant, then known as Santandrea, lived on the edge of the Vucciria Market, one of Palermo's liveliest (and seediest) public spaces. For decades the Bisso family fought a silent battle against the Mafia, refusing to pay *pizzo* (protection money) in an area where organized crime still simmers. After a series of escalating threats, the restaurant was burned badly one night in 2015, leaving the owners to escape out the back door with fifty guests under police protection as firefighters fought the blaze. "We were an absolute anomaly for the 'law' in this neighborhood," patriarch Pippo Bisso told *La Repubblica* shortly after, declaring the restaurant dead.

Bisso Bistrot is its reincarnation, found a few blocks down the road in the space that once housed Libreria Dante, the bookshop of choice for the city's literati. From early afternoon to midnight, the place is packed with a mix of stylish *palermitani* and happy tourists, either smart or lucky. The name sounds French, but the food is pure *palermitano*. The Bisso family matriarch, Anna Maria, handles the cooking, dispatching plates of artichoke *caponata* and swordfish *involtino* to the chattering masses. The fact that you may need to drink a few glasses of zibibbo on the sidewalk before your table is ready says something beautiful about the Palermo spirit: you can bomb it, you can blackmail it, you can push it to the brink, but it can never be defeated.

You'll find trattorie brimming with the spirit of Sicily no matter which direction you head from the Four Corners. At Zia Pina, you will find no menu at all, just Pina and her helpers cooking up great piles of stuffed sardines, baby octopus, and fried red mullet. At Trattoria Basile, you take your ticket and build your meal piece by piece: a few stuffed eggplant, a plate of spaghetti and clams, maybe a bit of grilled sausage. If you can eat more than €5 worth of food, you may secretly be Sicilian. At Osteria Mangia & Bevi, guests eat *pasta fritta*, a crunchy revival of yesterday's tomato-slicked spaghetti, on checkered tablecloths, on bar stools made from wine boxes, on any surface they can find.

The reason the trattoria is so important to Sicilians, though, has little to do with the food itself. It's because meals here are meant to be stretched out over the course of hours, and the trattoria format—appetizers followed by pasta followed by a main course, all washed down with bottles of inexpensive wine—makes a marathon meal feel like a leisurely jog. One of the better meals I eat in Palermo is a three-hour bacchanalia with a pair of Sicilians at the bustling Ferro di Cavallo on Via Venezia, a block east of the Quattro Canti. Waiters press glasses of prosecco into the palms of young *palermitani* gathered out front. Streetlights cast a gentle glow over the sidewalk tables. The menus are printed directly on the tablecloths: €4 for antipasti, €5 for pasta, €7 for meat and fish.

All of this could fall flat, feel too much like a caricature of a Sicilian trattoria, if the food itself weren't so damn good: *arancini*, saffron-scented rice fried into crunchy, greaseless golf balls; *polpette di pesce spada*, swordfish meatballs with a taste so deep and savory they might as well be made of dry-aged beef; and a superlative version of *caponata di melanzane*, that ubiquitous Sicilian starter of eggplant, capers, and various other vegetation, stewed into a sweet and savory jam that you will want to smear on everything. Everything around you screams Italy, but those flavors on the end of the fork? The sweet-and-sour tandem, the stain of saffron, the grains of rice: pure Africa.

The pasta: even better. Chewy noodles tinted jet black with squid ink and tossed with sautéed rings and crispy legs of calamari—a sort of nose-to-tail homage to the island's cherished cephalopod. And Palermo's most famous dish, *pasta con le sarde*, a bulge of thick spaghetti strewn with wild fennel, capers, raisins, and, most critically, a half dozen plump sardines slow cooked until they melt into a briny ocean ragù. Sweet, salty, fatty, funky—Palermo in a single bite.

Yet somehow, even with this lovely bounty before us, the food is overshadowed by the conversation at our table. As we plod our way through the meal, Alessio Genovese, a journalist from nearby Trapani, talks about Palermo's polemical mayor, about Sicily's ambivalent relationship with the rest of Italy, about the microdialects and cuisines found all over the island: "You can move from one village to the next and find that the food and the language have changed completely."

Four times the server comes by to pick up the plate of pasta, and four times she is sent back empty-handed—each time with an increasingly intense waggle from Genovese's finger. I put my fork down an hour earlier, but the two Sicilians push forward, eating, drinking, and talking in such a perfectly balanced manner that time seems to stop moving altogether. The oil from a pasta, the last drops of wine, the final thought in a conversation: crumbs are precious in Palermo, and they will be eaten—with the tines of a fork, the heel of a baguette, or the tip of an index finger.

On the opposite side of the Quattro Canti, back in the heart of Ballarò, a different type of dinner-table conversation is taking place, one that could help reshape Palermo into the twenty-first-century city Mayor Orlando imagines. Moltivolti is not your typical trattoria: founded in 2017, it's a co-working space and kitchen with owners from six different countries. It's a space where refugees can learn Italian, accumulate job skills, share stories with Sicilians. It's also a fully functioning restaurant with a menu that reads like an edible distillation of the Ballarò mosaic: couscous with chunks of braised lamb, spicy Afghan chicken, Greek moussaka, and *pasta alla Norma*, penne with sweet tomatoes, eggplant, and salty ribbons of aged ricotta, the most Sicilian of all pastas.

As I work my way through the Middle East and up through northern Africa, a group of young black men filters through the entrance. One by one they take their seats at a long communal table as bowls of pasta come trickling out of the kitchen: thick noodles with meat sauce heaped well above the brim of the bowl. They arrived last month from Gambia, where so many of Palermo's newest faces come from. "They're not used to eating so much pasta," the server tells me, "but it's growing on them."

Mohamed Shapoor Safari, a chef at Moltivolti, escaped from the Taliban in Afghanistan in the early 2000s and made his way by land and sea to Sicily—an excruciating four-year journey. Now he cooks for one of the restaurant world's most diverse clienteles: well-heeled *palermitani* share communal tables with wide-eyed tourists and recently arrived refugees. Along with his sous chef, a Gambian refugee, he cooks traditional Afghan cuisine, plus Moroccan and sub-Saharan African specialties. He also cooks Sicilian classics: *caponata, pasta con le sarde,*

Moltivolti, where Palermo's past
and future break bread.

arancini—the kinds of dishes whose flavors originally migrated across the Mediterranean. But here in Ballarò, the flavors begin to bleed into one another—the sardines in the pasta get a hit of chili, the slow-braised vegetable curry is enriched with Parmesan, the béchamel in the moussaka is lightened to better match Palermo's steamy climate. "I've learned all the Sicilian classics, but I like to put my own twist on them."

I can tell—from the rapping of his foot on the floor, from the way his eyes never leave the table when he speaks—that he saw a lot on his road to Sicily. Too much. Pakistan, Iran, Turkey, Calabria, searching for something that he found ten thousand miles from Afghanistan, in the heart of this city. "I came to Palermo because it's open to a lot of cultures," says Shapoor. "This is the first place I've found that feels like home."

At the table next to us, a Sicilian-Gambian couple take turns spooning their baby bites of couscous. In the corner classroom, two young students rip a beatbox while the Italian teacher spits out rhymes in Sicilian. Last night Moltivolti hosted women from seven African countries cooking dishes from their respective corners of the continent—a way for them to share and give back to this city they call home, and a lesson for its denizens about the food that will shape its future.

Of course, assimilation has not been so smooth all across Italy. In response to the surge of immigration and the rise of tourism, cities have begun to enact laws "to protect tradition and Italian cultural typicality," as one new ordinance in Verona reads. There, as in Venice, the government has banned kebab shops and other "takeaway ethnic foods." As of 2016, seventy percent of food sold in Florence's city center must be "local food." Some point out that other fast-food operations have been banned as well, but the laws and the local commentary make it clear that immigrant-run restaurants pose a threat to the most sacred cultural institution of all: Italian food. Culinary nationalism is nothing new, but both the tidal wave of immigration and the enduring pride in unembellished Italian food will challenge the country's kitchen landscape for years to come.

For the moment, Moltivolti is an outlier, a rare example of how to turn crisis into opportunity. More than a restaurant, an NGO, or a silver bullet, Moltivolti is an active conversation, one in which everyone from the college professor to the butcher to the war-hardened refugee can participate. In Palermo, those conversations always go down best at the table, surrounded by the tastes and textures that have stitched together the island's disparate cultures for millennia.

❦ 🥕 🍷

That's not to say you can't, you know, do something while you're in Palermo beyond binging. You can tour the city's magnificent churches and museums—from the grand mosaics and golden walls of Cappella Palatina to the jumble of arches and angles and foreign influences reflected in the central cathedral—and make a down payment on the gluttony Palermo is sure to provoke.

You can retreat to the shores on either side of town, to posh places such as Mondello, where the mentholated waters of the Tyrrhenian Sea will accept your bloated body without judgment, just as they do their Sicilian sons and daughters. You can take in a show at Teatro Massimo, as Michael Corleone did at the end of the Godfather trilogy, and hope that your night goes a bit better than his did.

You can seek out market life in the morning and death in the afternoon. At the Catacombe dei Cappuccini, you'll find eight thousand corpses fully dressed, some disconcertingly well preserved, their final thoughts still reflected in their faces. What began as a traditional burial ground for friars in the sixteenth century soon turned into a status symbol for wealthy Sicilians who learned of the catacomb's uncanny ability to preserve bodies; the two-year-old Rosalia Lombardo, the last body to be buried here ninety-two years ago, looks as though she just lay down for a nap.

For a more contemporary reminder of the tragedies trapped within this city, look to the memorials for those who have given their lives fighting the Mafia: one, a sleek black marble column in central Palermo for all of those who have died, the other, just outside of town in Capaci, for one man, Judge Giovanni Falcone, the patron saint of the anti-Mafia movement, who dealt a critical blow to organized crime in Sicily during the Maxi trials of the 1980s. (He operated alongside Orlando, but the two fell out after Orlando made claims about Falcone's collusion with the Mafia.) Falcone traveled with three bodyguards and talked openly about his imminent death; Salvatore "Totò" Riina, a ruthless mob boss, was all too happy to oblige. Riina had a half-ton bomb planted on the highway outside Palermo, which blew Falcone, his bodyguards, and his wife out of existence.

In the months and years to follow, the murders of Falcone and his fellow crusader Paolo Borsellino served to galvanize Sicilians, turning popular sentiment against the often romanticized thugs and murderers of the mob—a reminder that even death has a certain vitality in this town.

Of course, the whole damn island of Sicily is a treasure trove of discoveries, both natural and man-made. Coastal enclaves—Cefalù, Taormina, Siracusa—lay claim to some of Italy's most potent combination of pristine seascape, staggering history, and superlative seafood. On the slopes of Mount Etna, some of Italy's most talented winemakers produce potions of vexing deliciousness. Mountain towns such as Ragusa and Noto will break you with their beauty, their hospitality, their perfect little restaurants. From the ancient chocolate traditions of Modica to the magnificent mezze-and-couscous culture of Trapani to Catania's late-night street feasts of grilled horse and bad decisions, a road trip around the island will leave you love struck for Sicilia.

But as much as I long to venture out across this majestic island, it's hard to escape Palermo's gravitational pull. To fall under the city's spell, you don't need a car, a map, or even much of a plan. You just need to move your feet. In the waning moments of the afternoon, light splinters its way through every orifice in the old part, shooting through cracks, bending around corners, slipping through the great stone arches at the edge of the port. Follow the light and see where it leads you.

It will take you past a street corner where men gather to eat simmered offal from clandestine street carts. (Don't fill up before dinner!) Past the window of a workshop on Via IV Aprile, where inside an old man with wild hair whittles wood into magnificent little toys. (NO PICTURES! an exasperated sign reminds you.) On to Via Alessandro Paternostro, to places such as Bar Salvatore, where people fill the streets in the early hours of the evening for an *aperitivo*, that much-beloved Italian way to warm up for dinner with free bar snacks and booze. (Make it a spritz: prosecco, Aperol, and soda water, the closest thing to a Sicilian sunset in a glass.)

It's not all postcard pretty, of course. Much of Palermo can feel like an archaeological dig suddenly suspended: ancient buildings roped off and abandoned, corridors of plywood that stretch on without

meaning. On the street corners of even the nicest parts of the city's historic district, you'll find garbage stacked up in mountains of stench and decay—a by-product of southern Italy's penchant for strikes, labor disputes, and Mafia mischief making. When I walked by one such prodigious pile on Via Butera, one of Palermo's most elegant streets, and snapped a photo, a man in an apron came out of the corner bar and barked at me, "Great, there you go! A beautiful memory of Palermo!"

By now you probably need another drink. If you're up past midnight and thirsty, you'll find your way to the Vucciria—a small piazza with a few snaking tributaries where the city funnels its hungriest and thirstiest citizens. During the day, when the Vucciria Market stalls line the streets, pushing everything from swordfish to Grana Padano to fake Prada, you can slip in to Taverna Azzurra, sip a €1 glass of marsala from the bodega barrel and listen to the old men talk about Silvio Berlusconi and Serie A in a language no other Italians would understand. (Sicilians—

palermitani in particular—speak a dialect that bears only a passing resemblance to the language spoken on the mainland.)

But on a weekend night you'll find the piazza transformed into a pulsating street party. Grills set up around the sunken piazza sizzle with the scent of *stigghiola*, goat or lamb intestines wrapped around leeks and cooked until they crackle. Music pulses from parts unknown. There is no apparent order: drinks appear magically, music arrives from sources unknown, and smoke, a mixture of charred crustaceans and African hash, hangs thick in the air as throngs of young, drunk *palermitani* and a few lucky visitors push the night until it buckles.

🦐 🍴 🍷

"Palermo is changing. You can see it everywhere," says Nicoletta Polo Lanza Tomasi, the duchess of Palma. We're sitting in the patio gardens of the seventeenth-century Palazzo Lanza Tomasi, the former palace of Giuseppe di Lampedusa. He lived upstairs in the 1950s as he went from café to café in

Palermo, stitching together the scenes that would finally become one of the great masterpieces of Sicilian literature, *The Leopard*.

He would not live to see it published. In fact, just days before succumbing to a tumor on his lung in the spring of 1957, he received his latest rejection letter from the Italian publishing world, a final injustice in a life that had accumulated more than a few as it ground to a halt. He had left his beloved Palermo for Rome, hoping for a cure that would never come. Before setting off for his deathbed to the north, he left a letter to Gioacchino Lanza di Assaro, a distant cousin who had grown so close to Lampedusa in his later years that he had been adopted as his son. He knew his days were numbered:

My dearest Giò,
I am anxious that, even with the curtain down, my voice should reach you to convey to you how grateful I am for the comfort your presence has brought me these last two or three years of my life which have been so painful and somber but which would have been quite simply tragic were it not for you.

He goes on to implore dear Giò to find a publisher, a desire echoed in his tersely worded will ("Needless to say, this does not mean having it published at my heirs' expense; I should consider this a gross humiliation"). Giò did just that; a few months after Lampedusa's death, Feltrinelli Editore in Milan bought the manuscript—and the rights to one of the best-selling novels in Italian history.

For anyone looking to better understand Italy before it was Italy (and Sicily before it was part of Italy), *The Leopard* could be your history book. Set in southern Italy in 1860, in the final throes of the revolution that eventually unified the disparate city-states into the Kingdom of Italy, it grapples with crumbling order, class warfare, and the challenges of a world on the verge of irreversible change. The novel's eventual hero, the dashing liberal Tancredi, is based on none other than Gioacchino himself.

Back then, Gioacchino was one of Palermo's most promising young men—of a respected family, fiercely intelligent, a rising talent in the world of classical music. In 1972, he was named the director of Teatro Massimo, and eventually he went on to run many of Italy's most important opera houses (Rome, Bologna, Naples), as well as the Italian Cultural Institute in New York.

Like most of Palermo's upper class, he left Sicily for the better part of four decades, but in the 1980s, Gioacchino returned with his wife, Nicoletta Polo, and the duke and duchess set about restoring Lampedusa's port-side palazzo, bombed by the Allies in 1943, to its former glory, including converting the extra apartments downstairs into Butera 28, one of Palermo's finest accommodations.

"Thirty years ago, when I arrived, Palermo looked as if the war had just finished," the duchess tells me over afternoon tea in the garden. "Most people had moved into the new part of town. The old part was abandoned. Now we're seeing the rebirth of the historic center. Architects, artists, contractors are all buying and refurbishing this area."

It makes for a great story, one you've

probably heard before: an ancient city fallen into disrepair suddenly rising like a phoenix from the ashes of its former self. Sounds lovely, but no narrative in Palermo is ever so linear. Change is under way here, as it is everywhere, but traditions die hard: the offal still simmers, the old couples still shuffle over the cobblestones, the trash still builds up in impossible piles. If there is one striking change to Palermo, it's the one Mayor Orlando heralds: Ballarò and the blooming of an immigrant nation.

The duke is less optimistic in his assessment of the city. I climb the stairs to see Gioacchino one evening around midnight. Whiskey in hand, he shows me the art gallery and library, the penciled Picasso sketch of his mother ("one of the most beautiful women in Palermo"), and, of course, the original manuscript of *The Leopard*, now kept in a glass case with its own lighting system. I tell the duke I'm rereading the novel, inspired by my stay in one of the downstairs apartments. He smiles broadly. "It is a magnificent work, isn't it?" He says it with the emotion of someone who keeps it on his nightstand. "Remember, it's not a historical novel, it's a psychological one."

The conversation turns toward the city buzzing down below. "The man has lost his wit," he says about the mayor and his more grandiose visions of a new Palermo. "We are in a moment of great change. Italians don't want to be peasants anymore. Tourism one day will be the great business of Palermo, but not now. Not yet. The old city is still abandoned."

The duke tells me that 250,000 people once lived in Palermo's *centro storico*. Today, even with the recent uptick, that number is closer to 25,000, and most of those are immigrants. For the duke, much of the challenge starts with a lack of deep-pocketed citizens who could fuel a revival. "Many of the rich left. They went to Manhattan to buy real estate. That's why we're left without an upper class."

We step out into the warm, sticky humidity of the Sicilian summer. The upstairs palace terrace overlooks the gardens below and, below them, the line of trattorie and gelato shops that runs adjacent to the port.

The duke and duchess of Palma.

And beyond them, the Mediterranean and the bobbing lights of fishing boats and merchant ships trafficking these waters. I imagine one of them to be an official vessel dispatched from Lampedusa, filled with the latest cast of anxious migrants blinking expectantly into the night as the lights of the city grow brighter.

We stand there, covered in sweat, talking quietly under the din of passing traffic, as if sharing state secrets, uncertain when to call it a night.

"I hope he can get it together," he says after a long silence, referring to Orlando. "There's so much work to be done."

Just what that work is depends on where you're standing: on a blanket in Ballarò or above the palace gardens? That's the thing about Palermo; its beauty bends to the eye of the beholder. What is it: a hobbled old man or a wise and elegant matron? a broken promise or a dream still in the making?

Or both?

Lampedusa saw this coming decades ago, immortalizing the central paradox of Palermo in *The Leopard*'s most famous line, spoken by the brave Tancredi, the character the duke himself inspired:

Se vogliamo che tutto rimanga come è, bisogna che tutto cambi.

If we want things to stay as they are, things will have to change.

FOOD
FIGHTERS

Preserving the traditions of Italian cuisine

Manna in the Madonie Mountains, Sicily

THE MEDICINE MAN

Best known as the celestial sustenance God gave to the Israelites during their desert sojourn, manna is the rarest of ingredients, an esoteric sweetener mined from the flesh of ash trees. Manna-rich forests that once covered northwestern Sicily disappeared in the vapors of the twentieth century, but a few fighters, people like Giulio Gelardi, have helped keep manna production alive. Giulio harvests his trees in July and August, cutting a groove into the tree bark to expose a resinous stream, which crystallizes into a sweet stalactite under the heat of the Sicilian sun. More than just the world's top manna producer, Giulio is an evangelist, a passionate exponent of manna's healing properties (good for diabetes, intestinal problems) who starts each day with a chunk. (You can try some at Fud in Palermo and Catania.) "It almost died completely, but there's hope. The youth see it as something magical. And it is."

Amazing Shit

IN THE MIDDLE OF NOWHERE

Great meals are all about context. You'll find excellent food on most city blocks across the country, but you won't always find an experience—a journey that transports you to a world beyond the food on your plate. These are the meals that count, the ones that follow you for the rest of your life. There are hundreds of far-flung feasts worthy of a pilgrimage in Italy, but these four rural gems are as good a place to start as any.

Trattoria La Madia, Brione, Lombardia

BACKROAD BACCHANALIA

To get to La Madia, you'll need to peel off the A4 midway between Milan and Venice, wind your way along the SP19, slicing through villages and Franciacorta vines, until a final series of dramatic switchbacks brings you to the three-street village of Aquilini, where one of Italy's great rural restaurants waits as your reward. Be prepared, because the food comes fast and frequent: a table-swallowing antipasti spread—polenta swaddled in creamy mountain cheese, roast beef with charcoal salt, chicken liver parfait; boundary-pushing pastas, like spaghetti theatrically dressed with molten bone marrow sawed and scooped tableside; and a series of genre-bending *secondi* and *dolci* that will leave you deliriously happy. From dry-aged meats to housemade salumi to an over-the-top coffee service, all of this is way better than it needs to be, way better (and cheaper) than it has any right to be.

Terre di Himera, Termini Imerese, Sicily
ISLAND EDUCATION

Pinched between the Madonie Mountains and the crystalline coastline of Cefalù, Terre di Himera channels the greatness of Sicily's food traditions into one five-room agriturismo. Husband-and-wife team Fabrizio and Maria bake their own bread, press their own olive oil, and produce dozens of local specialties with ingredients either they or their neighbors grow. Spend a day at the beach and return to Maria's remarkable cooking—from category-killing vegetable dishes like eggplant Parmesan and minestrone built with the day's garden yield to local beef and whole fish grilled over a wood fire set beside the olive orchard. Get a good night's sleep, because you have a big breakfast in front of you: fresh ricotta cake, prosciutto and melon, fresh-baked bread and an encyclopedic spread of local meats, cheeses, and fruits. (Seriously, this feast to the left is breakfast for two.) A few days at Terre di Himera is more than a world-class escape, it's an edible education in the traditions and terroir of Sicily.

Osteria Sali e Tabbachi, Lago di Como

OSTERIA DREAMS

Imagine waking up to a life in a tiny village in a quiet corner of Italy, the kind of cozy place foreigners write memoirs about. Now imagine the village osteria, where the old-timers and the *giovani* gather in the mornings for *caffè* and Serie A recaps, in the afternoons for grappa and gossip. Come mealtime, you choose between postage stamps of roasted pumpkin or whatever the fisherman brought in the back door this morning, between a homemade chocolate cake or a local fruit tart, between a last glass at the bar or a nap before sunset. What you're imagining is Ostería Sali e Tabbachi, the sole restaurant in the quiet lakeside hamlet of Maggiana, perched well above the shimmering blue waters of Lago di Como. It's a place worth daydreaming about.

Antichi Sapori, Montegrosso, Puglia

THE GARDEN OF EATING

Down a dusty backcountry road, you come upon a farm: tangles of tomatoes, crawling vines of chlorophyll, a clucking coup of chickens. Past boxes of herbs and leaves, you enter the restaurant and are greeted by a chalkboard menu of the day's vegetables: they will be the stars of your meal, and you're welcome to grab a basket and pick them yourself. Anywhere else in the world this would feel too precious, but Puglia is a place that has long lived from garden to table, and every course from plant whisperer Pietro Zito and his team will be a love letter to the soil of southern Italy: the tomato sauce that jumps off the pasta, the squash blossoms stuffed with ricotta still warm from the morning's production, the eggplant so dense with flavor it tastes like meat. Antichi Sapori is the ultimate expression of Puglia's particular genius, where necessity and skill have turned vegetables into treasures.

RISTORANTE DUOMO

Ciccio Sultano is the island's mad
genius chef, and Ristorante Duomo
is the lab where he stretches the
boundaries of modern Sicilian
cuisine. Expect the unexpected.

PANIFICIO GIUMMARRA

You'll find Ragusa's handheld hero
scaccia, a pizza roll-up with geologic
layers of bright tomato sauce and
caciocavallo cheese, everywhere in
town, but this is the one you want.

RAGUSA

On an island of heartbreaking villages, Ragusa breaks the hardest. It's not just the old city that rises like a baroque stone staircase above a valley of green, or the storied history that brought wave after wave of would-be conquerors, or the fact that, block for block, it's one of the most delicious towns in Italy. It's the whole damn package.

GELATI DIVINI

Sicilians may not have invented ice cream (credit is due, as is so often the case, to the Arabs), but they did perfect it. Divini specializes in wine-based flavors, but does everything well.

LA CASA DEL GELSOMINO

A hall-of-fame B&B, with a lush terraced garden, stunning views from nearly every angle, and a breakfast that will be the high point of your day.

Chapter Five

NAPLES

——

What is the best pizza you've ever eaten? Close your eyes and take a few nibbles in your mind. Was it that picture-perfect pie from the new "artisanal" spot that racked up two dozen likes on your Instagram? The thick and greasy pepperoni-pocked slice from the street-corner shop scarfed down seconds before a taxi swept you home? The wafer-thin pizza at the white-linen restaurant you ate with a fork and a knife and a nice bottle of Nebbiolo? The frozen mini-pizzas Mom would serve as an after-school snack before she pushed on to the night shift? The puffy-rimmed beauty you ate in the warm wood-oven glow on your honeymoon in southern Italy?

If you're anything like me, the question will invite a flood of sweet memories—the exclamation point on a game well played, the umbrella in stormy weather, the scratching of an insatiable itch—but not an answer. That's because it's impossible to answer. Impossible to separate quality from context. Too many slices, styles, shapes, emotions, circumstances. Too many big moments. What is the best pizza in the world? If a tree falls in the woods? The sound of one hand clapping? If anything, it's a bizarro Zen exercise—not to clear your mind but to fill it with warm, toasty, cheesy memories.

But there is one place in the world where pizza isn't a memory. Where it isn't a special occasion or a promise fulfilled or a moment of weakness. Where it isn't even an event. The place where it's life.

Pizza marks the city of Naples in a way that no food in the world has ever marked a civilization of this size: in the pizzerias, 8,200 in total in greater Naples, that line every avenue, every alleyway, every piazza and pedestrian artery; in the tiny glass-windowed carts parked outside bars and cafés filled with bare-bones marinara pizzas ready for a quick snack and the gleaming metal canisters that house *pizzette*, small, barely dressed pizzas baked at dawn and sold throughout the day; in the low, colorful windows in the *centro storico* known as *bassi*, through whose swinging shutters the women of Naples once sold *pizza fritta* directly from their stovetops to hungry passersby; in the ubiquitous statues of the masked Pulcinella, the patron saint of pizza, who watches over the *pizzaioli*, the pizza makers, and blesses each day's batch of dough; in the smell of wood fires and fermentation that, combined with diesel and daydreams, make up the scent of this city.

In the people themselves, the inimitable *napoletani*, the mass of local citizenry powered by pizza—who knife-and-fork it at sit-down restaurants, devour it on sun-bathed street corners, and move about the city clutching *libretti*, simple, lightly dressed pizzas folded into four to make them edible on the run.

Pizza's very DNA is built into the city, and this city into it. Pizza comes with its own economics, its own vocabulary. You can have a *pizza a otto*—eat a pizza today and pay for it in eight days—or opt for a *pizza sospesa*—eat one pizza and pay for two, leaving a surprise for a less fortunate soul to enjoy.

Yes, emblematic dishes have long played outsize roles in the fabric of great cities. Even so, it is entirely possible to think about Philadelphia without thinking about cheesesteak, to drive ten minutes in Valencia without seeing a paella restaurant, to travel to Marseille and not sink a spoon into a single bouillabaisse. But it is not possible to talk about Naples without talking about pizza, to separate one from the other.

From zero to pizza
in sixty seconds flat.

I discovered this all in the most immediate way possible, in 2011, a few days after my thirtieth birthday, when I enrolled in a professional pizza-making course at the Associazione Verace Pizza Napoletana. The AVPN is the closest thing to a governing body in the world of pizza, founded by a coalition of revered pizza makers in Naples who recognized in pizza's global popularity an existential threat to the creation they consider uniquely theirs. They have since trained thousands of upcoming *pizzaioli* and added their official stamp of approval to new pizzerias that meet their strenuous guidelines.

Baked into the charter of the AVPN is a strict definition of *pizza napoletana*, which it regulates down to the last millimeter of its puffy, leopard-spotted crust. To wit:

From the centre the thickness is no more than 0.4 cm (variance ct10% tolerated), and the border that is no greater than 1–2 cm, forming a frame or crust. The crust known as "cornicione" is one of the identifying features of the product. . . .

The cooking of the "Verace Pizza Napoletana" . . . must be done exclusively in a wood fire

oven which has reached the cooking temperature of 485° C, (905F). . . .

Cooking time should not exceed 60-90 seconds.

The consistency of the "Verace Pizza Napoletana" should be soft, elastic, easy to manipulate and fold. The crust should deliver the flavour of well prepared, baked bread. This mixed with the slightly acidic flavour of the densely enriched tomatoes, and the respective aroma of oregano and garlic or basil and the cooked mozzarella ensures that the pizza, as it emerges from the oven, delivers its characteristic aroma—perfumed and fragrant.

The professional course lasts two weeks and includes a handful of different components to ensure that its students learn what it takes to represent Neapolitan pizza around the world: daily lectures on history and theory, visits to producers of the elements of pizza (tomatoes, mozzarella di bufala, "oo" flour), intensive practice sessions guided by exacting professors, and, finally, an apprenticeship in a local pizzeria.

I had recently left a magazine job in New York, settled in Spain, and considered giving up journalism entirely. I had enrolled in the course with the hope of fulfilling a lifelong dream to be a professional pizza man. As a teenager, my earliest kitchen experiments had involved dressing up frozen pizzas with cacophonous spice blends or making my own atop English muffin crusts with bottled tomato sauce and blankets of crispy-edged pepperoni. When I graduated from college in Los Angeles, the blueprints for a grilled pizza business with my girlfriend were scrapped at the last minute when my relationship dissolved and with it my dreams of selling Angelenos $18 fig-and-prosciutto pies with a flame-tickled cracker crust. But my fascination with pizza continued to ferment like a slow-rising, high-hydration ball of dough. I feasted on pizza blogs and forums that discussed topics such as mozzarella moisture content and canned-tomato acidity levels and familiarized me with the parlance of pizza: the *cornicione*, the puffy crust of a Neapolitan pizza; the *panetti*, the balls of dough used to make individual pizzas: the upskirt, named for the lusty glimpse given

to the undercarriage of a pizza (the leopard spotting being the sign of a well-made pie). I spent late nights on websites looking at pictures of pizza ovens. At thirty, I was losing a yearlong battle with writer's block and thought it was time to finally fulfill my wood-fired fantasy.

The AVPN classroom is housed in the basement of a run-down office building on a narrow street adjacent to Poggioreale prison, one of Italy's most overcrowded jails. There are a handful of desks, a whiteboard, two waist-high benches for kneading and constructing pizzas, and, most critically, two thick-domed wood-burning ovens built by local legend Stefano Ferrara. My classmates were a motley mix of international pizza aspirants: Manuela, with a shock of fuchsia hair and a look of mild bemusement frozen on her face ("I'm just here because my boss wants the AVPN certificate in his pizzeria," she said during our round of introductions); Danilo, a smooth-talking Napolitano expat with boy-band good looks and a dream of owning a battery of pizzerias in Toronto, his adopted home; Anliang from Taiwan, quiet and thoughtful, with a wife and kid and a pizzeria waiting for him back in Taipei, who looked at the class as a necessary step on his way to becoming a respected *pizzaiolo* in the Far East. And my favorite of the group, a Korean named Lee Yu Woo, who spoke just a few words of English and even fewer of Italian but managed to articulate his big heart and broad ambitions through a mix of animated facial contortions, wild note taking, and constant photo snapping.

Our professor was Roberto Di Massa, a Naples-born *pizzaiolo* in his late thirties, with the patience of a virgin and the boyish good looks of Michael Corleone just as he took over the family business. Roberto was born to teach pizza—the mixture of earnestness and intimacy he brought to the role convinced us all that we were exactly where we needed to be. He'd start each morning at the whiteboard, teaching us the foundations of Neapolitan pizza philosophy, a mixture of hard science and propaganda that aimed to instill in us the belief that there are two kinds of pizza in the world: Neapolitan and all others.

Roberto would demonstrate the core techniques over and over. Just as a sushi master knows that sushi is 90 percent rice and 10 percent fish, Roberto taught us that pizza starts and stops with the *impasto*, the dough. Anyone can buy good mozzarella or high-quality canned tomatoes, but only a master knows how to handle the nuances and complexities of *impasto*.

Here's how you build a Neapolitan pizza: Place a 250-gram ball of dough on a flour-dusted bench, form your hands into a triangle, and press the dough with your fingertips until a thick circle takes shape. Then, planting your right fingertips in the center of the dough to hold it steady, pinch the perimeter with your left hand and pull. A flick of your right wrist rotates the dough 90 degrees at a time while your left hand does the stretching. Done properly, it's a fluid, nonstop motion of rotating and stretching—no tossing, no fancy tricks, just careful, controlled stretching until you have a shell of uniform thinness. Next, deposit a ladle of hand-crushed San Marzano tomatoes (seasoned with nothing but salt) into the center of the pie and use the back of the ladle to gently work the fruit across the surface of the dough. The pizza is finished with a light scattering of buffalo mozzarella cut into thumb-size chunks, a few scattered leaves of basil, and a figure-eight swirl of extra-virgin olive oil drizzled from a copper pourer. After carefully sliding the raw pizza onto the wooden peel, the *pala*, deposit the pizza onto the oven floor with a quick snap of the arm—a push-pull motion that allows the pie to slide cleanly off the board. Use a metal pizza peel to gently lift the edges of the pizza and rotate it 45 degrees at a time so that it cooks evenly. A properly heated oven burns at 800°F or more, which can turn a raw pizza into a blistered, melted masterpiece in under sixty seconds.

Given the utter simplicity of the ingredients themselves, there is nowhere to hide technical flaws within the puffy-rimmed perimeter of a *pizza napoletana*. Everything comes down to technique, and, as I soon learned, there are a dozen critical junctures along the way where shit can go terribly wrong.

The cooking of a Neapolitan pizza is all about managing moisture. Because the cooking temperature is so high and the cooking period so short, everything needs to be carefully calibrated. Too much water in the dough, and it will rise in ways you can't control at such a high temperature. Not enough flour on your board, and the dough will stick and tear as you stretch it. Too much, and the excess flour will burn and carbonize in the heat of the oven. Distribute the tomatoes poorly, and exposed dough will burn and oversauced areas succumb to the one-two punch of weight and moisture. Water is everywhere on a pre-oven pizza—from the medium-hydration dough (Neapolitan pizza dough is more than 50 percent water by weight) to the tomatoes (almost always canned, always added uncooked to the pizza with nothing more than salt) to the cheese, either *fior di latte or mozzarella di bufala*, both of which come packed in water and weep ivory-colored tears when cut into. Your goal is

Pizza hounds wait for a taste
of the legendary Starita.

to calibrate those levels so that the tomato concentrates, the cheese melts and bubbles, and the dough colors, cooks, and gently crisps all at approximately the same time—no small feat when the heat of the oven can singe your arm hairs from three paces.

Roberto made the creation of a *pizza Margherita* look as ghee-whiz simple as tying your shoes. But on the first day of practice, as he fed the fire with chunks of wood stacked in the corner of the classroom, I quickly realized just how little my previous pizza experience meant in this new arena. I struggled with the moisture levels of my dough, tore holes through it with clumsy stretching, over- and undersauced and -cheesed my pizzas in ways that compromised their integrity. My work inside the oven was even worse: more than once, the pizza stuck to the peel or folded over on itself as I tried to slide it into the oven, burning the cheese and sauce on the heat of the floor, producing great clouds of black smoke that sent students and teachers alike into fits of coughing, and signaling to everyone in the vicinity that a novice was at work.

My classmates all came directly from pizzerias, and though they had their own battles to fight, they were producing respectable pies by the end of the second day in class. My quest for pizza competence would take quite a bit longer, and the idea of the final exam stirred in me a tremendous sense of anxiety. To pass the class and receive the coveted AVPN certification, each student must make two pizzas—marinara and Margherita, Naples' most emblematic creations—and submit them to a panel of judges consisting of the oldest and most-respected *pizzaioli* in Naples. I would need to get my shit together, or my quest to become a certified Neapolitan *pizzaiolo* would incinerate on the oven floor.

🌿 🍃 🍷

Pizza is the world's most popular food. Show me a human being who doesn't enjoy pizza and I will show you a troubled soul. You will find pizzerias in every country and on every continent across the planet—by some estimates, more than a million the world over. There are seventy-five thousand pizzerias in the United States alone, selling $40 billion worth of pizzas every year. Island in Vietnam: pizza. Ghost town in the Midwest: pizza. International Space Station: pizza. (For real: In 2001, Pizza Hut delivered a six-inch salami-topped pie aboard a Russian rocket to astronauts in the International Space Station.)

Pizza is the world's most democratic food. Christians, Muslims, Jews, Hindus; black, white, brown, yellow; omnivores, herbivores, vegans, celiacs: everyone eats pizza in one form or another.

Pizza is the most versatile food. It can be eaten with a knife and a fork at a dinner table, folded and devoured on a street corner, scarfed from a napkin right out of a toaster oven. It can be grilled, baked, fried, and frozen. It can please a crowd of hungry schoolkids, a couple on the verge of romance, a pack of men in suits.

Pizza is the most regionalized food. In Italy, a country not known for its culinary flexibility, pizza takes on nearly as many forms as there are regions, from wafer-thin crusts in Rome to thick, spongy rectangular slices in Sicily. The United States is home to at least a dozen unique regional styles: New York coal-fired pizza, Detroit pan pizza, Milwaukee bar pie, to name a few. Travel around the world and you'll find that the size, shape, and very nature of pizza evolve as you cross borders, time zones, equator.

And depending on whom you talk to, pizza is the most desecrated food. No food has been the vessel for more cultural idiosyncracies than pizza. Chicagoans make it on top of an inch-thick flotilla of flour and oil and layer it with so much cheese, sauce, and toppings that it eats more like a casserole than a pizza. Iranians dip slices in ketchup. South Koreans have an entire pizza subculture dedicated to peculiar pies—sauced with strawberry, topped with snails, housed in crusts cut with cream cheese and sweet potato. If you want to watch an Italian turn San Marzano red with rage, order a Hawaiian pizza, invented by a Greek Canadian restaurateur. Whereas much of the world sees pizza as a cultural canvas, an adaptable disc of dough upon which they can graft their own unique tastes and proclivities, Neapolitans in general and the AVPN in particular don't share this generosity of vision. They view pizza as a product uniquely tied to Naples' history and culture, and they seek to protect it in the same way UNESCO tries to preserve the Parthenon.

No one can deny Naples' preeminence in the evolution of pizza and its dissemination around the globe, but the history of pizza is not linear. It didn't even start in Naples. Humans have been topping flatbreads with various ingredients since Neolithic times, when Neanderthals cooked slips of dough over hot stones and topped them with oil and herbs. Since then, many of the world's greatest civilizations have been powered in part by flatbreads with stuff on top. The ancient Greeks ate *pita* (the most likely etymological root of the word *pizza*). The Persian armies of Darius cooked flatbread on scalding shields and topped it with cheese and dates to nosh on before battle. Traveling west across the Mediterranean, the Catalans and Valencians created *coca*,

crispy, oil-enriched flatbread layered with garnishes both sweet and savory, still very popular today. That some of them developed concurrently in relative isolation underscores the fact that pizza, in its most primitive state, is less an invention than an inevitability: societies geared toward efficiency would eventually find that flatbread made the perfect edible plate. Like nearly all the world's greatest culinary achievements, pizza was not birthed spontaneously in a moment of immaculate conception but evolved over time by circumstance and little bursts of human ingenuity.

Naples took those early, crude beginnings and added shape and substance. With New World tomatoes firmly ensconced in Mediterranean cooking (they gained a foothold in Neapolitan cuisine toward the end of the seventeenth century), it was only a matter of time until they found their way on top of flatbread. Most scholars mark 1734 as the birthday of the *pizza marinara*, still the most fundamental pizza of all, topped with crushed tomatoes, olive oil, oregano, and garlic, its name a reflection of the fact that the pizza was served to seafaring men at the port of Naples. Shortly afterward, Antica Pizzeria Port'Alba, which most food historians consider to have been the world's first official pizzeria, set up business, first as a roving stand for street pizza. A century later, it moved into a brick-and-mortar location on the corner of Via Port'Alba and Via San Sebastiano, where it still serves pizzas today. The emergence of Port'Alba and similar pizza operations also coincided with the arrival of the true protagonist of our story, the *pizzaiolo*, a dedicated craftsperson, a sign of the evolving complexity of the product—not just bread annotated with an extra ingredient or two but a seamless amalgamation of wheat, fat, and produce requiring the touch and dedication of a single producer.

By the turn of the nineteenth century, pizza all but dominated the street culture of Naples. According to Antonio Mattozzi's *Inventing the Pizzeria: A History of Pizza Making in Naples*, a remarkably thorough study, records from 1807 show more than fifty pizzerias operating in Naples.

Alexandre Dumas came to southern Italy sometime later and eagerly reported on the pizza scene unfolding on the streets of Naples: pizza with lard, pizza with cheese, pizza with anchovies. The *lazzaroni*—Naples' rough-edged lower class — that captured Dumas's imagination and pen were the progenitors of pizza culture. Without kitchens and in many cases bathrooms in their humble homes, they took to the streets to spend the little money they had on Naples' emerging staple—one that packed in calories for pennies. As Dumas astutely observed, "A pizza that costs two *centesimi* is enough for a man; a pizza that costs two *soldi* can satisfy a whole family."

The *lazzaroni* cemented pizza's early and enduring reputation as humble food, and with it came the types of social stigmas that kept Naples' upper crust from joining the party. That changed dramatically in 1889, the most famous date in pizza lore, when Raffaele Esposito of Pizzeria Brandi served King Umberto I and Queen Margherita of Savoy his fabled creation: a tomato-and-mozzarella pizza crowned with a few bright leaves of fresh basil, a nod to the brand-new Italian flag, just twenty-eight years after the unification of Italy. In truth, versions of the newly dubbed *pizza Margherita* had existed for more than a century before, but every great hero needs a spectacular birth, and the pizza's basil dalliance is a birthday befitting of pizza's hulking stature. More than a culinary act, *pizza Margherita*'s embrace of the red, white, and green of the Italian flag was a political act, an affirmation of the unification of Italy through one of its most humble regional foods.

In 1905, Gennaro Lombardi, an immigrant from Naples, opened the first pizzeria in the United States, on Spring Street in New York's Little Italy. The coal-fired pies shared much of the spirit of the Neapolitan pizzas they imitated: blistered bottoms, high-temp cooking, restrained toppings. Pizza caught on with the Italian population in and around New York, and just as the rest of regional Italian food evolved through the immigrant experience, so, too, did the Neapolitan staple. As Italian immigrants found success in America, the restrained food of

the poor took on new dimensions: crusts grew thicker, toppings became more abundant, cooking temperatures went down, and cooking times went up.

Pizza's popularity remained primarily contained within two parts of the world for the first half of the twentieth century: Campania and the US Northeast. It wasn't until after World War II, when Allied troops serving in Italy discovered a palate for pizza, that it began to find a broader audience. The United States' role in the global pizza explosion is a controversial one among food historians, one that inevitably releases a flood of nationalist postures and transatlantic recriminations. What can't be disputed is that through American technological evolutions and marketing prowess, pizza began to find a broader audience and a more efficient means of export. From that point, pizza's rise to the top of the food chain was all but inevitable.

Of all the great acts of alchemy executed in kitchens across the world, pizza may be the greatest. Flour, water, yeast, tomato, cheese—on paper, it reads like a shopping list for a household lacking imagination. On the palate, it reads like one of humankind's greatest achievements. Food scientists study a concept called amplitude, the ability of a single food to blend the five major taste groups: sweet, sour, salty, bitter, and savory. I'm no scientist, but I'd bet the farm that no popular food in the world holds a higher amplitude than a Neapolitan *pizza Margherita*. Sweetness and umami from the tomatoes, sour from the lactic punch of real buffalo mozzarella, salt from the dough, and an undercurrent of bitterness from the leopard blistering that marks any wood-fired pizza.

As pizza gained popularity around the world and began taking on new shapes and complexions, the old guard of pizza barons in Naples decided to band together to stake their claim on the global sensation. The AVPN, formed in 1984 by a group of twenty of Naples' most vaunted *pizzaioli*, started by defining the very dimensions of pizza—"from the centre the thickness is no more than 0.4 cm (variance ±10% tolerated)"—then, with the support of the Naples gov-

ernment, set up a system of training and certifying *pizzaioli* in the official creation of "true Neapolitan pizza."

Pizza napoletana may be the original form of pizza as we know it today, but for some—for those who like their pizza with textural contrast, who don't consider pizza a knife-and-fork proposition—it doesn't always deliver. Neapolitan pizza can be a violent enterprise—the high temperatures, the aggressive blistering, the miasma of cheese and sauce and rendered fat that leave the center of a pizza almost soupy. The resulting pizza is relentlessly soft, yielding, fickle, unforgiving. It is a game of centimeters and seconds—the difference between a subpar pizza and a superlative one is a blink of an eye in the mouth of the oven.

Anthony Mangieri, the infamously cantankerous *pizzaiolo* of Una Pizza Napoletana in San Francisco, once told me that only 10 percent of his pizzas were truly exceptional. And this from a man who has dedicated his entire life to making little more than *pizza Margherita*. The pizza world is filled with people—professionals and civilians alike—

who believe Neapolitan pizza to be over-rated. Neapolitan pizza detractors started to surface nearly as soon as the creation itself. In his 1847 story collection *Napoli in Minia-tura*, Gaetano Valeriani wrote, "Sometimes raw tomatoes are put on top . . . sometimes fish, sometimes cheese . . . and prepared like this they are put in an oven and burned. Heaven help us! All one's digestive forces are in difficulty for half a day with this undi-gested weight occupying them!"

The AVPN's principal mission is to ensure a baseline of quality for any pizza bearing the Neapolitan branding. Antonio Pace is the founder and president of the AVPN: thick glasses, pizza maker mitts, deadly serious demeanor, all wrapped up in a dark suit and tie. He has presided over the organization since its onset, during an immense surge in global interest in true Naples-style pizza. Today, you'll find AVPN-certified pizzerias in twenty-nine countries, more than 650 establishments in total. The bulk of those are found in the United States, Japan, and Australia, but AVPN-certified pizzas can be enjoyed

by the fine people of Brasilia, Taipei, and Evansville, Indiana, as well.

To maintain quality, Pace and a delega-tion of pizza luminaries travel the world, promoting Neapolitan pizza and ensuring that member pizzerias maintain the high standards set by the AVPN. "We protect *pizza napoletana* from imitations. We pro-tect the origins of pizza, which are intrinsi-cally linked to the heart of our city." Pizza may go to many places beyond their reach, but the world should never forget who in-vented pizza culture and who perfected it.

Today the AVPN has an app you can download to your smartphone that pro-vides both a database of reliable and "au-thentic" pizzerias around the world and the ability to flag pizzas that don't deliver on the organization's strict definitions and standards of quality. Upload a photo of a suspect pizza and the AVPN will inves-tigate: the pizza police, to protect what's served. "We have to be one hundred per-cent certain that they follow our rules," says Pace. "If they don't, we'll take back their membership card. It's our property."

DRESSING

Thin-crust, quick-fired pizzas don't have the structural integrity to withstand heavy toppings. *Pizzaioli* must have a light hand.

STRETCHING

No fancy tossing—just methodical hand-stretching. One hand rotates the dough, the other gently pulls.

COOKING

A proper wood-fired oven burns at 480°C, turning a pizza from raw to blistered in under 90 seconds.

SLIDING

Moving the pizza from the counter to the peel requires a delicate touch. This is the last chance for the *pizzaiolo* to stretch the dough and adjust the toppings.

Why so serious? Can't people just cook what they want and let eaters vote with their forks and wallets? Wrapped up in this is a broader discussion about culinary ownership and appropriation that will only grow more complicated as food continues to evolve in its journey around an increasingly borderless world. Culinary authoritarianism is fraught with potential perils, but the AVPN rightly recognizes that the stakes are high. Pizza is a $100 billion business, and those who helped create it want their fair slice. But, more important, pizza is their heritage, their DNA, and they'll be damned if some Yankee with a can of pineapple and a slab of bacon is going to fuck it up.

"Pizza in most of the world is a thirty-year story. In Naples, the story is two hundred years old," says Pace. "The important thing is that they don't call it *pizza napoletana. Napoletana* is a valuable brand, and it can't be devalued. If they can't maintain our high standards, they'll need to call it something else."

The AVPN is on the move and looking to expand. It has a branch in Los Angeles that handles certification for many of the North American outposts, but Pace says it's looking to open schools elsewhere. "We want to expand our reach and take the pressure off our Naples facility." With the expanding worldview has come the slightest crack in the traditionalist stance: "When innovation creates a better product, we adapt it; if it compromises quality, we reject it."

But despite the flexible posture, Pace is a purist at heart, as I imagine all ranking members of the AVPN are. "The most extraordinary invention ever was the *Margherita.* Sometimes I eat pizza with anchovies, sometimes I eat marinara. But if I eat 300 pizzas a year, 295 are Margherita."

I got my shit together. Slowly. It started in the classroom, through the penetrating rhythms of repetition. Knead, shape, stretch, dress; insert, rotate, remove—over and over, dozens of pizzas every morning flying out of the ovens before lunchtime. We worked in teams, taking turns as *piz-*

zaioli, on the bench making pizzas, and as *fornai*, sliding the pizzas into the oven and cooking them. Roberto taught us that Neapolitan pizzas are cooked via a trio of heat sources, radiant, ambient, and convection: the heat of the fire itself plus the heat accumulated on the oven floor and the mass of swirling heat built up inside the oven dome. With so much energy moving about, it's not enough to simply insert a pizza, then remove it once it's done; you must rotate it, expose bare parts directly to the flame, ensure that each centimeter is evenly subjected to the three forms of heat. Roberto liked to say that a good *fornaio* is every bit as vital as a good *pizzaiolo*—and if you've ever seen a pizzeria in full Saturday-night mode, with a *fornaio* juggling five or six pizzas at a time in a ferocious oven, you'll understand why.

Kids from the middle school next door to the AVPN classroom knew the routine. Around 11 A.M., when the oven ejected blistered pies every sixty seconds, they would take their places at the doorway and mix pleas for pizza with running commentary on the quality of our work. In some ways,

they were our toughest critics, young, picky *napoletani* who knew nothing of pizza theory or science or history but knew down to the millimeter of crust and the grain of salt how a pizza should look and taste and feel.

We made dough as every *pizzaiolo* in Naples did—first proofing it in a huge, unwieldy mass, then separating it into *panetti*, 250-gram balls (the standard weight of a Neapolitan pizza) before a second proofing. Every day the dough would emerge in a different state—from taut and compact to wet and flaccid, depending on whether it had rained overnight, the residual oven heat had lingered longer than normal, or there had been small, imperceptible differences in the way we had kneaded it by hand. Roberto would keep us calm, and teach us the little tricks of working with a bad batch—the dusting of flour or the flick of the wrist that brought order back to a chemistry of chaos. His assistant, Paolo, was everything that Roberto wasn't: loud, brash, narcissistic, *napoletano*. He spent the better part of the class telling stories of pizza exploits and performing dough-spinning tricks as we feigned excitement and tried to go about our business.

At all times, Naples purred in the background. At first the city feels like a shapeless mass, a miasma of traffic and noise and animated activity running on a steady diet of oven-baked wheat and oil-thick espresso. One of the many disputes between the city government and the sanitation industry, controlled by captains of the underworld, had gripped the city, and bags of trash were piled high and filled the streets with light notes of decay, mitigated only by the cool winter weather.

But slowly, as the days ticked off, the city began to take shape. What first appears as abject chaos—in the way cars move, the arguments had across apartment balconies, the way citizens order food or drink at a bar—reveals its own inner logic. The city's many idiosyncrasies slowly morph from frustrations to charming eccentricities to fundamental markers of a civilization surviving and thriving by its own far-fetched rules. Naples, as no other city I know, has swagger, and swagger goes a long way, espe-cially with history and culture to back it up.

There are few European civilizations that haven't set up shop in Naples at one time or another: The ancient Greeks founded it in 2000 B.C. and eventually shaped it into one of the most important cities in Magna Graecia. The Romans eventually came along and stuck around until their empire crumbled in A.D. 485. The Byzantines took over soon after, creating the Duchy of Naples, an independent state governed by military command that lasted for nearly five hundred years, until the Normans conquered the city and made it part of the Kingdom of Sicily.

During the ups and downs, the temporary residents each left a footprint in the wet cement of Naples: the Hohenstaufens created the University of Naples, one of the oldest and largest in the world; Charles I, king of Sicily, ushered in an era of Gothic architecture that still defines the cityscape today; and under the Aragonese, Naples became a center of the Italian Renaissance, establishing the city as a creative stronghold for centuries to come.

The Spaniards couldn't get enough of Naples—they made it one of their principal ports in the sixteenth and seventeenth centuries, and under their rule from across the Mediterranean, the city prospered. The arts and academics flourished as Naples grew into the second largest city in Europe, after Paris. But not everyone shared in the good times equally, and eventually the citizens, incensed by high taxes, rose up against the Spanish crown. The two struggled back and forth until 1656, when a plague wiped out half of the city's population, and Naples slipped into decline.

By the eighteenth century, Naples was on the rise once again. In 1734, the two kingdoms united into one ruled by Charles of Bourbon, thus initiating the reign of Bourbons and the Republic of Naples. In 1806, Napoleon disrupted the Bourbon party, but only temporarily: with the help of the Austrian Empire, the Bourbons defeated the Bonapartes in the Neapolitan War and reinstalled Ferdinand IV as king of Naples. It wasn't until late 1860, when Giuseppe Garibaldi's volunteer army defeated the Neapolitan forces in the last major battle before Italy's unification, that Naples found a measure of political stability.

Today, with a population of a million strong, Naples is Italy's third largest city and its most densely populated. You'll find a staggering 448 churches in Naples, and the historic city center, the largest in Europe, is a UNESCO World Heritage site. As the seat of Campania, it stands sentinel over one of the country's most astonishing displays of geography: the grape- and grain-covered hills of the interior, the pulse-racing cliffs of the Amalfi coast, and always the outline of Vesuvius lurking in the background, the shadow of all that's beautiful and tragic about this land. It doesn't take much imagination to understand where its most infamous idiom comes from: *Vedi Napoli e poi muori*. See Naples and die, because once you've seen Naples, you've seen it all.

During the few hours of downtime we had in the early afternoon, we'd wander as a crew—me, the redhead from Bologna, the Taiwanese Jedi, and Lee the big-hearted Korean—through the narrow, chaotic streets of old Naples, devouring pizzas from the most renowned ovens in the city. We tried *pizza fritta* at Di Matteo, where framed pictures of the owner and Bill Clinton greeted the swarms of clients waiting for their seats. We beat the crowds at L'Antica Pizzeria Da Michele, among the most famous pizzerias in the world, only to be disappointed—a cheap, solid pizza made with middling ingredients. We made a pilgrimage to Pizzeria Brandi, where that first fateful *pizza Margherita* was served, and washed down the history with a round of Peronis. Combined with the Margheritas and marinaras we ate during class, I was consuming seven or eight pizzas a day.

One day we visited a buffalo mozzarella producer on the outskirts of Naples. The cheese makers screened a video of hump-backed animals eating grass and spurting milk, then brought out massive mounds of still warm mozz, which we devoured with plastic forks. Another day, we hit the Antico Molino Caputo flour factory on the outskirts of the city. Caputo, more than any other product, is the lifeblood of

Naples pizza culture. Its fine-milled "oo" flour is the grain that forms the base of nearly every slice you consume in the city, and if you own and operate an AVPN-certified pizzeria elsewhere in the world, it's all but guaranteed that you have a contract with Caputo. *Pizzaioli* the world over wear Caputo caps and aprons and stack their red-and-blue sacks of Caputo flour head high in the kitchen. It's a badge of sorts, an assurance that someone understands the inexorable bond between Naples and pizza with a thin, puffy crust.

Our field trip to Stefano Ferrara's pizza oven factory produced no small amount of product lust among the students. We hungrily cased the massive warehouse, moving from one gorgeous oven to the next, convincing ourselves that one of those beauties was all that stood between us and pizza greatness. Danilo, the Italian expat with plans to open multiple pizzerias in Toronto after graduating from the class, began to negotiate with a sales rep right there on the spot, and by the time he departed Naples, his oven was in a crate on a boat bound for

AVPN, class of 2011.
The author is at the far right.

North America. For my part, I spotted a lipstick-red midsize *forno* with a dimpled dome like a breast with goose bumps and, in my head, began to build my future pizzeria around its gentle curves.

But I still needed to pass the class, which was no easy task at my current rate of evolution. I had myself pegged as the worst *pizzaiolo* of the group at the onset and was fighting to climb out of the cellar. I had trouble working the dough into consistent, uniform circles; I struggled to deposit it cleanly on the oven floor; I burned or flipped or misshaped nearly half the pizzas I made—a ratio that would not serve me well in the one-and-done final exam.

The pizzeria internship is the final component of the AVPN class, and the organizers dispatched me to Pizzeria Vesi, a midlevel operation with four outposts across the city. A more Neapolitan pizzeria you wouldn't find anywhere in the city—not in the camera-ready rustic pizzeria sense but in its status as a bare-bones restaurant that fed the neighborhood its daily dose of carbs and fat, whose employees approached their jobs with something between mild amusement and outright contempt. They projected a similar cocktail of contempt onto the young Californian suddenly clogging up the arteries of the kitchen.

The head *pizzaiolo*, Nino, was a fast-talking, fast-moving local in his early thirties just showing the first signs of a pizza-and-beer belly beneath his faded Caputo shirt. At first he seemed annoyed to have to worry about an extra head, and he dispatched me to the basement of the kitchen every evening to make dough. On a weekend or a night of a big soccer match, Vesi might sell 150 pizzas or more, and the workers typically made their dough in a massive machine that looked like an industrial cement mixer. But Nino insisted that I make every batch by hand, and he would come down occasionally to smoke cigarettes and smirk while I struggled to wrap my skinny arms around a ball of flour and water the size and composition of a small waterbed. Most nights, by the time I made it back to my *pensione*, I could barely lift my arms to get the key into the door.

Vesi, like most pizzerias, served pasta and salads and a few other side dishes, but the main business was pizza, a good percentage of it takeout or delivery. They served the standard range of Neapolitan pies: nearly three dozen in total, ranging from restrained (marinara, diavola, funghi) to the more enterprising (topped with fresh arugula, prosciutto crudo, sautéed greens). My favorite, the one I made for myself at the end of every shift, was quintessential Campania: *salsiccia e friarielli*, the bittersweet edge of the cooked greens playing perfectly off the warm, salty fat of the rendered sausage.

In the down moments, all talk turned to S.S.C. Napoli, the sacred soccer team of the city. If soccer is a religion in Naples, as it is everywhere in Italy, Diego Maradona, the hard-charging Argentine who brought the city its greatest moments of joy during his eight-year run as the team's divine striker, is its god. The fact that Maradona had been such a disaster personally—including his friendship with both cocaine and the Camorra—only seemed to amplify his heroic status, especially among my pizza partners,

who took to playing old clips of the short, stocky striker weaving through defenders, coked out of his mind. They'd pause it on moments when he'd rub his nose or wipe it across his forearm and collectively lose their minds. "*Vedi! Vedi!* I told you!" Everything Maradona did, from leading Napoli to its first Serie A championship in 1987 to the *mano de Dios* World Cup goal that he scored with his hand, he did with verve and swagger and contempt for the letter of the law, a trait that made him a true *napoletano* in the eyes of local worshippers.

Eventually Nino took pity on me and brought me up from the basement. I told him in my broken Italian that I needed desperately to pass my exam, and to do so I would need to practice with the pressure of a real restaurant. Somewhere along the way he hatched a plan to open a wildly lucrative pizzeria in Barcelona, with me as his conduit, which suddenly increased his interest in seeing me succeed. He didn't have the patience or the skill of Roberto, but his lessons on speed and the balance between being perfect and being good enough more closely approximated what life in a pizzeria would be like. When orders slowed down, he'd tell his *fornaio* to take a break and let me step in to handle a few of the pizzas. We devoured my early mistakes, but eventually, the pizzas began to emerge from the oven looking like something customers might—and indeed did—pay for.

The day of the big exam loomed large on the horizon. Nino gave me pep talks at night, peppered with romantic visions of our burgeoning Barcelona business and enough local dialect to leave me both inspired and confused. Roberto's guidance proved more measured and reliable: "You have just two pizzas to make. Check the oven temps carefully before starting, flour your boards, work quickly but calmly."

On the morning of the exam, with the pizza dignitaries dressed in suits and gathered around the judging table like the heads of the Five Families, we retrieved our containers of dough and opened the lids to find a ghastly scene staring back at us: a mixture of heat and humidity had melted the rows of individual balls into one large, almost indistinguishable mass. For a split second, Roberto's face went pale and a few foul words escaped under his breath. Then he regrouped, pulled out a spatula, and began to carve out individual pieces of dough from the blobs before us. We huddled around him, shell-shocked players looking up to the rock-steady coach for our final marching orders. "Breathe," he said, perhaps as much to himself as to us. "You've worked with dough like this before. You have just two pizzas to make. Check the oven temps carefully. Go lighter on tomato and cheese. Keep everything well floured."

I went second. I scooped my sagging dough from the container, deposited it on the board, hit it with flour, took a deep breath, and went to work. I started with the marinara, in principle the easier of the two. But there's also nowhere to hide technical flaws on a marinara—no cheese or toppings to cover up imperfections. I took extra time spreading the sauce across every centimeter (unsauced real estate will burn in the oven), placed five thin slices of garlic in the sea of red, then hit it with a fistful of dried oregano. It wasn't beautiful, more ovoid than circular, but I delivered it with a smile to the judges and went back to my station before they could react.

While they dissected the marinara, I turned to the Margherita. I took the same care ladling the sauce, gave the cheese a few shakes to wick off any extra moisture, swirled a perfect figure eight of olive oil over the top. But those were precious seconds I was adding to an already fragile process, and by the time I wrapped my fingers underneath the pizza to initiate the slide onto the peel, I could feel that something was wrong. I gave it a light tug, but it didn't budge from the board. Another pull: nothing. Stubborn, obstinate, stuck. I tried to shimmy it off the board with some extra wrist action, but just as it looked to be releasing, a hole ripped through the center of the pizza—and right through the center of my future as a *pizzaiolo*.

Roberto wasn't going to let it end this way. He turned to the judges, told them about the dough struggles, how we couldn't be blamed for the severity of the situation,

and pleaded with them to give me another shot. After exchanging a few whispers with the others, the president gave me a reluctant nod. I didn't make the same mistake the second time: I threw down a thick coating of flour on the board, stretched and dressed the dough as quickly as possible, got it onto the peel and into the oven. What emerged, shockingly enough, looked like a textbook Margherita. The judges found only one fault—the excess flour on the bottom had carbonized in the oven and given the pizza a lightly bitter background. "Beyond that, it's a very good pizza. *Complimenti*."

I passed.

🌿 🍃 🍷

In the years that followed, my fellow alumni spread the gospel of Neapolitan pizza culture around the world. Danilo took his Stefano Ferrara oven and built around it a pizzeria of instant success in downtown Toronto. Anliang returned to Taiwan and began to build out his own empire across Taipei. Manuela took her burgundy locks and her acerbic wit back to Bologna, where she makes honest pizzas for takeout and delivery on a side street in the old city. The AVPN certificate hangs on the wall, even if the owner doesn't want to spend the money to do true Neapolitan pizza. And Lee, after clocking an extra internship in Naples (to make it really count), returned to Seoul and, with his mixture of passion and precision, soon took up the throne of pizza king of South Korea. Years later, I visited Spacca Napoli on a frigid Saturday night, standing in a line of young Koreans that stretched deep into the winter darkness. After eating a few of the finest Neapolitan pizzas I'd eaten anywhere—the soppressata crisped and curled around the edges, the San Marzano tomatoes as bright as a desert sunrise, the swollen, fire-pocked crust exhaling breaths of yeasty steam as I tore into it—Lee and I embraced, took selfies backlit by the red glow of his jam-packed oven, and drank wine and talked pizza deep into the next morning.

The only student not to parlay the AVPN certificate into a career was me; I am a *pizzaiolo* by decree only. Nino, ecstatic when he learned the result of my final exam, sent me a handful of emails over the following months, asking about the pizza scene in Barcelona. I looked at some spaces, thought about what it would be like to spend twelve hours a day stretching dough, scattering cheese, and feeding the oven, and decided I didn't have the fortitude for it. As I got back to writing full-time, I turned pizza into a side project, worthy of intense study, constant at-home practice, and the type of bookish obsession that can ferment only at a comfortable distance.

I traveled the world, finding the Neapolitan footprint growing deeper everywhere I turned. In New York, the wood-burning ovens of new joints inspired by Naples lit up lower Manhattan like an urban bonfire. A *pizzaiolo* in Portland made me a Margherita worthy of the queen herself from an oven resting on a truck bed. In Japan, I saw why one of the AVPN's ranking members once whispered to me that the Japanese, not the *napoletani*, make the best *pizzaioli*. I found maddeningly good Neapolitan pizza not just in Tokyo but on a side street in Hiroshima, on the second floor of a Kobe office building, in a cabin in the woods in Hokkaido. Blackout good.

The one place I didn't eat Neapolitan pizza: Naples. I left a few hours after claiming my diploma and posing for pictures with pizza royalty, and haven't been back since. But throughout it all, I've felt a gravitational pull from Campania, from those wild, pizza-paved streets, as if I've left some important unfinished business behind. I've been told that change is afoot in the pizza world there, which has only fueled my longing to go back. What once appeared a totemic and immutable part of the Neapolitan fabric shows signs of slow alteration: new ingredients, new techniques, new tenets that slowly mutate the once untouchable approach to pizza.

I learn most of this from a new friend, a pizza partner in crime par excellence. I meet Luciana Squadrilli in Rome, ostensibly to discuss pasta and the new Roman kitchen, but once our mutual muse spills out onto the dinner table, it's tough to put it back into the box. Luciana is a food writer who is based in Rome but grew up in the center of Naples and who knows as much about Italy's pizza culture as anyone working today. Her book *La Buona Pizza*, coauthored by Tania Mauri and Alessandra Farinelli, is a stirring love letter to the food of her childhood. It tells the stories of ten of Italy's most influential *pizzaioli* and is a generous view of the country's regional pizza culture, though Luciana's heart (and stomach) belongs to Naples.

Luciana can tell you where Enzo buys his cheese. Where Salvatore sources his wood. How long and at what temperature Franco ferments his *impasto*. Her phone rings every few hours with a call from another top *pizzaiolo* around Naples, ready to dish the fire-roasted gossip of the day. If there is a controversy stirring—and controversy in the pizza world is as constant as the rising dough—Luciana will be the first to know about it. She has also spent the better part of the last two years traveling Italy, tasting and studying the regional differences of Italy's pizza masters, so she has a

PIZZA'S VERY DNA IS BUILT INTO THE CITY, AND THIS CITY INTO IT.

unique trait that eludes many Naples pizze-rati: perspective. Together, over a bottle of prosecco and Roman cracker-thin pizzas, we hatch a plan to travel south together.

We convene in Naples on a brilliant spring morning. Luciana wants to get right to the heart of the matter, so we start in the molten center of the city's pizza culture, Sorbillo at 32 Via dei Tribunali. While the first diners gather outside the restaurant door, an hour before the first pizza will come out of the oven, Gino Sorbillo invites us next door to La Casa della Pizza, an apartment that doubles as an office and pizza clubhouse, complete with newfangled tools and ingredients, stacks of pizza paraphernalia, and a gorgeous wood-burning oven.

"My pizza is good. Nothing more." It's one of the first things Gino tells me as I take a seat across the desk from him. He says it again while we sip espresso, and later over lunch. *È una pizza buona e basta.* He says it so often that it feels like a nervous tic, a way of deflecting the world's attention, a way of apologizing for the unyielding crowd gathered on his doorstep, for his saucy line

of pizza-related products, for his star turn on *Master Chef*, where he makes and breaks the futures of Italy's young chefs. For being the most famous *pizzaiolo* in the world.

It's not all his fault, of course. Many forces must conspire to allow someone to become internationally famous for making pizza. In Gino's case, those forces include impeccable timing, savvy self-promotion, and coming from a long line of *pizzaioli* that established a beachhead for the Sorbillo family in the center of Naples back in 1935.

"My pizza story is a story of courage," he likes to say. Not just his own courage, but that of his grandfather and father. Luigi and Carolina Sorbillo had twenty-one children, all of whom went on to work in the pizza industry in some way—including the firstborn, Esterina, who spent sixty-three years working for the family pizzeria, and the nineteenth-born, Salvatore, Gino's father. Together they maintained a successful family pizza operation during a time when nobody ran a small business in Naples without paying their dues to the mob. But the Sorbillo clan, despite all the evidence to the contrary, thought it best to deny the criminals their share. That was an unthinkable act of defiance at the time, and, ironically enough, it enabled both the pizzeria and the family to survive and prosper.

But it was Gino who made the Sorbillo name synonymous with Neapolitan pizza excellence. He added to this legacy of courage and determination an ambitious fervor, a spark of marketing genius, and a boundless supply of charm that provided just the right kindling to his wood-fired rocket ship. The fact that he brought those elements to bear right as the world's obsession with pizza was hitting a fever pitch only added to his stardom.

He found a platform on social media and through the press that no *pizzaiolo* before him had tapped into. He served as a judge on Italy's hugely popular *Master Chef*. He ran for mayor of Naples. He published politically charged editorials about the mafia in national newspapers. In response to southern Italy's relentless corruption, he hung a sign from the pizzeria window: AT MY RESTAURANTS, PIZZA FOR POLITICIANS

COSTS 100 EUROS. FOR THE NORMAL CITIZEN, 2. He's been known to write political messages—"Up with gays, down with the Mafia!"—in mozzarella before baking it in the pizza and sharing it with his 175,000 followers on Facebook and Instagram. Gino's brand of pizza populism has made friends in high places; in 2015, Pope Francis publicly blessed a Margherita from Sorbillo.

It's also made him a few powerful enemies. In 2012, a fire burned down a large part of Sorbillo. Most believe the Camorra started the blaze in response to Gino's very public refusal to pay kickbacks. Three days later, Gino had the oven firing once again, making an already beloved *pizzaiolo* even more famous in Naples and beyond.

The role of the *pizzaiolo* has changed dramatically in the past decade. For most of pizza's history, the *pizzaiolo* was among the hardest-working figures in the restaurant industry—responsible for making dough by the ton, building and feeding a steady fire, and shaping and cooking anywhere from dozens to hundreds of pizzas in a shift, all of which required a mixture of physical strength, mental fortitude, and if not a love of, at least an abiding respect for, repetition. Such pizza makers still exist, to be sure, but just as chefs have climbed out of the kitchen and into the role of speakers, philosophers, and rock stars, the most accomplished *pizzaioli* have become public figures, influencers, preachers with a ravenous pulpit.

"It used to be that the *pizzaiolo* wasn't supposed to speak," says Gino. "My father didn't say a word. He got behind the counter and did his thing. That's changed. Suddenly *pizzaioli* have a voice, and with that voice comes responsibility."

Now he has his own pizza palace in the heart of Naples where luminaries of the pizza world and beyond come to pay their respects, drink artisanal Sorbillo beer, tell war stories, and push the boundaries of what it means to be a *pizzaiolo*. The kitchen is filled with rare oils and esoteric flours and ingredients that producers hope to squeeze onto the Sorbillo menu. Photos of Very Important People eating pizza cover the walls; desks and tables house pizza tchotchkes, including Gino Sorbillo action

figures. To underscore the trajectory, Gino shows me his original office downstairs, a sweaty, claustrophobic space no bigger or cozier than a phone booth. "I started in here fifteen years ago. Imagine!"

We make our way through the traffic jam at the front door and into a restaurant buzzing with a full-throttle lunch crowd that won't relent for another three hours. We circle through a massive prep kitchen, Gino's unbridled enthusiasm pouring out at every turn. He speaks quickly and constantly, powered by half a dozen espressos and a reservoir of pizza passion, punctuating his points with hand chops and facial contortions. He shows us the dishwasher and the walk-in fridge and the cutting boards used for prep. At one point, he feeds pizza crusts down a new-age garbage disposal with the wide-eyed wonder of a kid melting a plastic action figure with a magnifying glass.

The centerpieces of the operation are two bright red Stefano Ferrara pizza ovens, lined up side by side like two Ferraris at the starting line, ready to whisk their passengers from raw to blistered in sixty seconds flat. Gino stands before them, his hands on his hips, the red curls of fire reflected in his spectacles. "This is our war machine. Fifteen hundred pizzas a day." He says it as if he still can't believe the number.

Before we eat, I ask Gino if he'd mind if I stood in the kitchen and watched his team work the busiest pizza service I've ever seen—in Gino's estimation, a relatively quiet Thursday afternoon. Two *pizzaioli* man the benches, stretching and dressing pizzas at a speed that would require slow motion to fully pick apart. Once dressed, a *fornaio* appears, unprompted, with a ready peel. The two guys working the peels say nothing to each other; each knows from instinct and body movements imperceptible to the naked eye exactly what the other is going to do next, so that the pizzas remain in a state of constant motion—from the bench to the peel to the oven floor to a cooler part of the oven floor to the peel to the serving tray, never spending more than fifteen seconds in a resting state. The performance is orchestral in its synchronicity, its instinctual complexity.

As in most busy Naples pizzerias, servers themselves take on a vital role in the cooking process, drizzling oil, applying arugula, laying out veils of prosciutto crudo and other delicate garnishes as soon as the pizzas emerge from the ovens. From that moment on, every second counts, the half-life of a Neapolitan pizza as short as the walk from oven to table.

A sentence in all caps red type runs through the center of the Sorbillo menu: IN HOMAGE TO THE ONLY FAMILY IN THE WORLD COMPOSED OF 21 CHILDREN, ALL OF THEM PIZZAIOLI. The pizzas below it bear the names of Luigi and Carolina's twenty-one offspring. The Ciro: buffalo ricotta, extra-virgin olive oil, basil. The Rodolfo: cherry tomatoes, smoked provolone, prosciutto di Parma. The Vittorio: tuna, wild oregano, Taggiasca olives. We take a seat at a countertop looking out onto the street. Guidebook-clutching passersby peer in with hungry eyes. Gino disappears into the kitchen and reemerges minutes later with a *pizza fritta*, the Naples specialty, a sealed half-moon stuffed with ricotta lightened with a wisp of lemon rind. State-fair food of the highest order. *Pizza fritta* is one of the earliest pizza evolutions in the city, a form that didn't require an oven and a cord of firewood to make. Surely movie fans remember a hot and bothered Sophia Loren in *L'Oro di Napoli*, Naples' sacred cinematic treatise, selling *pizza fritta* on the street from her bubbling cauldron.

Next comes Gino's Margherita, the edible flag, the measuring stick for *pizza-ioli* the world over. It swallows the plate whole, its zebra *cornicione* touching the table, the undercarriage almost sticky with the aggressive union of grain and heat. If you landed in Naples from Berlin or Boise and came straight here, this pizza would be a seminal life moment, the kind that gets its own shelf in the food archives of your mind.

The final pie falls into the camp of pizzas of provenance, built around a roster of ingredients that come with their own geo tags: yellow and red cherry tomatoes of Technicolor intensity, black olives from

Matese, chunks of anchovies from Cetara, *fior di latte* from pampered water buffaloes. It's a punched-up play on what non-Naples pizzerias might call the *napoletana*, the brightness of the tomato combo and the acidity of the buffalo mozz keeping the intense bursts of salt from the olives and anchovies in balance.

For Gino, pizza is instinctual. Making it and sharing it are acts of love and generosity. "Pizza shouldn't be technical. It should be enjoyable. I thought it was a bit banal, all of the tiny details—whether you spread your tomato in a circle or in an eight, how you add your cheese. I'm not concerned about those things. I make a good pizza. That's it." He pauses for a moment, then gestures toward the pie between us, oblong like a classic Sorbillo pizza. "I mean, my pizza isn't even a circle!"

Nobody around us seems to mind. Pizzas come flying out of the oven at a breathless pace. A thicket of outstretched arms captures midslice selfies. Diners use hunks of charred crust to sop up tomato streaks and mozzarella strands. And every few seconds, someone lines up behind us to ask for an autograph or a photo or simply to pay respect to the man whose pizza is merely good.

Enzo Coccia doesn't settle. Not for the second-best tomato. Not for a perfectly good *fior di latte*. Not for the type of flour a rival pizzeria could procure with a single phone call. Nothing comes out of the oven that isn't meticulously researched, tasted, tested, and approved by Signor Coccia. He approaches these matters with the earnest intensity of a doctor reviewing clinical studies for a new cancer drug.

When Luciana and I walk into Pizzaria La Notizia, 94, one of three pizzerias Enzo owns in Naples' Via Caravaggio district, he is seated around a table with three middle-aged men and a battery of ingredients. They taste olive oils from little shot glasses, take notes on tomato samples and pH levels, argue about soil composition and other matters of terroir that feel almost

comically out of place in a pizzeria.

As I soon find out, Enzo approaches every matter with this type of atom-splitting intensity. He learned the pizza trade the way most of his colleagues did—at the elbow of his father, who still runs the family pizzeria just down the road. But young Enzo didn't see pizza as a vocation, he saw it as a calling. "I grew up on my father's *banco di pizza*, but that was just my launch pad." At twelve, he was selling pizzas for the family on the streets, but already plotting out his own path. After his family apprenticeship, he went on to serve as the first secretary of the AVPN, back when the organization was little more than a handful of foreward-thinking pizza men. But his devotion to pizza grew well beyond the confines of the AVPN charter.

For Coccia, pizza isn't a discipline based on instinct and repetition; it's a subject to be studied over a lifetime. It's a carnival for the curious mind, a discipline that combines physics, chemistry, engineering, architecture, and, increasingly, no small measure of artistry. If they gave out PhDs in pizza,

Enzo Coccia, the pizza professor.

Coccia would be the one on the stage shaking the hands of the new doctors. The professor.

His book, *La Pizza Napoletana*, may be the least sexy pizza book ever published, a dead-serious study dedicated to the science of pizza with all the textual and aesthetic appeal of a dishwasher manual. But for a serious student of pizza, there may be no more helpful book in print today, assuming you know how to decode the dense jargon and complex science of gluten formation and refractory heat transference. If you are interested in, say, rheological properties or Chopin Alveograph wheat analysis, this is your book. Not surprisingly, Enzo operates a pizza academy—Enzo Coccia's Pizza Consulting—where he tries to distill three hundred years of pizza history into one hundred hours in the classroom. The course lasts a month, and to ensure that his lessons are fully absorbed, he takes on just four students at a time.

The spirit of Enzo's pursuit of perfection runs counter to the established culture of Neapolitan pizza, which is largely content to rest on the general awesomeness of the original creation. Since its inception, the economic model for pizza in Naples has been based on quantity. In the nineteenth century, *pizzaioli*, pressured to earn their keep in pedestrian-dense areas such as Via dei Tribunali or along the port, would bake hundreds of pizzas a day to eke out a meager profit. They had neither the time nor the resources to worry about the provenance of their ingredients.

Much of that mentality carries over today. Luciana explains that most *pizzaioli* in the city don't fret over ingredient quality, fermentation methods, or advancement of equipment and technique; they learn to make a solid, respectable pizza and leave it at that. It's understandable, especially given the fact that for most local clientele, pizza comes with a fixed price tag. *Pizza napoletana* has always been a food for the everyman, the daily bread of the *lazzaroni*, and despite the boundless potential to refine and elevate the product, you won't find many *napoletani* willing to pay more than four or five euros for a margherita, regardless of the pedigree of the pomodoro or the complexity of the double-proofed dough. To sell at that price point and make rent, many *pizzaioli* choose to use seed oils instead of the great olive oil of Campania; instant yeast instead of a natural starter; basic *fior di latte* instead of the growing array of artisanal cheeses made by small, local producers; standard canned tomatoes instead of the exalted Pomodorino del Piennolo grown in the volcanic soil of Mount Vesuvius.

"It's created a feedback loop of mediocrity," Luciana says. "If your neighbor is making pizza this way, if your *father* made pizza this way, why would you make it any different?"

As seen across Italian food culture, there's a fine line between preserving tradition and resisting change. One is based on an ethos, the other on inertia. At some point over the past decade in Italy, pizza crossed from being a cheap, delicious staple into being a vessel for culinary ambition. Not surprisingly, this transformation was spearheaded by forward-thinking Italians safely removed from the strictures of

Naples pizza culture. Gabriele Bonci, the iconoclastic force behind Rome's Bonci, makes dough with wheat grown and milled specifically for him, then uses the ethereal, crispy-tender base as a canvas upon which he creates sophisticated pictures using everything from rosy slices of seared tenderloin to grilled octopus as his paint. Simone Padoan, the captain of i Tigli in San Bonifacio just outside Verona, runs his establishment with the discipline of a Michelin chef, his corps of young toques working in quiet unison to create some of the most precise and esoteric pizzas on the planet: with roasted suckling pig with wilted greens, raw red shrimp, and wild arugula. A pizza can cost more than €30.

Endless debates can be had—have been had, are being had—about what constitutes pizza. When does it stop being pizza and start being something else? Is it the thickness or heft of the dough? Tell that to the Sicilians, who eat pizza that could be confused for cake. Is it the style of toppings? I've eaten pizzas in AVPN-certified places topped with canned corn, slices of industrial hot dogs, frozen vegetables. Is it the method of cooking? One of Naples' most famous pizzas, the Montanara from Starita, starts in a bath of hot oil and finishes in the oven. Every point has a counterpoint; every rigid stance opens you up to the potential of hypocrisy and backpedaling. How do you "protect" something that is constantly evolving?

Enzo Coccia may have started as a secretary at the AVPN, helping to define and enforce a narrow vision of pizza, but today he may be the *napoletano* who is most aggressively and convincingly altering the parameters of pizza. He applies his brand of technical and material mastery to create superlative versions of Naples' standbys—an assertive *quattro formaggi*, a punchy *capricciosa*, a simple and restrained Margherita. But here, at his more modern pizzeria, he pushes the concept of *pizza napoletana* into previously uncharted territory.

After adjourning the ingredients forum, Enzo takes a seat at our table. "What should we give you?" he wonders aloud, rubbing his forehead, running through a mental check-

list of the various projects in the works. "The salt cod?" his manager suggests from behind the cash register. "No. Not ready yet. But I know what we'll feed him." He walks back toward the oven, talks with his *pizzaiolo*, then goes to a fridge housing dozens of Italian microbrews and selects an appropriate vintage. (Pizzas of this caliber require thoughtful pairings, says Enzo.)

A few minutes later, the first pizza arrives: baby zucchini and ribbons of smoked pancetta spread across a pale green puree of spring asparagus. The base itself is flawless—firm enough to pick up by hand, light and tender enough to collapse as soon as it touches your teeth, with light sour notes of natural fermentation, plus the bittersweet balance that comes from controlled blistering of an expertly proofed and cooked *impasto*. The base may be the Platonic ideal of a Neapolitan crust, but the combination of smoke and layers of natural spring sweetness register as something entirely unique—pizza in shape and size, but its spirit is on some higher plane.

The second creation strays even further

213

EVOLUTION
of Pizza

THE FLATBREAD GENESIS

Wood-fired flatbreads have
existed for millennia, but it
wasn't until Neapolitans added
tomatoes in the mid-eighteenth
century that it became pizza.
Pizza marinara (tomato, garlic,
oregano) is considered the
genesis of pizza as we know it.

PIZZA UNBOUND

In the past decade, the
floodgates of creativity have
opened in the pizza world. For
masters like Enzo Coccia and
Franco Pepe, that means using
impasto as a canvas upon which
they paint challenging, esoteric,
soulful pictures.

LONG LIVE THE QUEEN

Eventually, Naples' favorite street snack and Campania's nascent mozzarella culture combined to create the cheese pizza. In 1889, *pizzaiolo* Raffaele Esposito added fresh basil to celebrate Queen Margherita's Naples visit, creating the namesake pizza.

BEYOND TOMATO AND CHEESE

The twentieth century saw an explosion of pizza permutations, from classic (*quattro formaggio*, prosciutto and arugula) to the controversial (pineapple and Canadian bacon). Pizza toppings began to reflect a broader global love of the pie.

from the path of prosaic pizza: burrata—plump balls, one per slice—gently oozing beside planks of smoked eel, nubs of toasted walnuts, and fine ribbons of fresh basil. On paper, it seems like a dubious combination at best, but the union of smoke and tang, supple flesh and crunchy seeds, threads an impossibly small needle—both elegant and deeply comforting, technically precise but soulful. This pizza would be at home on the menu of any Michelin-anointed temple in Europe.

When it comes to defining pizza, I'm firmly in the camp of those who are willing to accept a broad and liberal definition, but the one virtue that all great pizzas share is that the whole is greater than the sum of its parts. Enzo's creations speak of a generosity of vision and precise engineering wherein each ingredient acts like a force multiplier, there to concentrate and amplify the flavors of everything that surrounds it. Remove one ingredient and the high-wire balancing act comes to a tragic end.

In between pizzas, Enzo drops knowledge. We talk *impasto* (*pizzaioli* spend hours each day discussing dough—Enzo's *impasto*

ferments at room temperature for sixteen hours), the symbolic power of ingredient choice ("We need our ingredients to represent not just the best of Campania but the best of Italy"), and the role a more refined pizzeria such as La Notizia plays in the dining landscape ("The world economic crisis changed the dining world—that give us an opportunity").

"The pizza in Naples is much better today than it was ten years ago. It's not just about better technique, but people know more about their products now, too." His parents, his original masters, still run their pizzeria not far from Enzo's mini-empire. When I ask him how their business is doing, he shakes his head. "Not well. It's been tough going." A heavy silence falls over the table. "I might ask them to come work with me." This will not be an easy conversation.

He asks us for permission to bring out one last pizza. I'm six deep on the day, but incapable of saying no to whatever might come next. My mind races through a catalog of possible candidates—raw sea urchin from the Adriatic, maggot cheese from Sardinia—but after two journeys well beyond the realms of Planet Pizza, we finish where pizza started, with a simple Margherita but one with a lifetime of wisdom and practice packed into its perimeters. Mozzarella from water buffaloes treated like deities, tomatoes concentrated like red diamonds, the sheen of green-gold oil shimmering on the surface extracted by the ancient stone presses of Puglia. It's like tasting pizza for the first time—the acidity of the tomatoes sunrise bright, the just-melted mozz like little depth charges of lactic richness, the yeasty breath of the dough as warm and pure as a mother's love.

"We don't make perfect pizzas," says Enzo. "We try to make less imperfect pizzas."

The final dish, the majestic Margherita, is possibly the least imperfect pizza I've ever eaten.

✦ ❦ ❦

Nothing about the Pepe in Grani experience fits the standard Naples pizza formula. To start, it's not in Naples but in Caiazzo, a village fifty kilometers to the north. Fifty kilometers might not seem like much, but in Italy, where cuisine, dialect, and culture shift from one street to the next, it might as well be another country. To get to Caiazzo, you need to weave your way through Caserta, the heart of Campania, home to the ornate Royal Palace of the Bourbon kings of the eighteenth century, later a hotbed of nebulous Camorra activity. You brush by patches of earth pocked with industrial waste and mafia mischief, flash past rolling farmlands and orchards, once again flush in the decline of the local underworld, pull through picturesque small towns where men play cards on café terraces in the afternoon sun, and eventually ascend into the Alto Casertano until you come upon the hilltop village of six thousand souls. A few years ago, its streets were sedated, shops shuttered, population dwindled as the youth left Caiazzo in search of opportunities in Naples or elsewhere. But as Luciana and I stroll through the narrow streets in the town center at dusk, we see people everywhere—in bars, in newly opened boutiques, on the sidelines of pickup soccer games played against church walls. They come from Rome, Milan, the United States, and while they wait for their table—a wait that can stretch to three hours on a summer weekend—they breathe new life into Caiazzo.

The restaurant itself does not resemble any pizzeria you've ever seen. Down a winding stone staircase in the *centro storico*, surrounded by medieval churches and dimly lit piazzas, you'll find an eighteenth-century palazzo converted into a four-story fortress of pizza excellence. Everything, from the dramatic stone setting to the pizza lab with troves of dough in various stages of proofing to the garden growing fresh herbs and the terrace with ample views of the Alto Casertano, gives the restaurant the stature of a place worthy of a journey. And should you need to fall into a deep, postprandial pizza slumber, there are a few stylish rooms on top of the palazzo, ready to receive you.

Then there's the man himself. Franco Pepe—wood-frame glasses and a soft skirt of gray hair, more psychiatrist than pizza man at first glance—comes from a family built on bread. His grandfather was the village baker, who turned the grain from the countryside and the water drawn from the Caiazzo well into daily bread for his neighbors. Franco's father took those baking skills and transferred them to pizza, establishing Antica Osteria Pizzeria Pepe in the town's central piazza as a local institution. But, like Gino and Enzo back in Naples, it was Franco who realized the full potential of the family's pizza dynasty. He and his two brothers worked at their father's side for nearly forty years, but when they finally inherited the family pizzeria, they didn't agree on a path forward. Franco wanted to push against the parameters of pizza, to seek out the best ingredients and to continue to evolve and innovate at any cost; his brothers wanted to run a solid traditional pizzeria befitting of a hilltop town of 5,700 residents. When the differences proved irreconcilable, Franco left, bought the old palazzo a few blocks down the road, and began to construct his dream: running the greatest pizzeria the world had ever seen and, with it, expanding the very nature of pizza itself.

But Franco's version of pizza advancement is less about moving forward than about embracing the best practices of the past. He likes to call his kitchen wireless, a reference to his aversion to technology in pizza making. He and his corps of cooks make the dough for four hundred pizzas every day by hand in a *madia*, the traditional wooden box in which pizza dough has been proofed and stored for more than a century. No recipes—his father and grandfather never worked from recipes—just a lifetime of experience that tells him how much sourdough starter, how much beer yeast, how much flour, and how much time fermenting a day's given slate of variables will demand from the dough. "You need to listen to the dough with your hands," he says.

Franco's return to time-honored traditions started not in the kitchen but in the soil of the Alto Casertano. Since opening Pepe in Grani, he has worked directly with small producers to adhere to the principles of *kilometro zero*—the practice of hyperlo-cal cooking popular in the upper ranks of Italian cooking but rarely if ever embodied in a pizzeria. As the supply chain continues to splinter, *pizzaioli* are left having to make the same decision that other chefs and restaurant owners do: whether to work with the industrial farms and mass producers who provide cheap, consistent product in a single trackable delivery or to embrace the small, local producers who are trying to revive old traditions and bring a level of intimacy and integrity to the food chain.

Franco made his choice the day he decided to leave the family pizzeria behind and strike out on his own. His isn't a tepid foray into "farm-to-table" cooking; it's not an asterisk on the menu or a talking point at the table; it's the foundation of everything he does. Rather than find ingredients to showcase his pizzas, he makes pizzas to showcase his ingredients. His extra-virgin olive oil comes from a tiny producer just down the road; buffalo mozzarella is pulled fresh every morning at eleven from a *caseificio* the next village over; he builds his sourdough crust from Grano Nostrum,

Franco Pepe and his *pizzaioli*
still make dough by hand.

a varietal of wheat out of use for fifty years before Franco brought it back from the dead. He creates entire pizzas to support a single esoteric ingredient. The Alife onion, for example, has a history that stretches back to ancient Rome, when gladiators rubbed it on their bodies to strengthen their muscles. A century of wars and urban flight brought the onion to the verge of extinction in 2010, when a few local farmers worked with Slow Food to revive its cultivation. Franco paired it with *scamorza* and pancetta and turned it into the star of one of his most popular pizzas.

We start our meal in the kitchen, right beside the blazing oven, where one of Franco's cooks chops a filet of local grass-fed beef into rough cubes and dresses it with olive oil and wisps of lemon rind. A puffy disc of dough emerges from the oven, which Franco cuts into wedges before heaping it with mounds of this restrained tartare. The union of warm, smoky bread and cool, grassy beef is enough to make me want to camp out in the kitchen for the rest of the night.

Later we head to the upstairs dining room, humming with the chatter of local families and wide-eyed out-of-towners, the cooing of young couples more lost in the *impasto* than in each other. Franco proposes a pizza-tasting menu of sorts, which starts with what he calls his *Margherita sbagliata*, the "mistaken" margherita. It arrives like a piece of abstract painting, the tomato transformed into four perpendicular racing stripes, the basil rendered into green splotches of oil: the same guest list but a whole different party.

The role of the *pizzaiolo* has always possessed a certain theatricality, the oven strategically positioned by the restaurant's entrance to give clients and passersby an enticing view of the work. As with so many parts of the pizza process, Franco takes the next logical step, broadcasting the action on larger screens for everyone to absorb. One table on the second floor offers a glass window into the kitchen for a bird's-eye view of the oven-blasted ballet.

There is a mystical, intangible magic that Franco tries to recapture at every turn: pizza not as a meal but as a feeling.

He's a man driven by smells: the earthy breath of his grandfather's slow-proofed, wood-fired breads; the grassy aroma of fresh-picked garden herbs. By visions: dough kneaded by hand and fermented in wooden boxes; the *libretti* he ate as a kid, now baked in his oven in the morning and sold to locals from a gleaming metal canister for €1.50 apiece. The unplugged kitchen, the ancient gladiator onion; the agronomist he works with to identify local ingredients in need of attention—they may seem like excesses or affectations, but Franco is a man who believes wholeheartedly that every tiny detail matters, that if pizza is to be elevated from a food to an experience, from a meal to a memory, every piece of input must be considered.

For the guys back in Naples, Franco's intensity poses an existential threat to the old guard of pizza making. When *Gambero Rosso*, Italy's influential culinary guide, added a three-slice pizza rating to its review process, Franco Pepe's was the only pizzeria in the region to receive the top honors the first year. The *pizzaioli* of

Naples were apoplectic. "That was a major turning point for *pizza napoletana*," Luciana says. The next year, the Naples Chamber of Commerce sponsored the guide, and suddenly six Neapolitan pizzerias were awarded three stars.

The endless stream of fawning international press dedicated to Franco's "perfect" pizza is understandably a serious buzzkill for the Naples establishment; the number of "world's best pizza" articles that clog up the Internet these days says as much about the modern mob mentality as it does about the poetry of Franco Pepe. But whether the *napoletani* will admit it or not, it was in large measure Franco's sudden fame that shook Naples from its slumber.

The pizzas keep coming: *parmigiana di melanzane*, planks of eggplant mixed with tomato and Parmesan, roasted in the wood-fired oven until dense and sticky with flavor, then used to crown a pillow-soft disc of dough; *la pinsa conciata*, a poetic union of pork lard and fig jam and an ancient goat cheese once on the brink of extinction; *calzone con scarola riccia*, a featherweight shell of blistered *impasto* stuffed with wilted escarole and anchovy and a tickle of dried chili.

It's a dizzying procession of tastes and temperatures and textures, filled with bites of brilliance and a range of emotions that line up one after the next, like a series of waves, holding you in the grip of a massive natural force: nostalgia (for every time a pizza made me deliriously happy), doubt (a lifelong dislike of eggplant called into question), hope (if the union of flour, tomato, and cheese can be this good, what can't humans accomplish?). It's mystic pizza, the work of a sorcerer capable of conjuring up the type of magic simply not accessible to other *pizzaioli*, even the most ambitious ones. The kind of pizza that memories are made of.

Is it the best? Is Franco's pizza the best in the world? Is it the best I've ever expe-rienced? What about those rectangular, thick-crust sausage slices I'd bring home at 2 A.M. after a long night at the office to devour in bed with no one but the Sopranos to keep me company? Or those extra-large every-thing pizzas my family inhaled in Auck-land after thirty-six hours of international travel, the one we still talk about every few Christmases? Or the minipizzas my brother Ryan used to make for me during our days as bachelor roommates, those four-bite, pesto-slathered English muffin pizzas, a blood bond, a bridge between two islands adrift in a vast ocean? Or the magnificent Margherita I pulled from the AVPN oven, the first one that looked and tasted and smelled of true *pizza napoletana*, the one that caught Roberto's eye from across the class-room as he mouthed a single word: *Bravo*?

Is it better than that?

MAMMA MARIA LUISA

NAME: Maria Luisa Belli

CITY: Genova

REGION: Liguria

SPECIALTY: *Trofie di Reco* with pesto, a Ligurian classic.
I also love to make *torta pasqualina*, a local tart
with artichokes and eggs, a recipe I learned from
my grandfather.

KITCHEN MEMORY: My birthday this year. I had all my friends
and family bring ingredients to cook a vegetable dish.
I called it sixty Shades of Green. It looked like a
Master Chef episode.

PHILOSOPHY: Dare to do what you can with the ingredients
you have. In Liguria the food is poor but incredibly rich.

The
CURE

SALUMI SELECTOR

01. PROSCIUTTO DI SAN DANIELE

Hind leg of pork cured in salt for at least eighteen months.

02. LARDO DI COLONNATA

Pork fat seasoned with herbs and spices and cured in Tuscan marble

03. COPPA

Pork shoulder salted and aged for up to one year.

04. MORTADELLA

Emulsified pork speckled with fat, pepper, and pistachio.

08

07

06

05

05. PANCETTA
Cured, unsmoked pork belly.
Eaten raw or cooked crispy.

06. CULATELLO
The heart of the hind leg of a pig,
cured in a pig or cow bladder.

07. FINOCCHIONA
Tuscan salami seasoned with
fennel and red wine.

08. BRESAOLA
Lean legs of spiced beef air-dried
up to four months.

BRODETTO

ANATOMY
of a dish

FISH SOUP FOR THE SOUL

Like French *bouillabaisse*, Greek *kakavia*, and Catalan *suquet*, *brodetto* (also known as *zuppa di pesce* in parts of Italy) came about in the days before refrigeration as a way for fishermen to use up the unsold catch—usually small, cheap fish.

A TASTE OF THE SEA

What started as a humble soup grew over the years into an increasingly complex and regionalized dish. The one common denominator: a heady broth that expresses the fullness of the sea at any particular port.

A SEA OF CONTROVERSY

"The only element about *brodetto* that is always the same is that it is never the same," said the great Waverley Root. Red wine or white? Crustaceans or mollusks or both? Just a few fish, or an entire aquarium? There are no wrong (or right) answers.

ONE FISH, TWO FISH

The most famous fish soups come from the Adriatic coast, especially Le Marche, where cooks use thirteen fish to honor the Last Supper diners. Livorno, with its justly famous *cacciucco*, is the Mediterranean *zuppa* capital.

MATERA

The story of Matera is a meandering tale of beauty and tragedy, death and rebirth. Once a vibrant but impoverished community of sixteen thousand souls living in an intricate system of caves, the Italian government forced the people of Matera to move to state housing in the 1950s, a move with deep socio-political ramifications. Today the abandoned caves are alive once again, and old residents have returned to usher in a new era of underground culture, making Matera one of Italy's most magical destinations. Go now.

⦿ L'ABBONDANZA LUCANA

A beautiful introduction to the joys of Basilicata cooking, served up in a multitiered restaurant fashioned from old caves. Start with the antipasto sampler and move on to the list of handmade pastas.

⦿ CASEIFICIO BONTÀ DEL LATTE

Basilicata and nearby Puglia are two of Italy's great cheese regions, so plan to eat your weight in buffalo mozzarella, burrata, and ricotta while here. Start at this excellent family cheese shop.

📍 SOTTOZERO

A fine place for a beer and a bit of Basilicata-style street food, including the emblematic *panzerotto*, a golden pocket of dough stuffed with fresh mozzarella and fried in olive oil.

📍 IL BELVEDERE

New cave hotels are opening up every month in Matera, but the stylish Belvedere has been doing it right for years, with big subterranean rooms and first-rate hospitality.

Chapter Six

SARDINIA

—

SPAGHETTI ALLA MARINARA ALLA SARDEGNA

- 400 grams dried spaghetti
- Copious amounts of cold-pressed olive oil
- As many wild mussels as you can find, scrubbed
- 4 handfuls of wild sea plants
- 2 cloves garlic, thinly sliced
- 1 bucket Mediterranean water
- Special equipment: vintage forty-foot sailboat, guide to wild Sardinian herbs, bathing suit, Michelin-starred chef

INSTRUCTIONS:

Load the sailboat with bottles of white wine, olive oil, fishing rods, and yeasty, dark-crusted bread. Work your way carefully out of the narrow channels of the Cabras port on the western shore of Sardinia. Set sail for the open seas.

Navigate carefully around the archipelago of small boats fishing for sea bass, bream, squid. Steer clear of the lines of mussel nets swooping in long black arcs off the coastline. When you spot the crumbling stone tower, turn the boat north and nuzzle it gently into the electric blue-green waters along ancient Tharros. Drop anchor.

Strip down to your bathing suit. Load into the transport boat and head for shore. After a swim, make for the highest point on the peninsula, the one with the view of land and sea and history that will make your knees buckle. Stay focused. You're not here to admire the sun-baked ruins of one of Sardinia's oldest civiliza-

—

tions, a five-thousand-year-old settlement that wears the footprints of its inhabitants—Phoenicians, Greeks, Romans—like the layers of a cake. You're here to pick herbs growing wildly among the ancient tombs and temples, under shards of broken vases once holding humans' earliest attempts at inebriation. Taste this! Like peppermint, but spicy. And this! A version of wild lemon thyme, perfect with seafood. Pluck a handful of finocchio marino, *sea fennel, a bright burst of anise with an undertow of salt.*

With finocchio *in fist, reboard the transport vessel and navigate toward the closest buoy. Grab the bright orange plastic, roll it over, and scrape off the thicket of mussels growing beneath. Repeat with the other buoys until you have enough mussels to fill a pot.*

*In the belly of the boat, bring the dish together: Scrub the mussels. Bring a pot of seawater to a raucous boil and drop in the spaghetti—*cento grammi a testa. *While the pasta cooks, blanch a few handfuls of the wild fennel to take away some of the sting. Remove the mussels from their shells and combine with sliced garlic, a glass of seawater, and a deluge of peppery local olive oil in a pan. Taste the pasta constantly, check-*

ing for doneness. (Don't you dare overcook it!) When only the faintest resistance remains in the middle, drain and add to the pan of mussels. Move the pasta fast and frequently with a pair of tongs, emulsifying the water and mussel juice with the oil. Keep stirring and drizzling in oil until a glistening sheen forms on the surface of the pasta. This is called la mantecatura, *the key to all great seafood pastas, so take the time to do it right.*

Serve with a bottle of ice-cold Vermentino. Pat your belly. Fight over who gets to fare la scarpetta *with the dregs of sauce from the serving bowl. Say something vague and fuzzy and warm such as "bella Sardegna" that nobody at the table can possibly disagree with.*

This is what we do the first morning I meet Roberto Petza. I roll out of bed in a stranger's house in Cabras, a small fishing town on Sardinia's west coast, and find him sitting at the kitchen counter, slicing cheese. I don't know much about Petza, only that he's the only chef to have held a Michelin star on the island in the past thirty years and that a close *consigliere* of mine in the

Italian food world, the kind of guy who knows every trattoria in Trieste and where to buy *'nduja* at midnight in Calabria, told me that the only way to fully appreciate the island is with Roberto Petza and subsequently made the introduction via email. I have been given only vague instructions about what my wife, Laura, and I will be doing while on the island by Roberto's right hand, Domenico Sanna, a man whom I have been emailing for weeks in hopes of extracting a few details about the week ahead. Thirty-seven emails later, I still know nothing. "Don't worry. We take care of everything."

Well, not quite everything. When Laura and I show up the day before the mussel pasta feast at the mysterious rendezvous point, a house down a tiny street in Cabras, Daniela, a tall, tan blonde, greets us with a look of abject confusion. She doesn't know any more than we do about the itinerary. The three of us stand there stupidly blinking into the light until Daniela suggests that we drink some wine and slowly piece together the plan. Daniela is a

cook at Roberto's restaurant. Daniela has a boat. Daniela will be taking us and Roberto out on the boat tomorrow morning. But first we need to eat dinner, so after our wine she drives us down to Ristorante i Giganti, a local seafood restaurant, and tells the owner that I am a food writer and he should feed us accordingly. "It doesn't look like much," Daniela says before peeling off in her van, "but trust me. This is where you want to eat tonight."

As soon as we take our seats, a sequence of six antipasti materialize from the kitchen and swallow up the entire table: nickels of tender octopus with celery and black olives, a sweet and bitter dance of earth and sea; another plate of *polpo*, this time tossed with chickpeas and a sharp vinaigrette; a duo of tuna plates—the first seared and chunked and served with tomatoes and raw onion, the second whipped into a light pâté and showered with a flurry of *bottarga* that serves as a force multiplier for the tuna below; and finally, a plate of large sea snails, simply boiled and served with small forks for excavating the salty-sweet knuckle of meat inside.

As is so often the case in Italy, we are full by the end of the opening salvo, but the night is still young, and the owner, who stops by frequently to fill my wineglass as well as his own, has a savage, unpredictable look in his eyes. Next comes the *primo*, a gorgeous mountain of spaghetti tossed with an ocean floor's worth of clams, the whole mixture shiny and golden from an indecent amount of olive oil used to mount the pasta at the last moment—the fat acting as a binding agent between the clams and the noodles, a glistening bridge from earth to sea. "These are real clams, expensive clams," the owner tells me, plucking one from the plate and holding it up to the light, "not those cheap, flavorless clams most restaurants use for *pasta alle vongole*."

Just as I'm ready to wave the white napkin of surrender—stained, like my pants, a dozen shades of fat and sea—a thick cylinder of tuna loin arrives, charred black on the outside, cool and magenta through the center. "We caught this our-selves today," he whispers in my ear over the noise of the dining room, as if it were a

Roberto Petza, wild sea fennel, and the ancient ruins of Tharros.

secret to keep between the two of us. How can I refuse?

It is a staggering display of the Sardinian sea from a little town with no one to feed but its own—a glimpse of what everyone keeps telling me about this island, that there are very special things happening in every corner of Sardinia.

But what Roberto offers the next afternoon out at sea is a different taste of Sardinia entirely: raw, spontaneous, simultaneously rustic and refined. A dish I'll use as a decoder ring to better understand this island and this man.

"People love to talk about kilometer zero," he says as we're scraping up the ghost of lunch with heels of bread. The boat sways gently with the swells. Seagulls glide above, eyeing our crumbs. "You can't do kilometer zero in Barcelona. You can't forage in New York. *This* is kilometer zero. *This* is foraging. It's not a trend—it's part of our DNA."

This is the first of a dozen meals we will eat together and the beginning of a thesis he builds mysteriously but effectively to

answer one simple question for me: What is Sardinia?

This is not just his Sardinia; this is the Sardinia of the cheese makers and bread bakers, the foragers and shepherds, the fishermen and wine hounds. And he wants to share it all with me. And you.

As the ancient Greeks once told it, when the gods were done creating the world, they scrounged together the leftover scraps—inhospitable mountains and barren soil—tossed them into the middle of the Mediterranean, then stepped down on the resulting mass. They called it *Ichnusa*, Greek for "footprint," a dark and difficult impression in the middle of a brilliant sea.

Despite being surrounded by water, Sardinia does not have a storied Mediterranean history. The *sardi* have long looked at the sea with suspicion, as a source of disease, invasion, and other existential threats to the island's survival.

They had good reason to worry. Beyond

being a breeding ground for malaria, the Sardinian coastline became a welcome mat for pirates, miscreants, and would-be conquerors. The first recorded civilization remains one of Europe's most mysterious, the Nuragics, a Bronze Age tribe who built more than seven thousand stone settlements, among the oldest known manmade structures, that still dot the island today. The Phoenicians touched down in the ninth century B.C., hoping to tap into some of Sardinia's rich mineral deposits. They were more interested in trade than in conquering, but they found the Sardinians immune to both. The Carthaginians faced a similar challenge three hundred years later; they controlled the coastline but had no one to rule but themselves. Everyone came—the Romans and Byzantines, Goths and Saracens, Genoese and Pisans—but nobody stayed, finding Sardinia devoid of many resources to extract and populations to govern.

The only thing this diverse body of Mediterranean misfits had in common was how little of an impact they had on Sardin-

ian culture. The *sardi* were too busy living in the mountains and the central plains to be bothered by the coastal visitors. Unlike Sicily to the south, where the impact of its invaders can be felt everywhere in the island's multicultural milieu, as the Sardinians stymied one would-be conqueror after the next, their native culture remained largely intact. When Italy finally emerged as a country in 1861, the newly unified government did what nearly everyone else before them had done and what too many continue to do today: it let Sardinia be.

Today the population has begun to fill in around the coastline—from the 150,000 living in the capital, Cagliari, to the gilded resorts of the Costa Smeralda, where the rich and beautiful of Europe come to be rich and beautiful when the mercury rises.

But twenty years of shifting demographics can't unravel thousands of years of hardwiring, especially on an island as obstinate as this one. The soul of Sardinia lies in the hills and mountains of the interior and the villages peppered among them. There, in areas such as Nuoro and Ozieri, women bake bread by the flame of the communal oven, winemakers produce their potions from small caches of grapes adapted to the stubborn soil and arid climate, and shepherds lead their flocks through the peaks and valleys in search of the fickle flora that fuels Sardinia's extraordinary cheese culture. There are more sheep than humans roaming this island—3 million in total—and sheep can't graze on sand.

On the table, the food stands out as something only loosely connected to the cuisine of Italy's mainland. Here, every piece of the broader puzzle has its own identity: *pane carasau*, the island's main staple, eats more like a cracker than a loaf of bread, built to last for shepherds who spent weeks away from home. Cheese means sheep's milk manipulated in a hundred different ways, from the salt-and-spice punch of Fiore Sardo to the infamous maggot-infested *casu marzu*. Fish and seafood may be abundant, but they take a backseat to four-legged animals: sheep, lamb, and suckling pig. Historically, pasta came after bread in the island's hierarchy of carbs, often made by the poor-

est from the dregs of the wheat harvest, but you'll still find hundreds of shapes and sizes unfamiliar to a mainland Italian. All of it washed down with wine made from grapes that most people have never heard of—Cannonau, Vermentino, Torbato—that have little market beyond the island.

Roberto grew up in San Gavino Monreale, a small industrial town forty-five kilometers north of Cagliari. One of six boys, he had a knack for building things with his hands, leading his mother to enroll him in a master carpentry school. But Roberto turned his talent for tinkering to the kitchen, secretly taking cooking classes at a local trade school until his future was written. At seventeen, he knew he wanted to be a chef, but he also knew that Sardinia didn't have the kind of restaurant infrastructure to match a man of his ambition. "I took my beat-up suitcase and set out in search of something. I remember coming out of the subway and seeing the Eiffel Tower and thinking 'Holy shit, I'm not in Sardinia anymore.'" He started in Paris: two years cooking everything from classic French to Chinese to Mexican cuisine. He spent those early days in a hostel, one of sixteen bunked up in a small dormitory. "Every night all sixteen would say good night in their own language: German, Spanish, Taiwanese. *Bello.*"

He kept moving. Corsica. South of France. Catalonia. England. Switzerland. The Isle of Man. Dozens of restaurants, each one a memory and a lesson. In northern Italy, at Osteria della Bullera, he found his mentor in Stefano Rigoni, who taught him perhaps the most valuable lessons of his world tour: how to work within the seasons; how to make *salumi*, cheese, wine. How to do things right. How the restaurant is a bridge between the land and its people. "My experience there gave me the ability to understand a way forward."

Thirteen years, twenty-eight restaurants, and tens of thousands of miles later, he returned to Sardinia with a plan. "I knew two things: I wanted to open my own restaurant before I turned thirty. And I wanted to call it S'Apposentu after the room in my grandma's house I could never enter in as a kid." Because of the Sardinian bureaucracy, he missed the first goal by five days. In 1998, he opened S'Apposentu in San Gavino Monreale, his hometown, before transferring it to the grand Teatro Lirico, an opera house in Cagliari.

The dawn of the twenty-first century wasn't an ideal moment to open an ambitious restaurant in Sardinia. The mining industry that had fueled much of the island's economy during the late nineteenth and twentieth centuries—coal, zinc, silver—ground to a halt. Factories closed. People fled en masse to mainland Italy in search of opportunity. While many Sardinians lost touch with the island, Roberto was busy trying to reestablish his connection to his homeland. "I left when I was seventeen. I had to repatriate. I had to relearn my island."

Despite the challenges, S'Apposentu slowly bloomed into one of Cagliari's most important restaurants. Roberto brought with him the hundreds of little lessons he had learned on the road and transposed them onto Sardinian tradition and *terreno.*

THE SOUL OF SARDINIA LIES IN THE HILLS AND MOUNTAINS OF THE INTERIOR.

He turned roasted onions into ice cream and peppered it with wild flowers and herbs. He reimagined *porceddu*, Sardinia's heroic roast pig, as a dense terrine punctuated with local fruits. He made himself into a master: of bread baking, cheese making, meat curing. In 2006, Michelin rewarded him with a star, one of the first ever awarded in Sardinia.

But success breeds contempt and suspicion in small communities like Cagliari, and S'Apposentu's ascendance to the top of the totem pole gave birth to a group of vocal detractors—restaurateurs and chefs who resented the sudden rise of the young chef and his radical cuisine. Roberto's enemies went to work, pressing political friends to exert their power over problematic outsiders. In 2002, claiming a handful of building and licensing violations, the local government shuttered S'Apposentu.

With his name and his pedigree, Roberto could have taken off for the mainland—the "continent," as they call it here—and opened up an ambitious restaurant in Rome or Florence or just about

anywhere else his travels had taken him. He could have spread the Sardinian gospel through fancy, high-concept dishes to an eager audience of international diners. Instead, he chose to move his restaurant to Siddi, an hour north of Cagliari, a town of 350 people.

Siddi was once home to a well-known *pastificio*, a factory making artisanal pasta, but when it shuttered in the 1990s, many local people lost their livelihoods. Village life has been stripped down to the basics: a church, a post office, a single bar that lures the town's drinkers like a honey trap. It's the kind of place where watching the arrival of an unknown vehicle is a spectator sport, where stares of skepticism and bewilderment follow you as you walk the streets, looking for signs of life.

The restaurant name remained, but the concept evolved. For starters, Roberto traded the fancy Teatro Lirico location for a chic farmhouse once owned by the Siddi pasta barons. But more than the chance for a face-lift, the decision to move from a coastal city to an inland village came down to location: "I chose Siddi because it allowed me to create something more than a restaurant." Found in the area called Marmilla, a name given it by the Romans because the rolling hills reminded them of breasts, Siddi puts Roberto into direct daily contact with the people—the farmers, foragers, winemakers—who fuel his food.

Turns out that Roberto's enemies unwittingly gave him exactly what he needed: a new home in which to articulate an even more ambitious vision of Sardinian cuisine.

🌱 🍇 🍷

Day 2 of the unknown Sardinian adventure begins in the Mercato Civico di San Benedetto, an imposing two-story market in the center of Cagliari. San Benedetto doesn't have the infectious chaos of Palermo's Ballarò or the watercolor beauty of Bologna's narrow market alleys, but you'll find three hundred vendors selling everything the island eats under one roof, along with a thicket of local cooks hunting for dinner. Having made market runs with chefs

around the world, I skipped breakfast, and Roberto quickly confirmed my choice: We navigate the produce stands, plucking palms full of cherries from every pile we pass, chewing them and spitting the seeds on the ground. We eat tiny tomatoes with taut skins that snap under gentle pressure, releasing the rabid energy of the Sardinian sun trapped inside. We crack asparagus like twigs and watch the stalks weep chlorophyll tears. We attack anything and everything that grows on trees—oranges, plums, apricots, peaches—leaving pits and peels, seeds and skins in our wake. Downstairs in the seafood section, the heart of the market, the pace quickens. Roberto turns the market into a roving raw seafood bar, passing me pieces of marine life at every stand: brawny, tight-lipped mussels; juicy clams on the half shell with a shocking burst of sweetness; tiny raw shrimp with beads of blue coral clinging to their bodies like gaudy jewelry. We place dominoes of ruby tuna flesh on our tongues like communion wafers, the final act in this sacred procession.

Everyone in San Benedetto has been waiting for this moment. Around every corner Roberto incites a cacophony of pleas and provocations and disappointments: How much do you want to pay—how about twelve euros a kilo? *Che cazzo*, Robi! What do you expect from me? Where's my gift? Robi, Robi, over here, over here!

At the butcher counter, Roberto surveys the impressive spread of sheep meat splayed before us. "Sheep has always been the most important protein on the island," he says. We move to a stall specializing in viscera. "What the rich don't eat, the poor figured out how to cook." He buys a lobe of calf's liver, a thick femur bone caked with marrow, and a whole sheep's leg. I ask him if he's reconstructing some local franken-mammal. He winks.

It's a crash course—a rapid-fire survey of the farmers and flavors behind the island's food chain that stretches my taste buds and imagination like a rubber band. It's also a test. Roberto's not looking for canned plaudits about the glories of Sardinia. In truth, he buys most of his

vegetables closer to home, from an experimental farmer adjacent to the restaurant. He's looking to see if I can distinguish between the good and the bad, to make sure we're speaking the same kitchen language. There are pockets of brilliance scattered throughout the market, but not everything we eat is worthy of Italy's towering reputation for next-level produce. Some of that is due to the inherent challenges of Sardinian soil—historically a tough place for growing fruits and vegetables. But for Roberto, it's part of a systemic issue at the heart of Sardinia's food chain: lack of organization. "Sixty-five percent of the farmable land in Sardinia is untouched. Eighty percent of our produce comes from off the island. It's absolutely insane."

Two hours later, I'm seated at a table in the S'Apposentu dining room as Roberto and his team set about transforming our market haul into lunch. The work is a curious mix of surreal and prosaic kitchen detail. A *stagista* from Mexico covers roasted pigeon bones with water to boil for stock. A young man from Verona fills sun-dried tomato leather with horse tartar. Roberto debones sea anemones (did you know that sea anemones have bones?). Daniela, ruffled sailor's shirt traded for a crisp chef's jacket, peels and cleans the last of the season's artichokes until they're no larger than walnuts.

The quiet elegance of the dining room is a long way from the rough churn of the market: modern art on the wall, Billie Holiday on the speakers, brut rosé in the glass flute before me. My camera and notebook have their own stool. Domenico, my pen pal and the master of ceremonies, emerges from the kitchen in a cobalt suit bearing a plate of bite-sized snacks: ricotta caramel, smoked hake, baby artichoke with shaved *bottarga*.

The first course lands on the table with a wink from Domenico: raw shrimp, raw sheep, and a shower of wild herbs and flowers—an edible landscape of the island. I raise my fork tentatively, expecting the intensity of a mountain flock, but the sheep is amazingly delicate—somehow lighter than the tiny shrimp beside it.

The intensity arrives with the next dish, the calf's liver we bought at the market, transformed from a dense purple lobe into an orb of pâté, coated in crushed hazelnuts, surrounded by fruit from the market this morning. The boneless sea anemones come cloaked in crispy semolina and bobbing atop a sticky potato-parsley puree.

Bread is fundamental to the island, and S'Apposentu's frequent carb deliveries prove the point: a hulking basket overflowing with half a dozen housemade varieties from thin, crispy breadsticks to a dense sourdough loaf encased in a dark, gently bitter crust.

The last savory course, one of Roberto's signature dishes, is the most stunning of all: ravioli stuffed with suckling pig and bathed in a pecorino fondue. This is modernist cooking at its most magnificent: two fundamental flavors of the island (spit-roasted pig and sheep's-milk cheese) cooked down and refined into a few explosive bites. The kind of dish you build a career on.

Roberto invites us into the kitchen to watch the cheese course take shape. He boils forty-six liters of sheep's milk in a

A few dozen of the three million
sheep that roam Sardinia.

massive steel pot. An assistant, the young cook from Verona, stirs in rennet, and when the coagulant takes effect, he dips in plastic baskets and packs them full of soft curds. "This is why I came here," he tells me. "You won't find raw ingredients like this except in one or two kitchens in all of Italy."

Roberto goes through and marks each basket of fresh cheese. "Like good Catholics, we make the sign of the cross each time." Later he moves the cheese to a cellar, where the chef ages it for as little as a few weeks or as long as four years.

The cheese selection changes with the seasons—could be a spunky, bouncy one-month wedge with the faint whisper of wild herbs and flowers. Or a dense, four-year cheese that crumbles on contact and delivers wave after wave of electricity. There aren't many restaurants that make and age their own cheese, but there aren't many restaurants of this quality that have sheep farmers a few kilometers from their back door. You can smell their diet as you squish the salty granules between your fingers.

Pecorino made weekly from the neighbor's flock. Flatbread baked in a wood-fired oven. Surf and turf as only a *sardo* can imagine. Yes, each dish is a story—all food is a story. Sometimes it's prose, sometimes it's poetry. Sometimes it's not worth the plate it's written on. The story Roberto is telling belongs to another genre entirely—one in which he's both the author and the protagonist, straddling two distant worlds, one as old as fire, the other as fresh as today's batch of cheese.

🌿 🍃 🍷

For all its untamed beauty, Sardinia is an island of cars. There's no other way to go about traversing a land as vast and sparsely populated as this. If you want to dip your toes in the crystalline waters of the Costa Smeralda; if you want to see the sheep negotiate the sharp cracks and crevices of the Gennargentu range; if you want to take in the fifty-seven murals of political strife and artistic angst that wallpaper the buildings of the hilltop town of Orgosolo; if you

want to taste the microregional cuisine as it shifts from Sassari to Nuoro to Oristano; if you want to experience this island as it's meant to be experienced by an outsider, moving from sand to stone, peak to valley, cove to crest, staying and feasting at one amazing *agriturismo* after the next, you'll need to settle into the driver's seat and take to the open road.

On a broad level, your best strategy is to commandeer a vehicle as soon as you land, set your coordinates for an interesting village or idyllic stretch of coastline, and put your foot to the pedal. Like all driving in Italy, the first moments on the highways and back streets of Sardinia will stir consternation and helplessness in driver and copilot alike. Normal traffic laws are mere suggestions; directions appear contradictory; roundabouts transform into merciless gyres. But as the hours turn into days and the stream of mistakes into a static of white noise, a calm washes over you behind the wheel. Wrong turns become opportunities. Strangers become momentary friends. The highways lined with wildflowers flash by you in a blur of colors: *red yellow white, yellow white yellow, red yellow white pink yellow red*. From time to time, a vehicle parked on the side of the road proffers a concentrated taste of the season: a truck bed of cherries, a cargo van of peaches, an old Panda packed with tiny golden apricots. To truly taste Sardinia, be prepared to pull over at any second.

Roberto Petza spends a lot of time in his Citroën Nemo. To build his world and support his people, he sweeps across the island like a searchlight, driving from farm to vineyard to fishing port to any dusty corner where good food is happening.

Each new day in our Sardinian sojourn begins with a fresh sense of confusion.

"Where we going today, chef?" "Oh, you'll see . . ." Eventually I stop asking and surrender to the idea that we're victims of a benevolent kidnapping. The *sardi* have a long, tragic history of using kidnapping as a tool for intimidation and enrichment. Roberto and Domenico use it as a means of showing me as much of the island as possible without the interference of expec-

tations. And they pull it off to dramatic, dizzying effect. We spend the week oscillating between confusion and elation, from quiet contemplation to giddy revelation—a roller-coaster ride that serves to heighten the impact of everything we see and taste.

One by one, we meet the links in Sardinia's food chain, a nose-to-tail tour of the people—the grandmas, the butchers, the young apprentices—who give the island cuisine its DNA. In a more just world, this book would be about nothing more than Sardinia: *Bread, Sheep, Sea*.

We drive ninety minutes north to visit Panificio Sapori della Tradizione, a small bakery in the mountain town of Mamoiada. "It's a long way to go for bread," says Roberto over a gas-station espresso, one of ten he drinks a day to keep his engine running, "but this is serious stuff for Sardinia."

Flour and water, the foundations of Italian cooking, are what keeps this island fed. Sardinia was once called Italy's *molino*, the mill from which a bread culture of amazing depth and breadth originated. Slowly most of the mills have shuttered, and the local grain production has been replaced by imports shipped across the Mediterranean. But even if the industry of bread has dwindled, the culture remains paramount in the Sardinian diet and the island way of life.

If one food defines Sardinia, it is *pane carasau*, the flat, paper-thin, oven-baked circle of crispy wheat you find stacked high, casting shadows on market floors and kitchen counters the island over. Born more than three thousand years ago, it's not just a flatbread but a lifeline for shepherds, a pantry staple for bolstering soups and pastas, a fork for conveying the flavors of the island. Also known as *carta di musica*, it looks like an oversize communion wafer and eats like a cracker of divine provenance, and it sits at the center of any self-respecting Sardinian table.

Traditionally, this was a bread that brought the island together, its laborious production reason enough to join mothers and daughters, aunts and nieces as they kneaded and shaped and baked their way through another week's batch. But as the story goes with so many threatened food traditions, the time demands are too stiff for the modern family, and an island of family bakers has been reduced to a few large producers who keep *pane carasau* at the center of the Sardinian diet.

Daniela Gregu, the owner of Panificio Sapori della Tradizione, is a keeper of the flame. Her day begins at 4:30 A.M., hours before the first light hits the craggy peaks surrounding Mamoiada. She combines flour, water, yeast, and salt, working it by hand from a slurry to a paste to a shaggy heap to a smooth, resilient ball of dough. The mass is hoisted onto a long wooden baker's bench and sliced into individual pieces. Two women set up in front of opposing ovens and work small pieces of dough into flattened rounds with wooden dowels. In the heat of the oven the pockets of dough bubble like blisters before the cloud of hot air trapped inside escapes. Once removed, they're bisected horizontally while still hot, the two resulting disks stacked again for another round in the oven. Whereas the first pass in the oven produces a swollen sphere of dough, a puffy pitalike vessel, the second crisps the halved rounds into crunchy flotil-las ready to withstand the days and weeks between conception and consumption.

Like all serious bread baking, that of *pane carasau* is about rhythm, repetition so precise that you could keep time by it. All morning and into the early afternoon the women work, producing tower after tower, a city of crunchy carbs, two hundred pounds in total, each piece marked with the restau-rant or the family it is destined for. Every piece is slightly different: some have perfect outer rims toasted a gentle shade of caramel; others come out pale and oblong. Beyond the individual idiosyncrasies, the general shape and structure are remarkably similar for a product of *pane carasau*'s rustic roots: twenty centimeters in diameter, a quarter centimeter thick, with a gently toasted com-plexion and a crunch that keeps for months. By lunchtime, the bakery is filled with a metropolis of *carasau* towers enveloped in gentle wisps of woodsmoke. "It's time to move on," says Roberto, gently freeing me from the trance I fell into watching the women work the ovens.

Daniela packs up a box for Roberto, some to be taken back to the restaurant, where his team will heat the disks gently, crack them by hand into craggy triangles, drizzle them with peppery olive oil, and shower them with flecks of fresh rosemary and coarse salt. The rest will travel with me back to Barcelona, where weeks from now I can console myself with little bites of Sardinia.

One afternoon, Roberto and Domen-ico take us to a neighboring village to meet with Gianfranco, a local wine producer who grows Vermentino and Cannonau—the island's most ubiquitous grapes, both capable of thriving in rocky soil. Oeno-philes often dismiss Vermentino as too one-dimensional to make great wine, but Roberto isn't the type to solicit popular opinion. Vermentino needs another grape to add perfume and structure, but the chef doesn't like the options most winemakers have turned to. "It hurts to see people plant chardonnay on this island."

Together with Giuseppe Pusceddu, an experimental wine producer from the Costa Rei, they are working to create a new project with these stubborn grapes—a wine refreshing enough to drink on a summer afternoon but with enough character to serve to a guest at S'Apposentu. At 1 P.M., under a blazing sun in the middle of a row of Gianfranco's fruit, the two hold an impromptu meeting. "We'll do some tests, check the sugar and acid levels of the grapes, and work from there," says Roberto. The consensus: two experiments. First in the beginning of September, when the grapes are younger, more vibrant. Then a month later, when the fruit is more mature. Both bottles fermented with unknown potential and questionable market value.

With the parameters of their partnership set, we return to the farmer's house, where three generations of *sarde*—Gianfranco's mother, wife, and daughter—serve us a lunch of pure *sardo* stock: celery and artichokes in *agrodolce*; chickpeas stewed with garden vegetables; roasted snails covered in garlic, parsley, bread crumbs, and tomatoes sun-dried in the front yard; rabbit *alla cacciatora* with oven-roasted onions.

Today's spread paints the picture of abundance, but each dish is a different expression of Sardinia's *cucina povera*, recipes developed during a history of poverty. The snails come from the garden, a free source of post-rain protein; the tomatoes were picked last summer and sun-dried to last through the cold winter season; *lorighittas*, little twists of dried pasta strewn throughout the chickpeas, were traditionally made from the leftover wheat given to the poor at the community grain mills and added to soup to extend its impact on empty stomachs. "*Zuppa* is synonymous with poverty," says Roberto, "it's a way to hide what you don't have. That's why you'll find it in every *sardo* household but almost never in a restaurant."

More than defined techniques, these are rhythms developed and sustained season after season, from generation to generation, absorbed into the island at a molecular level. Put them all together and you have a cuisine of depth, diversity, and abiding deliciousness with only a passing resemblance to the food of mainland Italy.

"Sardinia doesn't have a deep restaurant culture," says Domenico. "It's a culture of eating in the home. And home cooking here doesn't change from one region to the next but between one village and the next. Sometimes from one street to the next."

Gian Piero Frau, one of the most important characters in the supporting cast surrounding S'Apposentu, runs an experimental farm down the road from the restaurant. His vegetable garden looks like nature's version of a teenager's bedroom, a rebellious mess of branches and leaves and twisted barnyard wire. A low, droning buzz fills the air. "Sorry about the bugs," he says, a cartoonish cloud orbiting his head.

But beneath the chaos a bloom of biodynamic order sprouts from the earth. He uses nothing but dirt and water and careful observation to sustain life here. Every leaf and branch has its place in this garden; nothing is random. Pockets of lettuce, cabbage, fennel, and flowers grow in dense clusters together; on the other end, summer squash, carrots, and eggplant do their leafy dance. "This garden is built on synergy. You plant four or five plants in a close space, and they support each other.

It might take thirty or forty days instead of twenty to get it right, but the flavor is deeper." (There's a metaphor in here somewhere, about this new life Roberto is forging in the Sardinian countryside.)

"He's my hero," says Roberto about Gian Piero. "He listens, quietly processes what I'm asking for, then brings it to life. Which doesn't happen in places like Siddi." Together, they're creating a new expression of Sardinian *terreno*, crossing genetic material, drying vegetables and legumes under a variety of conditions, and experimenting with harvesting times that give Roberto a whole new tool kit back in the kitchen.

We stand in the center of the garden, crunching on celery and lettuce leaves, biting into zucchini and popping peas from their shells—an improvised salad, a biodynamic breakfast that tastes of some future slowly forming in the tangle of roots and leaves around us. Finally our reverence is interrupted by a few unexpected guests in the garden. "Right now I'm locked in a battle with the grasshoppers. Maybe the chef would like to add a few to the menu."

One afternoon, between a massive lunch and an even larger dinner, Roberto takes me to visit a man he considers to be his greatest inspiration. When we pull into the town of Gonnoscodina, a dramatic hairpin drive up and over the hill from Siddi, Delfino Porcu (*sardo* for "pig") is sitting on the curb reading a magazine about saffron. There are shady spots all around, but he has chosen this exposed swath of cement, undaunted by the angry June sun pouring down on his bare, bronzed scalp. He shakes my hand, crunching my digits with his iron grip, then says matter-of-factly, "I've been reading about better ways to pick the stamens from the crocus." A pause and a grin: "The stamen is the part that counts."

He's dressed in military green from head to toe, with a silver eagle belt buckle and a tight V-neck shirt that strains to contain his chiseled upper body. "It's important to never stop reading. The mind needs to feed on new information every day. It's how I stay young." As an eighty-one-year-old who looks not a day over sixty-two, he should know.

Foraging was once a fundamental part of the Sardinian food system—both a necessary resource for a hungry island and an edible illustration of the deep connection between the people and the land. Delfino is one of the last of a dying class of foragers, who works the land not as a hobby or a weekend pastime but as a means of survival—physical, spiritual, and otherwise. He once fell in love with a woman who didn't love him back. Beyond that, his life has been dedicated entirely to the natural world—to learning as much about the flora and fauna of the island as possible. "When we were young, we took all of this for granted. Everyone knew what to do with these plants. We're losing our patrimony."

We follow him in his tiny Fiat back to his house, stopping every few hundred meters to sample one wild herb or another. He has lived on these fifteen hectares all by himself for decades. Not alone, exactly: there are five beautiful *sardi* dogs gathered near his shack, a dozen or so pigs over the hill, and a small but intensely beautiful sunken garden at the foot of the property. "Back before the

Delfino Porcu,
master of the Sardinian soil.

weather started changing, this was like the Garden of Eden. Absolute paradise."

As we walk around the property, Delfino treats his land like an old-timer treats a photo album, offering an anecdote or piece of intel for every plant we pass. "They used these leaves to numb teeth in the old dentist offices. . . . When you're feeling a bit off, add a handful of these seeds to a glass of hot water, wait ten minutes, and you'll sleep like an angel. . . . Doctors tell us to eat fish for the omega-3 fats, but this herb has even more. . . . *Portulaca oleracea*, this used to be the salad green of choice of the Romans. Then it fell out of favor." Delfino could explain the history of the world through a small patch of weeds.

Every few days, Delfino arrives to make a delivery to S'Apposentu, an ever-shifting selection of nature's menu *du jour*: thin, sweet stalks of wild celery, spicy *dragoncello* (tarragon), bitter bunches of dandelions. Whatever Delfino brings, Roberto folds into the day's menu. "There are lots of great farmers and producers around the island, but there's only one Delfino."

Delfino has turned his backyard into his pantry, his classroom, his pharmacy, his love. As I watch him move from one plant to the next, crushing the leaves below our noses, telling stories about dramatic confrontations with one species or another, and offering prescriptions for cholesterol problems and back issues, I keep coming back to the same thought: this man knows more about this patch of earth than I'll ever know about anything.

There's an old *sardo* parable that goes something like this: A farmer is working his land one day when his plow strikes something hard beneath the earth. He digs it out to discover a dusty gold lamp, and after a few rubs, out pops a genie, ready to grant him a single wish. "The only condition," says the genie, "is that whatever you wish for, your neighbor will get double." The farmer puts down his plow, wipes his brow, and, after a minute or two, looks at the genie and says, "I'll have you take one of my eyes."

Brutal. But any *sardo* you meet along the way will be all too happy to load you down with anecdotal evidence: the farmer who poisoned his neighbor's soil; the rival shepherd who kidnapped a few sheep from the next guy's flock; the restaurant owners who had their rival shut down. Italians say the Sardinians are more guarded and suspicious than their compatriots on the mainland.

Keep in mind, these aren't my judgments or even based on any extensive observation. In fact, every moment in Sardinia confirms exactly the opposite: that the Sardinians are possessed of a near-boundless generosity, that if they invite you over for a snack and a glass of wine, they mean a spit-roasted animal and a long afternoon of drinking, and if you're in the market for a new shirt, the ones right off their backs are there for the taking. Time and again I'm blown away by the hospitality of the *sardi*—Angelo, the rental agent from Europcar who calls around to his buddies at rival agencies to negotiate a car for us; Giovanni Montisci, the cult winemaker,

who soaks us in a series of bold, funky reds and stuffs us with *porceddu*, wood-fired suckling pig, one of the heroes of the Sardinian kitchen; the farmer's mother, Angelica, who walks me through each step of her family recipes with patience and pride in equal measure. People who I meet for minutes send messages asking when we'll be back. *Any day now!*

More and more, those dusty genie anecdotes speak to the island's past—when limited resources and a contentious history turned neighbors into rivals—but not to its future. The innate challenges of life on Sardinia are substantial. Physically and politically isolated from the rest of Europe, the *sardi* have made a history of figuring things out on their own. Enlightened locals have come to realize that no man is an island, that Sardinia is the kind of place that needs everybody to push in the same direction.

Roberto embodies this spirit down to his marrow. A dozen years and a million miles of wandering the globe stirred in him a connection to home that you won't find in a sedentary chef. The more he saw of the world, the more he recognized the riches of Sardinia, until it became as clear as the turquoise waters of Porto Giunco that he wanted to dedicate his life to supporting this island in whatever small ways he can.

Turns out those ways aren't so small. With each visit to a cheese producer or farmer or forager, I see why people talk about Roberto the way they do—about someone who is "much more than a chef." The word *chef* doesn't mean what it once did—a general who leads a team of cooks into battle every night. In our increasingly food-mad world, *chef* means philosopher, politician, author, entertainer.

For someone of Roberto's polished pedigree and prodigious talent, it would be easy to decide that Sardinia simply isn't big enough; on the contrary, he has calibrated his ambitions to the perimeters of this island and set about working fiercely within them. More than a celebrity or an iconoclast, he positions himself as a middleman, a catalyst for small, steady changes around Sardinia—the type that will have a lasting effect on how this

island feeds itself for decades to come. He is a creator not just of dishes but of communities.

In 2010, not long after transplanting S'Apposentu to Siddi, Roberto opened Accademia Casa Puddu, a culinary school designed to educate young Sardinian cooks and to keep the next generation of culinary minds on the island they call home. Classes include the typical tent poles of a culinary education—sauce making, meat fabrication, stock theory—but extend deep into the local DNA of the island, from foraging wild herbs to learning to work within Sardinia's microseasons.

One night, I eat dinner at S'Apposentu with Gianfranco Massa, the director of the Accademia. Bald head, strong jaw, broad chest, he looks like Hank Schrader, the DEA agent from *Breaking Bad*, only with a mission decidedly more benign than meth enforcement. "Our job is really about support. How can we convince the young kids to stay and work the land?"

When I ask about government support, he reaches over his shoulder and pats himself on the back. *"Bravi! Bravi!* That's all they do. They love to talk about us during an election, but then they're quick to forget."

There's an Italian term used to describe people like Roberto—*rompiscatole*, people who break structures, crush schemes, and, amid the wreckage and the rubble, build something entirely new. "Sardinia needs Roberto," Gianfranco says. "And more like him."

At this point Roberto delivers a dish—tiny ravioli stuffed with smoked eel, another little love letter. The chef pretends not to hear, but the blushing cheeks betray him. (So reticent is Roberto to talk about himself that after seven days traversing this island together, he fails to mention Sa Scolla in Baradili, his newly opened pizzeria, which serves pizzas built with seasonal Sardinian ingredients and washed down with local microbrews—an opening I only discover later online.)

"For us, it's all about virtuous cycles," Roberto says. "Plant a seed here in one part of the island, help to water it, and watch it grow."

Talk of preservation and regeneration echoes across the island—from Gianfranco's Vermentino vines to the aquaculture operations off the coast of Cabras. Usually it's applied to cheese, bread, wine; sometimes it means an entire community.

Nughedu Santa Vittoria is a town looking for a second chance. Located 100 kilometers north of Cagliari in the dead center of Sardinia, every turn through the village offers staggering views avross the island's rolling topography.

A small congregation of young, well-dressed men wait for us on the steps of the town church. These are Roberto's latest partners, a group dedicated to building their town into a sustainable tourist destination. Since the 1970s, as the mineral industry crashed and jobs began to disappear, towns such as Nughedu Santa Vittoria have watched as their youths have fled to the mainland in search of a life Sardinia can't provide. "Depopulation is an epidemic across the island, especially in the small villages," says Francesco Mura, the town's mayor, a man on a mission. "We are tired of watching young Sardinians leave the island."

We take a tour of the town—down one cobblestone road after the next, a village of picture-postcard beauty unfolds around us. Kids play hide-and-seek in the narrow stone streets. An old man invites us in for a taste of his homemade liquor. A seventy-year-old woman and her ninety-year-old mother take the late-afternoon *passeggiata*, stopping in front of the church to make the sign of the cross. If this were Tuscany, you'd find an army of Brits and Americans refurbishing villas and preparing to press their own olive oil. But we're a million miles from Montepulciano, so the residents have turned to Roberto with a plan to revitalize village life.

"We don't want to be another tourist stop," says Francesco. "We want to create an experience, share part of our culture, and that's something you can do only through community." The chef and the townspeople discuss cooking classes, special dinners in the homes of locals, cheese-making lessons. Through the town center runs a route

that locals call the Cammino di Santiago of Sardinia, a system of trails that connect the island's idyllic villages—a potential path forward for Nughedu Santa Vittoria.

Francesco and the townspeople want to give us a taste of their vision. In the small, spartan community center, a group of men stands around three large pots, beginning the preparations for dinner. This is the interior of Sardinia, where sheep outnumber humans ten to one, and these guys look to be doing their best to narrow the gap. Women do most of the cooking in Sardinia—with one notable exception: sheep, which are raised, killed, and cooked by men.

As we circle the room, one gentleman pulls a knife from his pocket and begins to cut up chunks of leg and shoulder. Another, unimpressed by his buddy's blade, unsheaths his own. "That's not a knife. *This* is a knife." In Sardinia, everyone carries a knife.

On the other side of the room, a man pushing ninety gives a master class in mutton: he sears large chunks of meat until they are mahogany colored, then stirs in

Tripe and tomatoes, part of the
magical home cooking of Sardinia.

onion, celery, sun-dried tomatoes, and 35 liters of water, skimming the fat as it slowly bubbles up from below. "This will take some time," he says as the stew settles into a simmer, "but the results will be magical."

Outside, young Nicolas sits on a chair and plays a soul-stirring melody on an accordion. A handsome couple dances the *ballo sardo*, a sequence with lots of tiny movements and elaborate choreography. A well-dressed boy approaches on the back of a white horse, clipping and clopping to the groans of the accordion. If at first the scene feels slightly stilted, a coordinated sequence of rural traditions to impress the urban guests, the organic energy of Nughedu Santa Vittoria soon takes over. A soft pink light clings to everything as the village comes to life in the cooling hours of dusk. One by one, the people of Nughedu Santa Vittoria arrive bearing gifts. A man cradles bottles of his latest batch of homemade beer. A woman slices up a wheel of pecorino she makes from her husband's flock.

We take our seats at a long communal table and the feast commences. *Mallored-dus*—small and chewy, Sardinia's most

ubiquitous pasta shape—come glazed in sheep broth and stained with saffron. Ravioli stuffed with potato and pecorino wear a coat of simmered tomato and crushed parsley. Finally, the stars of the evening: First, sheep boiled with potato and onion offered by a group of younger cooks, resistant but remarkably light. Then the old man's version, redolent of herbs and wisdom, the fickle flesh rendered defenseless by decades of practice.

Nobody enjoys the meal more than Roberto, who closes his eyes, nods his head, and generally looks as if he's tasting all of this for the very first time. "People just don't realize how damn good Sardinian food really is. There's only one Michelin star on the island, and it's tucked down a small street in Siddi. And that's a problem. If we had the five or eight we deserve, we'd have more people, more creative energy, a virtuous cycle we would all benefit from." A chorus of approval bounces around the table, though it's unclear whether anyone here knows or cares about Michelin stars.

Someone down the table, a visitor from

a distant land, asks for Parmesan and barely lives to tell the tale. *"Parmigiano? Niente! Sempre pecorino. Sempre!"*

Roberto, Francesco, and the rest of the men argue about wine. About local pasta shapes. About a bit of everything. The only point of agreement is the general supremacy of Sardinia in all matters of the stomach and heart, a proclamation the entire village drinks to. Promises are made about the next steps in Nughedu Santa Vittoria's resurgence, and Roberto looks tickled. "Put talented people in the same room, add wine and some sheep," he says, "and let them forge a future for the island."

After the plates are cleared, a bottle of local firewater materializes and the village begins to tilt. Our new friends share the type of sad stories known by too many, sing songs in a dialect known by too few. Someone suggests that I mount a horse. When the bottle is gone, we waddle down the hill to the local bar, the entire village behind us. The idea is to order espresso and be on our way, but nobody here looks ready to budge an inch.

At one point, Francesco catches me scribbling furiously in my notebook and smiles. "You sure you want to leave?" A few minutes later, Roberto comes up from behind, puts his hand on my shoulder, and motions to the scene before us—the dark outline of distant mountains, the crater and the lake lapping below, the piazza full of villagers lost in song and drink. *"Questo è Sardegna."*

This is Sardinia. It's a phrase that follows me like waves of sheep across the island. Lonely shepherd: *This* is Sardinia. Salty fisherman: No, *this* is Sardinia. Proud *nonna*: This is and this . . . and oh, this, too. Visionary chef: Don't forget about this, my friend. This is Sardinia, the island forged from the scraps of the gods. Hills like supple breasts, plains like cracked cake batter. *This* is Sardinia. Coastlines of transparent beauty. Rough pyramids of weathered stone. This is Sardinia. Holy bread. Mountain cheese. Altered beast. The island no one could conquer. A footprint in the sea. This is Sardinia. *This* is Sardinia! This!

FOOD
FIGHTERS

Preserving the traditions of Italian cuisine

Wood-Fired Pecorino, Basilicata

THE CACIO CUSTODIANS

Many of Italy's fiercest food fighters work to preserve a physical entity, an ingredient or a species threatened by the inexorable march of modernity, but what this couple fights for is even bigger: a rapidly vanishing way of life. Now in their seventies and living on the border of Basilicata and Puglia, they make cheese the way nobody else does anymore: They raise goats and sheep, then warm the milk over a fire of fig branches. This is cheese so elemental it doesn't have a name, just a description: fresh, three-month, six-month. The hard cheese makes a heroic hunk to drop on a dinner table; the soft, fresh cheese is there to be stuffed into ravioli or slathered on toasted bread with sliced figs or a drizzle of honey. To taste the sheep's-milk ricotta straight from the bubbling cauldron is to ruin yourself for all other ricotta going forward (a risk worth taking). "We don't do anything special. We just do it the way it's always been done." These days, that qualifies as something very special, indeed.

MAMMA DANIELA

NAME: Daniela di Giacinti

CITY: Vicenza

REGION: Veneto

SPECIALTY: *Ciambellone*, a soft cake made with cocoa powder. I also love to make pasta—it's what brings people together in my house.

KITCHEN MEMORY: We live near an American military complex and twenty years ago my friend Greg brought me a turkey. Since then I cook stuffed turkey every Christmas and serve it with antipasti and lasagne.

KITCHEN PHILOSOPHY: Italian food is healthy. Pasta saved us from burgers. People should learn how to make Italian food just because it's very easy and it has the power to make people happy.

ANATOMY *of a dish*

WHERE'S THE BEEF?

In a country where meat is more often used as a role player than as a dramatic centerpiece to a meal, this Tuscan T-bone is a rare example of protein-forward cooking. While pigs and sheep are more common in the south of Italy, Tuscany has a long, deep relationship with beef.

TUSCANY'S T-BONE

A proper *fiorentina* is a T-bone or porterhouse cut, the bone dividing a strip steak from a generous cut of filet. It should come from a Chianina, a Tuscan breed known as one of the largest and oldest in the world, prized for its lean, tender meat.

LA FIORENTINA

WHEN LESS IS MORE

A perfect example of Italian restraint—no marinades, no sauces, no distractions; just a giant piece of meat seasoned with coarse salt and cooked hot and fast over a wood flame (or on a cast-iron surface). At most your steak will get a drizzle of olive oil and a whisper of rosemary.

BEAUTY AND THE BEEF

Skip the antipasti, the pasta, and other distractions and focus on the big task at hand. A real *fiorentina* is three fingers' thick, up to six pounds of pure protein. It's best eaten with an empty belly, a bowl of creamy white beans, and a bottle of Chianti.

ODE TO THE AGRITURISMO

The place you see at night when you close your eyes and dream of Italy: a rural B&B where everything is beautiful and delicious and nothing hurts. Run almost exclusively by families with deep connections to the local terrain, the *agriturismo* is not just an affordable place to sleep and eat, but a window into local culture you won't find at a hotel. Depending on where you stay, you can press olive oil, see wine production, make cheese, and, of course, eat and drink like royalty. Pick your spot at agriturismo.it, or start with some of my favorites.

📍 AGRITURISMO CACCIAMICI

The sun-baked hills of Tuscany, the golden fields of grain, the boundless breakfasts and dinners built around local foods — Cacciamici is the platonic ideal of an *agriturismo*.

📍 LOCANDA DELLA VALLE NUOVA

Visit local artisan producers, hunt for truffles with a crew of canines, or explore the tiny villages and coastal cuts of Le Marche — all from this magical mountain hideaway.

LA TRAVERSINA

Like sleeping inside a lavish English garden run by two lovely Italians. Learn to garden, learn to cook, learn to do absolutely nothing but eat and wander the Piedmont for a few days.

AGRITURISMO IL PORTONE

A striking stone villa in the center of Majella National Park, Il Portone is a perfect point into Abruzzo, one of Italy's most overlooked regions for serious eaters.

Chapter Seven

PIEDMONT

—

Tuesday, October 11, 10:37 A.M.,
Eataly, Torino

It takes all of three minutes in the pasta aisle for me to reschedule the train tickets. We need to be in Bra for a meeting with a master trekker, but in front of me are the building blocks of a million marvelous lunches, and my imagination is boiling like a pot of salted pasta water. We have a long, strenuous journey ahead, and I want to be sure we prepare accordingly.

The journey in question is a seven-day hike through the Langhe, a hilly corner of Piedmont that is home to one of the most potent combinations of culinary excellence and natural beauty in Italy. I had spent

many sleepless nights wondering how it would be possible to pack the awesomeness of this very special place into a single chapter. Phone calls, emails, Hail Mary Google searches that stretched search-engine algorithms to the snapping point. "An old mustachioed chef in the hills of Sant'Antonino who may be Italy's most underrated culinary treasure!" wrote one enthusiastic friend from the area. There's a farmer raising trout in ponds around Cuneo using a method developed centuries ago. A magical truffle hunter who has spent his entire life perfecting an idiosyncratic technique for unearthing the white diamonds. It all seemed glorious, but no single story felt sufficiently broad to capture and distill the power of Piedmont into a few dozen pages. Then my wife, Laura (bless her 20/10 vision), had the lightbulb idea of the year: Why don't we walk? Four simple words with a lifetime of wisdom surging through their syllables. As we've learned over our years together, on excursions through Provence and Japan and northern Spain, walking brings you as close to the local terrain as possible, allows you to see and hear and devour a little bit of everything, a wild and varied soundtrack set to the marching metronome of one foot falling after the other.

I grew up backpacking in the High Sierras with my dad, who taught me the value of being able to carry your life on your back, and later with friends who lived to disappear into the wilderness for a few days of spiritual cleansing. Provisioning for a backpacking excursion usually means collecting a stack of freeze-dried stir-fries and space-age nutritional bars that pack a day's worth of micronutrients into the size of a domino. But this is a different kind of trip—not of sleeping bags and butane dinners but of B&Bs and tiny trattorie, and it requires a different form of provisioning: picnic provisioning. And with apologies to France and Spain, titans of the lavish larder, there is no better country in the world for picnic provisioning than Italy.

And so we find ourselves here, in the aisles of Eataly, the citadel of Italian food culture, with the whole of the country's greatest culinary treasures splayed out before us. Where to begin? The long corridors of regional pastas—*trenette* from Genoa, *paccheri* from Campania—with their appropriate sauces? The mountains of still-life vegetables and fruits front-lit like a theater performance? The basement bodega exploding with the most elegant wines and esoteric microbrews this country has on offer?

Down every aisle a single thought follows me like a shadow: Brand Italy is strong. When it comes to cultural currency, there is no brand more valuable than this one. From lipstick-red sports cars to svelte runway figures to enigmatic opera singers, Italian culture means something to everyone in the world. But nowhere does the name Italy mean more than in and around the kitchen. Peruse a pantry in London, Osaka, or Kalamazoo, and you're likely to find it spilling over with the fruits of this country: dried pasta, San Marzano tomatoes, olive oil, balsamic vinegar, jars of pesto, Nutella.

Tucked into the northwest corner of Italy, sharing a border with France and Switzerland, Piedmont may be as far from the country's political and geographical center as possible, but it is ground zero for Brand Italy. This is the land of Slow Food. Of white truffles. Barolo. Vermouth. Campari. Breadsticks. Nutella. Fittingly, it's also the home of Eataly, the supermarket juggernaut delivering a taste of the entire country to domestic and international shoppers alike. This is the Eataly mother ship, the first and most symbolically important store for a company with plans for covering the globe in peppery Umbrian oil and shavings of Parmigiano-Reggiano Vacche Rosse.

We start with the essentials: bottle opener, mini wooden cutting board, hard-plastic wineglasses. From there, we move on to more exciting terrain: a wild-boar sausage from Tuscany. A semiaged goat's-milk cheese from Molise. A tray of lacy, pistachio-pocked mortadella. Some soft, spicy spreadable *'nduja* from Calabria. A jar of *gianduja*, the hazelnut-chocolate spread that inspired Nutella—just in case we have any sudden blood sugar crashes on the trail.

I could live in these aisles, use the warm wood-fired focaccia as a pillow, slices of hand-carved *culatello* as a blanket. I could write thesis papers on the marketing genius of Italy's food factions, books on the forces that conspired to create such a magnificent confluence of culinary might. But there is a strategy meeting in Bra and, beyond it, a winding path through Piedmont. We must keep moving.

Tuesday, 4:45 P.M., Bra
Elio Sabena stares at me with a look of mild bemusement. Hard to tell if it's my mid-

dling Italian or the borderline-absurd plan I've posed to him.

"*Allora . . .*"

Elio is one of the Langhe's most experienced trekkers, recruited to help us craft a perfect plan for slicing up the region on foot. Despite the abundance of footpaths coursing through Piedmont like capillaries, it's not easy to understand how all the anatomy fits together. Elio, with the support of the local government, is working to change that. After decades of walking from one village to the next in every possible sequence, he created BarToBar, a seven-day, 124-kilometer journey starting and finishing in Alba, cutting through the two most famous wine regions (Barolo and Barbaresco, hence the name) and the high-mountain Alta Langa in between.

I reached out to Elio because I want to follow largely in his footsteps, but with a few twists and turns to meet a few special characters and maximize the potency of the food and wine offerings along the way. We cover the tables in the hotel lobby with detailed maps and topographical charts as Elio

gives me a full overview of the region. (For anyone serious about journeying through this part of Piedmont, his book *Scoprire le Langhe* is an indispensable resource.)

He listens to my questions patiently and responds politely to the strange sequences I begin constructing: "So what if we start in La Morra, move across the valley to Serralunga, then curl around to have lunch at Cesare Giaccone in Albaretto?" His favorite area, the rolling valleys around Barbaresco, just east of Alba, appears out of reach for this trip, but he assures us that nothing but excellence awaits us on the path ahead. When I tell him I'd like to visit two great wineries and two great osterie a day, plus meet a truffle hunter or two along the way, he smiles. "You could walk in any direction across the Langhe and do that." In the Langhe, you can't throw a hazelnut shell without landing on something delicious.

Two hours later, I have a rough route mapped out, but with the forecast in the coming days showing a heavy storm front rolling in, he warns me that I'll need to be

All roads lead to *vino*.

adaptable. As someone who books plane tickets on the way to the airport and outlines books on the backs of bar napkins, I assure him that adaptability will not be a problem.

"In the worst case, you can try to hitchhike," he says on his way out of the hotel. "You never know—maybe you'll get lucky."

With the plan secure—a taxi set to take us the first leg of the way, which Elio insists is unwalkable—we reward ourselves with a serious dinner downstairs at Osteria Murivecchi. I realize as I sit down that I've been here before—my first time in Piedmont, in the fall of 2011, on a truffle-fueled romp through the Langhe. Over the course of three days, two Catalan friends and I managed to eat every possible foodstuff—from eggy handmade pasta to beef tartare to mashed potatoes—covered in wafer-thin slices of *tartufo bianco*. The highlight of the trip was a hunting session at dawn with a retired police chief with a fondness for Spaniards. His sprightly cocker spaniel unearthed a dozen truffles, and when we went to say our good-byes, he pressed them into our palms. "I have enough already."

No truffles today. We need comfort, not class. I eat lentil soup ladled from a beautiful glass terrine. Laura orders gnocchi, celestially light, brought back to earth by a cloak of creamy Castelmagno, a mildly funky blue cheese made a few towns over. I finish with *brasato al Barolo*, beef braised to the point of collapsing in a bath of the region's most famous wine.

Sated and lightly buzzed, we stumble back to our room, stretch out across the bed, and fall immediately into a deep, dreamless sleep.

Wednesday, 9:47 A.M., Verduno
"*Buongiorno*. I am Bruno, it will be my pleasure to drive you today. Please, please, I will take your bags. *Prego*. So where did you say you're going? Oh yes, yes, Verduno, of course. Lovely town. Your friend is right, it is a difficult walk, but luckily I am here to drive you. And there is so much to see between here and there. To your left you'll find Slow Food's university. Imagine that: going to college to study food! *Che bello!* If you look to your right, you will see the

Tanaro River, which divides the Langhe from Roero. The Langhe has rich soil, fertile, some of the finest in all of Europe. Roero, *in cambio*, is harder, inhospitable, ungenerous. The Langhe is a paradise, a *giardino*: pears, apples, pomegranates, chestnuts. Everything you could want to eat falling from a tree. And above all, *nocciole*. You see those trees? Those are South American hazelnuts. Fatter. Rounder. There are also the smaller Turkish hazelnuts, but Ferrero Rocher uses the big ones to make Nutella. And wine—everywhere, wine. Barbera, Bonarda, Dolcetto, and the king, Nebbiolo, the king of all grapes. You've come to the right place. We've just officially crossed over into the Barolo area, the one you see in the books and magazines. You know we have UNESCO heritage status here, right? I'm not sure what that means, other than that this is a beautiful part of the world and we are all very proud of it. I am happy that we can all agree on this point. So you plan to walk around the Langhe, eh? Wow, that's ambitious. I myself say, why walk when you can drive?, but I'm sure you have your reasons."

On Wednesday morning, we find the narrow streets of this town of five hundred all but empty. The little action in Verduno emanates from the apex of the village, where Casa Ciabotto does the town's only discernible commerce. Coffee, wine, pasta, gossip—the kind of one-stop shop you need in a village like Verduno. We settle in for a cappuccino and soak up a bit of Verduno's languid pace. A couple wanders in, salutes the bartender like an old friend, orders a bottle of wine. Outside, the church clock tower strikes eleven.

"*Come va?* What's new?"

"*Niente.* Well, there's no *tartufo.*"

"Seriously? None?"

"Nothing so far. They say it's going to be a very difficult year."

"Of course. *Troppo caldo. Troppo secco.* How much they going for?"

"It's tough to say. There's not even enough to sell. My neighbor has a great dog, *molto bravo*, and he takes him out to the *nocciole* to hunt during the season. On a normal day, he has no problem finding four, five, six *tartufi*. He went out yesterday: *niente.*"

As promised, we find two exceptional wineries in Verduno, two of the dozens that carpet the hills surrounding the town. Next door to Ciabotto, Castello di Verduno was the wine-washed pleasure palace of King Carlo Alberto di Savoia in the mid–nineteenth century. Today, it operates as a winery, restaurant, and hotel—a typical trifecta in the Langhe, albeit in particularly stately digs. Raffaella shows us around the cellar, with its dank, ripe smell of fermentation and ancient history. Two small caverns house the current owner's most prized potions, including a few bottles that stretch back more than a century. During the tasting, lovely Raffaella apologizes for not having the type of florid wine vocabulary oenophiles like to toss around. I promise her that I don't mind, that as much as I love to drink wine I simply lack the type of analytical capacity to convincingly discuss subtleties and nuances. She sums up our shared philosophy on wine efficiently: "I know what I like, and I know what I don't."

Like many people we meet, she seems blown away by the area's ascendance into the upper echelons of wine culture. "I'm from a small village in Roero. My grandfather made his own wine, like so many people did back then. He added sugar to balance out the tannins, just like all the old-timers did. This explosion in the area has been unthinkable. A hundred euros for a bottle of Barolo—what local can drink that? It's all going to the United States, where they're happy to pay that much."

With a bottle in our bellies and another in my backpack, we head down the road to Fratelli Alessandria. Alessandro Alessandria, who runs the winery along with his brother Vittore, comes from four generations of winemakers. "We have always been family owned and always been very serious about our wine." To demonstrate, he gestures to a framed document on the wall. Researching in Slow Food's Wine Bank in nearby Pollenzo, he came across a remarkable piece of memorabilia: an 1843 award recognizing Fratelli Alessandria as Piedmont's Winery of the Year.

He breaks down the lay of Barolo: in a space no larger than a small city, you'll find more than 350 wineries. The microclimates of this part of the Piedmont make for great variety, even if everyone is mostly growing the same grapes. In the west, you find fruit with more subtlety and rounder tannins. In the east, around the steep slopes of Serralunga and Monforte d'Alba, the wines are more aggressive, with more tannin. In Verduno, the nearby Tanaro River gives off cold winds that lend the wines of the area deeper aromas—spices generally, black pepper specifically, which punches hardest in Verduno's esoteric and awesome varietal, Pelaverga. As Barolo and Barbaresco have ascended to the top of the international wine world, Pelaverga has remained one of the great underappreciated wines of the region.

In many ways, the history of Fratelli Alessandria mirrors that of Piedmont's wine culture. For four generations, production at Fratelli Alessandria continued with little change. But under the brothers' guidance, the winery has begun to make real changes in everything from the growing to the processing and aging. Alessan-

dro's father, like nearly all winemakers of his generation, wanted to maximize yield, which meant using lower-quality fruit. They used old oak barrels with no control over temperature or humidity. Now they grow less fruit, leave more leaves on the vines to protect the grapes. But more than what happens on the vine, Alessandro focuses his energies on everything that happens after harvest. "You can only lose quality once you pick the grapes." He stores the wine in newer, cleaner casks and controls temperature and humidity using the latest in technology.

"We have the tools and the knowledge to make better wine today," he says, "and I would be crazy not to use them. Even if the older generation doesn't understand. My father and I have fought a lot over the past twenty years. We've seen lots of changes, and he has his own ideas. We differ in our approach, but our goal is the same."

These changes, says Alessandro, reflect a similar movement across the region, where smart, young winemakers are using the tools and knowledge available to them

to modernize Barolo and the other big wines. "Tradition doesn't mean not evolving. It's not an excuse to preserve bad practices."

He views the rise of Barolo with a good measure of ambivalence. "Tourism and friendly competition and UNESCO have all helped. But we must be careful not to make the same mistakes other regions have made. We don't want TripAdvisor of wine. We can't make wine for guidebooks or specific critics. You make it for yourself first and foremost."

Another tasting, another lesson, another head full of juice. Verduno sparkles in the early-afternoon light. Only a few hundred steps into the trip, and I'm already rethinking the entire plan. Maybe we should stay for a night or two in this wine-soaked village? Maybe Alessandro would like some help with the harvest? Maybe I can buy this little fixer-upper on the outskirts of town and write a book about all the charming and hilarious misadventures that ensue?

But a meeting farther down the road

is enough to snap us out of the Pelaverga-driven fantasy and propel us forward.

Wednesday, 5:30 P.M., Barolo

In the United States, my friends and family call me a wanderer, a rolling stone. In Spain, they have a better name: *culo inquieto*—a restless ass. One who simply can't sit still. Generally the terms apply to a larger life philosophy, one defined by the next journey, but the engine that drives it, even on a daily level, is the need for new stimuli. A trip like this is made for someone like me. Sure, I can sit in a small town for a week straight doing nothing but watch a family hand-stretch mozzarella into ropes of ivory succulence (see chapter 2), but I'm much more comfortable on the move—in a situation where the panorama of stimuli is always being refreshed, a constantly morphing milieu of sights, sounds, tastes, and faces. Hence the walking.

Have you ever driven through an especially beautiful expanse of Earth—down Highway 1 in central California, say, or the Pan-American Highway in Chile—and felt the sudden urge to do something? Not just to gape, not to pull over and take photos, but to find a deeper connection to the land? To roll around in the grass? To take a bite out of the earth? It's an itch that can never be scratched inside a moving vehicle; the closest you'll ever get to taking a bite out of the land is putting your life on your back and walking directly through it.

There is something undeniably magical about moving yourself from one town to the next with nothing but the power of your own two feet. One village—its bars and restaurants, its ancient stone steeple, its castle towers and pregnant cantinas—disappear behind you just as another one grows nearer. Removed from traffic, from human interaction, from anything that would qualify as a modern distraction, your mind is left to stretch itself into new dimensions. I think of how the settlers planned the first villages, the land grabs and miniwars fought in these hills, the earliest evolutions of alcoholic fermentation. Most of the thought goes to food: the simmering sauces, the braising meats, the

285

mounds of flour and egg turned into a million different shapes across the Langhe's wheat-dusted surfaces. Just as I'm moving on to a virtual panna cotta and a few fingers of grappa, we arrive at our next destination.

We travel light, as there are no bulky sleeping bags to contend with, no tents to hurry up and construct before the sun goes down. Packing nothing but a few changes of clothes and bright neon rain jackets frees up space for the important stuff: stemware and cutlery, plus the growing collection of dried meats and aged cheeses and funky condiments we accumulate along the journey. And because tastings are free in most wineries across the region, and because it's good practice to buy a bottle wherever you visit, hardly a moment goes by when I'm not shouldering a few local vintages.

Drop me into the middle of almost any landscape and I'd be dead within days, starved and dehydrated and outmaneuvered at every moment by nature. But in Piedmont, where the land is so fertile that everywhere you step you feel like you're making marmalade beneath your feet, I

take no small comfort in knowing that we could survive drunk and happy underneath a hazelnut tree for at least a few days.

Of course, the last thing the Langhe needs is another foreign interloper occupying precious parcels of land. The Bassa Langa (Lower Langhe) is some of the most expensive real estate in the world. Nearly every square inch of it is given over to either wine production or hazelnut farming. It just so happens that verdant, near-vertical staircases of vines and rough groupings of hazelnut trees make for spectacular eye candy—a landscape so suggestive of the products it creates that wine and *gianduja* and truffle-strewn pasta feel less like ingenious creations than foregone conclusions. There is a powerful symbiosis at work here—humans and nature in a dance that neither leads for more than a few steps at a time. On a nearly hourly basis, I found myself turning to Laura, gesturing to the latest collaboration between human and nature, and asking, "Are you serious?"

No doubt this expanse stuns visitors twelve months a year, but fall is when this part of Piedmont is at the height of its powers. The vines sag with swollen fruit. The leaves turn so fast you can almost witness their transformation from green to yellow to red to dead in real time. The air delivers the scents of autumn at every turn—notes of roasted earth and burning branches and molecular transformation, the first whispers of decay.

But not everyone is so thrilled about the landscape these days. Carlo Marenda is one of four thousand *tartufai* working in Piedmont today—men, mostly, who spend the autumn days tilling the earth in search of the rarest and most expensive of culinary treasures, the white truffle. Just as we arrive in Barolo, a charming village whose tiny size belies the massive reputation of its namesake wine, Carlo pulls up in his Panda with his two shaggy dogs, Emi and Buk, pressed up against the rear window.

Carlo doesn't come from an ancient lineage of truffle hunters; instead, he learned the craft from Giuseppe Giamesio, one of the Langhe's legendary *tartufai*. The two grew so close over the years that when

Giuseppe passed away, he gave Carlo his two dogs to continue the hunt with. No matter how smart and experienced a truffle hunter may be, he is nothing without a dog with a nose for fungus. So important is the truffle dog that canine kidnappings are common in these parts. (In Roddi, aspiring hunters can enroll their dogs in truffle university.)

Unfortunately for Carlo, Emi, Buk, and the thousands of other humans and canines in the Langhe, there is less and less hunting to do these days. The wine industry and the truffle industry, in most ways, are fundamentally opposed—if not explicitly or philosophically, then in the nature of what each demands of the earth. Grapes want warm, dry summers and open spaces, while truffles require both trees, whose root systems breed the spores, and rain, which helps the spores develop and concentrates their heft and aroma. This past summer in Europe was the hottest and driest in modern history. Deep into October, nobody can remember the last time it rained.

The combination of bad weather and

shrinking forests means that 2016 shaped up to be one of the worst truffle seasons on record. Total wine-devoted acreage has tripled since 1967, much of it owned by foreign interests. After watching one patch of tuber-filled forest after another get swallowed up by vineyards, Carlo decided to act. "If we don't do something soon, Alba will lose its truffle culture entirely."

One afternoon while out hunting, Carlo met Edmondo Bonelli, an environmental consultant who shared Carlo's concern for the continued survival of the Langhe's truffle culture. They joined forces to form Save the Truffle, an initiative aimed at preserving as much of the remaining land as possible for the patches of poplar and hazelnut trees under which truffles grow. Much of that comes down to the individual owners, who can decide whether to clear-cut or to leave intact as much of the natural flora as possible surrounding their vines. Hoping to convince local landowners to do just that, Carlo sent out a letter to two hundred local wineries. He received two responses.

We wind our way up a small mountain road beyond Barolo and park the car. Carlo lets the dogs out to run, but he ends up leashing them every few minutes as we come across another tractor or another truck sagging with just-picked fruit. Carlo flashes me an exasperated look. "See what I mean?"

We descend the side of the mountain and plunge into a small patch of forest that Carlo calls one of his favorite spots in the region for finding fungus. "Around this time last year I found four or five truffles every time I went out around here. This year, so far, nothing. But maybe we'll get lucky."

Maybe. I cross my fingers, because the act of unearthing something worth a couple of hundred euros or more is genuinely thrilling—the modern man's search for gold. But I must admit, I'm skeptical of the truffle hype.

My first truffle experience came in New York in 2005, when I paid $80 for a golf-ball-sized tuber from Buon Italia in Chelsea Market. I had little idea of what to do with it, but with a group of friends eager to bask in its earthy funk, we slowly figured it out: neutral flavors, simple preparations, nothing to get in the way of its heady perfume.

The first night was a rousing success. We sat around for hours, turning over the mysteries of the universe, giggling like a dorm room full of stoners, all of us seemingly intoxicated by the truffle's powerful pheromones. A new ritual was born, an annual Truffle Fest that stretched on for the better part of a decade across state lines and continental divides. In that time, I've cooked dozens of truffle-larded dishes. Soft scrambled eggs. Scallops and salsify in parchment. Wild mushroom pizza. Butter-bombed risotto. Whole roasted chicken with truffle slices slipped like splinters under the skin. Above all, handmade pasta tossed with melted butter and anointed tableside with truffle—the finest vessel for the tuber's dreamy fragrance.

But like so much in the food world, truffles have gone from an occasional indulgence to a full-blown fetish—one whose consumption is worn like a merit badge on Instagram feeds of globetrotting gastronauts every fall. Along the way, prices and demand have risen and quality has fallen as the origins of the truffles grow more and more opaque. All of which raises the question: Are they worth it? I love the romance of them, the fact that humans themselves are clueless as to how to effectively cultivate or even locate the fickle fungi. It's a delicious reminder that for all of our technological advancements, nature still wins.

I don't think of myself as a culinary curmudgeon. I spend nearly everything I save on eating as well as humanly possible, but I still operate on a price-to-pleasure formula when I make food decisions. And the price and the hype have grown insufferable. As I type this, a pound of truffles goes for $2,000 in Alba, considerably more than elsewhere in the world. A single dish with truffles shaved on top can fetch three-digit prices in fancy restaurants. A hundred dollars for a cluster of spores shaved onto my pasta? *No, grazie.* If I'm going to pay a hundred dollars for something white that goes

A POWERFUL SYMBIOSIS:
HUMANS AND NATURE
IN A DANCE THAT NEITHER
LEADS FOR MORE
THAN A FEW STEPS.

—

up my nose, it had better hit harder than a plate of pasta.

Yet guys like Carlo (and dogs like Emi and Buk) have helped turn tubers into a $4 billion business. There are 16,000 truffle hunters in Italy, 25 percent of them at work in Piedmont. Alba basks in the international attention, turning its once quiet annual truffle show into an international bonanza. White truffles come from all over northern and central Italy, as well as a dozen other countries from Croatia to China. But the one everyone wants, the name that fetches top dollar in markets and restaurants across the planet, comes from right here: the Alba truffle.

As we dig about in the earth, coming up empty, proud vendors ready their goods for the big weekend market. But based on everything I've heard—from Carlo and the handful of other hunters I've been in touch with—the truffles on sale this Sunday won't be Alba truffles, at least not most of them. Head to social media in early October, the first official week of the season, and you'll see white-gloved servers in restaurants from Texas to Tokyo shaving truffles over delicate plates of pasta, all under the name of Alba. But in a year like this one, it's simply not possible.

"Macedonia, Croatia, Serbia," says Carlo. "Right now they're coming from everywhere but here." He tells me about the truffle sprays vendors use to increase the fragrance of foreign truffles, about the fact that the ruse is widely known and accepted by everyone along the way. Nobody—not the hunters, not the vendors, not the restaurants that serve truffles, not the local government, which banks on tourism and the marketing power of the truffle—wants to admit what's really going on. There's too much damn money at stake.

Emi and Buk work their way through the woods, bounding from one tree to the next with their noses to the ground. It's dark now, and we swoop our headlamps around the dense forest flora, searching in vain. An hour later, we reemerge from the woods empty-handed.

When Carlo drops us off at our hotel, it's hard not to feel a tinge of disappointment.

Despite my reservations about the truffle culture, it would have been nice to sleep with a diamond underneath my pillow.

Thursday, 8:39 A.M., Monforte d'Alba

Rain. Buckets of it, cold and constant—exactly as every single person we've met this week has predicted. I'd held out hope that the local prognosticators were as misguided as the ones in my town, but clearly the meteorology game in Piedmont is strong.

I stand on the balcony of our *agriturismo* and survey our prospects. Across the vines and orchards, a chorus of chickens, pigs, and dogs cuts through the pitter-patter. Good to see that the animals continue with business as usual. But for the humans of this part—the winemakers, the truffle hunters, the chestnut and hazelnut farmers—today will be a day of rest.

We don't have that luxury. There is juice to be swilled, *tajarin* to be twirled—we must push on.

In the central piazza of Monforte, in the one bar that seems to be open and active, we find a group of old men huddled around the counter, sucking caffeine from their mustaches and working out their collective ambivalence about the rain. The wine guys worry about its impact on the harvest, going on now throughout the region. The truffle guys do the math: rain today means more truffles in November means extra Christmas presents in December. Keep it coming.

Our math is simple: torrential rainstorm equals difficult journey ahead. No picnics, no naps under the vines, no panoramic perfection. With no signs of the rain letting up, we do the only sensible thing we can think of: we seek out a covered spot where we can drink wine. Halfway up the climbing village, we find a stone grotto carved into the side of the mountain that appears to be made expressly for this purpose: rustic stone table, benches, generous views of the town below. A bottle emptied and the rain still relentless, we make a bet: How long will it take us to hitchhike to Roddino, today's lunch destination? Laura, emboldened by the vino and the kindness of the *piemontesi*, bets five cars; I guess eleven.

We stand on a street corner heading out of town and wait. And wait. The first few cars slow down and look ready to let us in, but they are probably just trying to get a glimpse of the unknown characters hitchhiking in their little wine-soaked hamlet. Thirty minutes and twelve cars later, an old man in a Smurf-blue moving van pulls up and rolls down the window: "*Dove andate?*"

Renzo from Roddino leaves us on the doorstep of Osteria da Gemma, a Langhe culinary landmark in a village scarcely large enough to fill the restaurant. Before we can shake off the wet and the cold, before we can see a menu or catch our breath, the waiter comes by and drops a cutting board full of *salumi* between us. *Prego*. Then another plate comes out—*carne cruda*, a soft mound of hand-chopped veal dressed with nothing but olive oil and a bit of lemon, a classic warm-up to a Piedmont meal.

The plates continue, and it soon becomes very clear that we have no say in the matter. *Insalata russa*, a *tricolore* of toothsome green peas, orange carrots, and ivory potatoes, bound in a cloak of mayonnaise and crumbled egg yolk. *Vitello tonnato*, Piedmont's famous take on surf and turf: thin slices of roast beef with a thick emulsion of mayo and tuna. Each bite brings us slowly out of the mist of emotion and into the din of the dining room.

No menu ever arrives. We are allowed to order wine—a bottle of Barbera d'Alba "Vignota" from Conterno Fantino in Monforte, juicy and direct as a British tabloid—but otherwise we are at the whim of the kitchen of women cooking furiously behind us. We spot three generations—four, maybe, depending on how you squint—but they dance around one another as if they had all been born at the stroke of midnight.

Pastas come next: Piedmont's two most emblematic shapes covered in a meaty ragù: *agnolotti al plin*, rich veal-stuffed parcels, and *tajarin*, the thin, golden, eggy noodles of the region. These are the two most famous pastas of the Langhe, the type you will find on every single restaurant menu from Alba to Novello, but they both come alive in Gemma's kitchen. The *tajarin* are especially miraculous: being so thin and delicate, it's normally impossible to get a true al dente texture out of this pasta, but these golden locks possess a marvelous, enduring chew. Laura and I eat in silence until the last ragù-slicked strand vanishes.

There are no cigarette or bathroom breaks at this meal. The moment the pasta disappears, the *secondi* arrive: stewed rabbit *alla cacciatora* and *brasato al Barolo*, classic cold-weather comfort food, the kind designed to get locals through long winters working in the mountains. As the server clears the last of the dishes, Laura and I sit with that starry-eyed postcoital look stained on our faces. Maybe it's the rain, maybe it's the energy of this place, maybe it's the relief of not having to choose or think or even wait for anything. Maybe it's the generous soul who dropped us on this doorstep. But even before we've started to digest it all, I know this will be a meal I'll carry with me forever.

Here, thirty-five years ago, Gemma Boeri, now seventy years young, opened a *circolo sociale*, a social club where locals could

have a bite to eat. In 2005, she opened the doors to the public. Everything about the food and the service suggests someone not just born to feed but born to nourish. From the spread of antipasti to the savory, slow-cooked finale, lunch is a treatise on the beauty of the Piedmontese kitchen. Here you'll find Italy's most potent combination of power and finesse, where the ingredients aren't left naked on the plate but concentrated through time-honed techniques: kneading, braising, reducing, emulsifying. Think: *bollito misto*, hearty cuts of chicken, beef, and sausage simmered and served tableside from a rolling cart with a battery of condiments. Think: *polenta grassa*, sheets of creamy cornmeal layered with fontina cheese and baked until bubbling. Think: *finanziera*, a medieval stew of livers and kidneys and sweetbreads, mushrooms and truffles and peas, cooked in wine and butter and stock. Think: one of Italy's most satisfying and soulful food cultures.

By the time we finish our espresso, the busy dining room has all but cleared, save for a table of old-timers playing cards in

Gemma Boeri and her
golden tangles of *tajarin*.

the corner. Behind them, in a clean, well-lighted room framed by a long glass wall, Gemma is making pasta. A long bench, a pile of flour, a trail of empty eggshells in her wake. One long, deep yellow, un-broken sheet of pasta runs the length of the room, covering three tables—maybe twenty meters long from end to end. She folds it section by section and runs a long blade through the sheet, creating 12-inch-long noodles every bit as thin and exact as those of a Tokyo soba master. Every thirty seconds, she stops to separate the strands into little piles that build across the table like golden molehills.

I stare through the window, eyes glazed, jaw slack, arms goose bumped. Gemma spots me gawking, beckons me in. I step in cautiously, apologize for interrupting, but she keeps beckoning. *Vieni, vieni.* Come on in.

We talk pasta. I express my undying admiration for everything we just ate, above all the brilliant texture of her *tajarin.* "It's nothing, really," she says, dusting her hands with flour, preparing for her next move.

The nonchalance is not false modesty; for Gemma, making pasta is an act as routine as brushing her teeth or washing her face. I make pasta all the time, I tell her, but mine never tastes like yours. "Of course not. You are young," she says, as if the combination of egg and flour can feel the innocence in my fingertips.

Finally she gives a little. "If you want to know the secret, it's letting the pasta rest. Work it well, roll it out, then walk away. Come back in an hour and continue." And with that she gets back to work. Something tells me it's a bit more complicated than that, but for her it's not. And that's what matters.

I see in her precise movements, in her gentle grace, in the flour under her fingernails and the light creases under her eyes some ancient wisdom that cannot be taken lightly, as it was not accumulated lightly. It doesn't transfer to notebooks or blog posts or television programs. She has been on her feet since 8 A.M., braising beef, simmering ragù, cleaning vegetables—just as she has done for the past four decades. The fact that it's seventy-year-old Gemma standing here immediately after lunch service, transforming eggs and flour into a wellspring, and not one of the younger, experienced cooks in the kitchen, should tell you everything you need to know: this is not an art that transfers easily.

"Yes, I get tired. I'm tired every day. I'm tired right now," she says, her shoulders slumping ever so gently. "But I keep going because it's what I love most."

Friday, 5:45 P.M., Serralunga d'Alba

The downpour continues. We spend the better part of twenty-four hours barricaded in a room in an *agriturismo* a few miles beyond Gemma's. We drink wine and eat cheese in bed, waiting for the weather to turn, but this storm has taken on biblical dimensions. Our plan to push deeper into the Upper Langhe—to the milkshake-thick forests and sharp rocky peaks, the part that Elio called the most soul-stirring of the region—will need to be abandoned. If we hope to make it back to Alba by Sunday, we'll need to head north. But how? I study

Elio's topo maps, hoping to find in the psychedelic swirl of colors and textures some warp zone through this sopping mess. We grow restless. When the rain stops for a full twenty minutes, we throw on our plastic ponchos and hit the road.

For the first stretch, as we walk downhill on a quiet country road lined with pear trees and hazelnut groves, everything goes just fine. But as we begin to ascend through a vineyard, we find that the rain has transformed the trail between the vines into slopes of melted chocolate. Keep in mind that these aren't the gentle, rolling slopes of California wine country but exaggerated angles of earth and plants, turning a brisk climb into something closer to a mud-wrestling match between you and the Nebbiolo.

After an hour of fighting our way up the slope, mud sucking at our shoes like vacuum hoses, we finally reach a ridge, and through the trees and across a valley, Serralunga d'Alba appears like an oasis in the desert. Staircase vineyards surround the village on the hill, giving it the feel of an inverted amphitheater—with the dramatic twelfth-century Serralunga Castle as the star of the show. In the distance, behind fleeting holes in the storm, the first snows of the season cling to the peaks of the Alps.

Serralunga may just be the perfect Piedmont village: not too small, not too large, a Goldilocks civilization with everything you've ever wanted packed into a gorgeous hilltop hamlet of 507 inhabitants. There are two excellent restaurants—one traditional, the other with a smart touch of modern flair. Two wine bars of the caliber that will make your local wine bar almost impossible to return to. A few small, charming-but-not-too-charming stores selling produce, cured meat, and fresh pasta. World-class wineries waiting everywhere for your visit. Views for days. Looks to kill.

Serralunga means "long greenhouse"—a reference to the narrow, outstretched village resting on the top of this ridge and the dense, fertile world growing below it. Everyone in Serralunga earns a living doing one of two things: making wine or making

food. If that doesn't sound like a world you want to be a part of, I have no idea how you made it this far in the book.

It would be so easy for a place like this to be insular, uptight, or smug, to succumb to its own pastoral perfection, but Serralunga shows no signs of knowing or caring just how great it is. Despite the hills being covered with some of the world's most coveted fruit, the soil spotted with a billion dollars' worth of spores, you will find no airs in Serralunga beyond the umami air of fermented grapes and subterranean fungi. Everywhere we turn we are confronted with intense acts of kindness. A question about directions yields a story about the history of the castle. The old woman sweeping her steps in the early-morning light pauses for a *buongiorno* so heartfelt it burns off the autumn chill clinging to our bones. We see a young man we met a few towns back, in Monforte, who invites us to finish off the bottle of Barbera he is drinking pensively on a patio on the edge of town.

We stay the night at Azienda Agricola Guido Porro, a small winery with a handful of basic rooms above the cantina. Despite its reputation for making brawny, sophisticated juice, the operation couldn't be more low-key: Guido (fourth generation) makes wine, Giovanna (wife) serves Piedmont classics to guests, Fabio (fifth generation) waits in the wings. Before heading out for dinner, Giovanni (third generation) conducts what might be the fastest and most generous wine tasting ever—an accelerated ascendance from the humblest to the noblest grapes that leaves us both nearly too tipsy to make it to the dinner table. Down the road at the Massolino winery—as spiffy and refined as Guido is homey and informal—we climb the same Serralunga staircase the next morning for breakfast, from the fresh, sprightly Dolcetto to the powerful, brooding single-cru Barolo, but it's more of a leisurely walk than a full-on sprint.

In a matter of twenty-four hours, we manage to nudge our way to semilocal status at the small wine bar. We stop in for one last drink before continuing our path toward Alba, and as we get to chatting, I tell the barman that I may be in the market for *un piccolo tartufo*. We sit on the patio, sipping a bottle of local prosecco, figuring out what it would mean to abandon our apartment in Barcelona and take up residence in Serralunga (a disease commonly referred to as "What-If Syndrome" throughout Italy), when a father-and-son team of truffle hunters pulls up in a white Panda. We talk about how the year is going. "It's not going," says the father, brushing off a clump of dirt clinging to his gray jumpsuit.

I mention a pair of gentlemen who ordered a truffle at Cascina Schiavenza, the village's excellent trattoria, last night. Normally one can soak up a bit of vicarious pleasure in a restaurant raining truffles down on its clients, the dining room hot boxed with tuber aromas. The two diners last night sat at the table directly next to ours, yet when the server came around to shave the midsized *tartufo* they had selected, none of us could smell a thing.

"I know," the son says, shaking his head. "I sold it to them. It was the best I had found all season." The transaction, for all its seeming shadiness, represents the pressures on a market driven entirely by the whims of nature. Travelers with white diamonds in their eyes plan trips months in advance, and when they land at the table of any restaurant within sniffing distance of Alba, they want tubers, not excuses about the weather. Hunters sell whatever they can pull from the earth, and restaurant owners have little choice but to buy and serve it.

Before setting off, the father digs deep into his pockets and pulls out a white truffle the size of an orange. Even caked in dirt, it's an object of arresting beauty—its lunar surface, its mud-caked dimples, its meandering curves. He places his thumbs in an odd-shaped divot in the center, and before I can beg him to stop he snaps it in half, revealing a world of little bugs pulsing through its pores. *Vermi.*

"It's painful. Might have been worth a thousand euros in Alba," he says. His disappointment lasts all of thirty seconds before he shrugs his shoulders. "Oh well. Tomorrow, I think I'll go look for porcini instead."

Saturday, 11:48 A.M., Castiglione Falletto
After a few days of defiance, the sun makes its triumphant return on Saturday morning, shining with an intensity that feels almost apologetic. The dark tarp placed over the sky these past few days has suddenly been rolled up and stuffed into storage, and the colors and shapes beneath are so crisp and vivid it looks as though the Langhe picked up a fourth dimension overnight.

Suddenly the quiet roads and empty bars teem with locals and out-of-towners who flock to soak up every scrap of sunlight. On the terrace of La Terrazza da Renza in Castiglione Falletto gathers what appears to be half of northern Italy. Packs of *milanesi* clad in cashmere and turtlenecks reflect the valley through the dark lenses of their Gucci glasses. Why, yes, I'd love another *amaro, grazie.*

We settle for a corner spot in the shade, just beyond the beautiful people. There is no menu, and the server warns us that there are slim pickings after the lunch stampede. Nevertheless, our table soon overflows with plates of *carne cruda*, mixed charcuterie, olives, and a cornucopia of carbs, which we devour in silent concentration, scooping the soft, ruby folds of raw meat onto the ends of crunchy breadsticks like savory ice cream cones. Our server returns with a plate of shaved raw porcini, the first of the season, dressed with a rough salsa verde goosed with large chunks of anchovy. I see the couple at the table next to us eyeing the plate with envy, and I offer them a go at it. They invite us over, and we start a long, meandering conversation about the almost surreal excellence of Piedmont. By the time we pay the bill, we have made plans to eat *bagna cauda* in the mountains after the next snowfall.

In Italy, as in almost any civilization in the Northern Hemisphere, the stereotype goes that people in the south are warm and friendly, if a little less ambitious, while northerners are serious, industrious, and maybe a little bit cold. But none of those prejudices plays out during our time in Piedmont (or anywhere in the north, really). True, emotions may not spill out publicly here the way they do in Palermo or Naples, northerners may be a touch less effusive, but here, as much as anywhere else I've been in the country, a smile or a question or a plate of porcini is usually the first step toward friendship.

Our new pals offer us a lift to the next destination, but, emboldened by the mix of autumn sun and wild mushrooms, we forge ahead on foot. By the time we make it down the back side of Castiglione Falletto, we regret the decision. La Morra rises like a giant in front of us, with an ascent that looks more like scaling than walking. La Morra may be the most famous of all Langhe villages—for its central position, its famous vineyards, and the huge piazza perched at the edge of town with staggering views across the entire Langhe. Along with Barolo, it's the closest you'll find to a touristy village—one souvenir shop, two gelato spots, two ATMs—downright metropolitan compared to other villages in the area.

We passed through earlier this week after our Verduno adventure, but we've wound our way back for one reason: to visit the cantina of Elio Altare. Positioned on a ridge below La Morra, the legendary winery is among the most famous and influential in the region. From the terrace, you can see the layers of the Langhe line up one by one: little Annunziata in the foreground, Castiglione Falletto behind it, and there, standing tall in the background, *la bella* Serralunga and its magic castle.

If there is any true element of pilgrimage to our winding, muddy, agnolotti-fueled adventure, this is it. Elio Altare is one of the original Barolo Boys, the band of young men who forever changed the direction of winemaking in the area. I spoke with Elio's daughter, Silvia, earlier in the week to arrange a meeting our first time through La Morra, but she was unequivocal: "We're in the middle of harvest right now, and the rain is coming in. I can't have any distractions." When I offered Laura and myself as extra hands in the harvest, she didn't bite. "That's very sweet, but also illegal and unsafe. If you want to talk, it will have to be later in the week."

In 1976, twenty-six-year-old Elio decided to travel to France to see what his contemporaries to the north were up to. So worried were his parents about the trip that they called in the local priest from La Morra to come down and bless him before he departed. The real blessing was yet to come, as young Elio bounded from one winery to the next, soaking up the techniques of the wine renegades of Burgundy like a cask of new French oak.

When he returned a year later to Piedmont, Elio was a changed man. After seeing the advancements in French winemaking, he realized that Piedmont was trapped in the past. His father, Giovanni, had been making wine in the tradition of his ancestors, who had valued quantity over quality, not to mention hygiene. He kept cows and chickens in the same area in which he grew his grapes. He operated the bodega without running water. Barrels and tanks were cleaned once a year, if at all.

Elio wanted to modernize Barolo production. He cleared the patches of fruit trees on the property (back then, fruit still yielded higher profits than wine in the Langhe). He added hot water to

The Barolo Boy and his daughter:
Elio and Silvia Altare.

clean the equipment. The biggest change, though, came down to the barrels: he wanted to age his wine for shorter periods of time in new oak barrique instead of the long soaks in old casks more common in the Langhe, creating more vibrant, fruit-forward Barolo. In a moment that has taken on a mythical quality in the wine world, young Elio fired up a chain saw and sank its metal teeth into the old Barolo barrels his ancestors had so adored.

Giovanni didn't understand. What his son was proposing simply wasn't the way of Piedmont. Here, you made as much wine as you possibly could from the harvest and hoped that quality followed. A rift opened between father and son; they didn't speak for ten years. Giovanni finally had his revenge: on his deathbed in 1985, he changed his will to cut Elio out of his inheritance, giving the vineyard to Elio's sisters instead.

Elio didn't flinch. He worked hard to implement his new vision, eventually buying the land back from his sisters. Along with Enrico Scavino, Luciano Sandrone, and others, who applied the same new philosophy to their own family wineries, the Barolo Boys brought not just better techniques and more interesting wines to the region but a spirit of collaboration and community to a region where winemaking was once an isolated, secretive endeavor.

Tradition never dies quietly in Italy, and it was the same with Barolo. A rival faction of purists raised up in defense of Langhe tradition, accusing young Elio and his rebel conspirators of catering to foreign tastes and watering down the ideals of Barolo. The Barolo Wars ensued and raged on for years across the Langhe as Barolo grew into one of the world's most coveted wines. Today there is enough demand for Barolo that everyone has a place at the table, meaning that people with deep pockets can compare tradition and innovation side by side and make their own conclusions.

Today Elio Altare is one of the most famous wineries in the world, with new vintages that sell out long before they're drinkable and big-year bottles that command price tags north of $500. Elio's daughter, Silvia, runs the day-to-day operations now, and she shows no signs of slowing down the evolution of the family winery. During our tour of the cellars, she bounces from room to room and topic to topic, her mind reeling with history and anecdotes and technical observations. She officially took over less than six months ago but looks as though she's been building to this moment her whole life. "Of course I feel the pressure. But there's no longer a need for a revolution. My job now is evolution."

Upstairs, we sit around a table with a group of importers from London as Silvia takes us through a tasting: a bright, unfiltered, easy-to-down 2015 Dolcetto (in Piedmont they have a saying: "We don't drink water, we drink Dolcetto"); a soft, berry-suffused 2012 Langhe La Villa made from Barbera and Nebbiolo; and the king of the castle, a 2012 Barolo DOCG, an elegant, concentrated taste of Piedmont *terreno* and Altare philosophy, the kind of wine you strap on a backpack and a pair of hiking boots to drink.

Elio shows up with a rare bottle of his 2009 Cinqueterre made from fickle white grapes grown on the rocky Ligurian coastline—one of the many projects he's undertaken in his "retirement." (Others include making cheese and restoring an abandoned mountain village.) I am not by nature an oenophile, but everything that passes our lips makes me feel like one. Only the meager size of our backpacks keeps us from buying the full breadth of the Barolo Boy's legacy and lugging it across the valley.

Sunday, 1:45 P.M., Alba

On our last day of walking, somewhere between the meandering vineyard-lined paths around Roddi and the billboard-laden concrete leading into Alba, the pastoral Piedmont fantasy comes to a prosaic end. Alba is not a large city, but after five days in the pin-drop-quiet villages of the Langhe, it might as well be Manhattan. Compounding the chaos is the fact that Alba's world-famous Truffle Show, now in its eighty-fifth year, is in full swing, and the town swells to triple its population on Saturdays and Sundays from early October until late November.

On the outskirts of the city, the flashing lights and mechanical movements of a carnival crowd the skyline. A community center houses truffle-related attractions for kids. Stands line the main thoroughfares leading to the heart of Alba, offering cured meats and cheeses to the weekend warriors who made the trek to the truffle capital of the world. A vague medieval ambience hangs over the festivities. Knights and maidens in fantasy garb circle the streets. Old men show off antique wooden tools to wide-eyed children. We head for a drink to steel us but quickly retreat when we find the bar packed three people deep.

We take refuge at La Piola, one of the region's finest osterie, an outgrowth of Piazza Duomo, the Michelin three-star restaurant upstairs. Enrico Crippa is the celebrated captain of both, one of Italy's new guard of young, ambitious chefs stretching the old tenets of Italian cuisine into new dimensions. Upstairs you can eat deconstructed eggplant parmigiana and a fifty-one-ingredient salad in a dining room of pink pastels and abstract paintings—lovely, no

doubt, but a bridge too far for these two sweaty, exasperated pilgrims. We settle on the more casual outpost downstairs.

La Piola pulses with the electricity reserved for the most important meal of the week in Italy: Sunday lunch, a three- to four-hour communion with loved ones, a deep breath before plunging back into the cold waters of the workweek. For us, it's a simpler equation: *We're starving. Please feed us.* Servers swarm the room with white truffles and tiny digital scales to calculate the damage—at €4 a gram, the bill adds up, but it gives those looking for a light truffle fix the chance to indulge. Everything that comes out of the kitchen—from the rosy pink *vitello tonnato* to the agnolotti—is a category killer, the veal perfectly medium rare, the stuffing in the pasta parcels so dense with flavor it tastes like pâté. Before we leave, we book a table for the next night, just in case we decide to stick around Alba.

Outside, the chaos continues well into the evening. Humans make large quantities of fried dough disappear. Children climb on hay bales and hammer on the heads of their siblings. Wine stains the street like the French Revolution. At the heart of all of this is the market itself—a large tent housing a few dozen vendors of truffles and truffle-related products. Projections of truffles hang from the rafters, sharing air space with *tartufo* still lifes. Stacked everywhere are pyramids of truffle-infused oils, butters, creams, jams, meats, and cheeses. In the center of the milieu, a dozen truffle hunters house their treasures under glass domes. After the past five days, when every experienced truffle hunter I met told me the same thing, that the truffles had yet to arrive in the Langhe, I am surprised to see hundreds of truffles for sale. Some are small, dark, knotty—exactly as Carlo told me any true Piedmont truffle would be at this moment in the season. Some are black, the more abundant and less celebrated brothers of the white wonders. But most of the truffles are gorgeous—large, sturdy, and uniformly white. All of them— large and small, black and white—wear the same proud label: *tartufo d'Alba*.

I approach one of the stands. The vendor is holding forth in front of a group of Italian visitors, talking about the secret location to which he and his trusty dog return year after year to dig up the white diamonds. He lifts the dome, releasing an intense perfume. For a second, the fragrance overpowers my skepticism and I find myself being tractor-beamed toward the truffle. But then I remember Carlo's warning—that sellers in the markets use truffle sprays to keep their products smelling strong—and I snap out of it just in time.

I approach another hunter—young, bearded, distracted by his smartphone. His glass case is lined with pictures of him, his father, and their dog getting dirty in the forests around Alba. He has what may be the market's most impressive truffle: a baseball-sized wonder, dense as a block of cement, unblemished. I ask to hold it, bring it to my nose, try to divine just where in the world this specimen came from. How much? "A thousand euros." Tough year, no? "Yes, it's been tough, but we've been lucky so far."

Maybe they have been. Maybe the truffles of Macedonia are every bit the equal of the truffles of Italy. Maybe a great year in Serbia is better than a bad year in Alba. Maybe there is a secret stash of white truffles that only the people in this tent seem to know about. Maybe I should stop and smell the spores and tell my dubious dome to shut the hell up. Maybe it doesn't matter.

In the end, I decide to save my money. Instead, I buy a jar of *crema di tartufo* made by TartufLanghe, in the truffle by-product business since 1968. For €16, it has what almost no one else here does: 7.5 percent real Alba white truffle suspended in an emulsion of cream and whipped butter.

Next to a 2012 Barolo from Elio Altare, it should make a fine dinner, as pure and powerful an expression of Piedmont as you'll find anywhere.

In the days and weeks to come, yesterday's torrential rains will seep into the celebrated soil of Piedmont and do their magic on the timid spores struggling to coalesce beneath the surface of the Langhe, and Carlos, the men of Serralunga, and the other four thousand truffle hunters will plunge into their favorite forest of hazelnut trees with trusty dogs at their sides and hope their fortunes are rescued by the rain that nearly washed us out of the valley. But for now we'll drink the rebel Barolo, eat our *tajarin* with truffle butter, and give our feet a short rest.

MAMMA VICENZA

NAME: Vicenza Frialis

CITY: Francocci

REGION: Umbria

SPECIALTY: *Anatra in salmì* (braised duck with myrtle), an herb from Sardinia, where I was born. I try to bring a bit of home here to Umbria.

KITCHEN HERO: My mom and my *nonna*. I needed to learn to cook. I had twelve younger siblings and I cooked for all of them while Mom worked.

FAVORITE KITCHEN MEMORY: When we were able to eat a plate of pasta, because we couldn't always afford it. It was the biggest event when my mom cooked ravioli or polenta. These are my best memories, even if I was always the last one to eat, because my siblings came first.

Life Skills

DRINK LIKE AN ITALIAN

From a *crema*-rich *caffè* to a sparkling afternoon *aperitivo*,
this is what (and how) you should be drinking in Italy.

GET WITH THE SCHEDULE

Italians are famously fastidious about when they drink what. Sunrise to 11 A.M. is cappuccino time, the early afternoon for espresso (milk is anathema after 12 P.M.). Early evenings are for *aperitivo* — wine or beer, with snacks — and after dinner is time for the stronger stuff: grappa, a cocktail, or a *digestivo*.

LEARN THE LINGO

Order a "grande latte" and you'll get a giant glass of milk and the stink eye. Everything starts with espresso, more commonly called *caffè*. Order a *ristretto* for a shorter, concentrated shot; a *lungo* for a longer, gentler one. A *macchiato* gets you a little steamed milk, and a *cappuccino* gets you a lot more.

03

TAKE A STAND

Few things can be more egregiously overpriced in Italy than drinking at a pretty table outside. The price of *caffè* at the bar is capped by the government, but all bets are off when you step outside. Don't be surprised to pay €6 for a cappuccino in a piazza with a privileged view.

04

KEEP IT QUICK

Coffee culture here isn't one of slow sipping and lingering. Italians don't drink venti mochas in to-go cups; they drink four to five *caffès* spaced throughout the day, like cigarettes, to scratch and itch and break up the demands of the day. Find a bar you love and keep going back to the counter.

SIP A BETTER BIRRA

Most people don't make it past the wine in this country, but Italy's long been at the forefront of the global craft beer movement. Producers like Baladin and Birra del Borgo blend old-school Belgian inspiration and American creativity to craft beers nuanced enough to carry you through a meal or a long afternoon on a sunny terrace.

MAKE A MEAL OUT OF IT

Italians rarely drink on an empty stomach, and a glass of wine or a spritz is usually a bridge to a free bite. In Venice, feast on small snacks called *cicchetti*; in Milan and Bologna lavish spreads put out for *aperitivo* can easily double as dinner. If you're not getting something to eat with your glass, you should find a new place to drink.

07

DRINK LOCAL

Just as you don't eat pesto in Palermo
or carbonara in Campania, you shouldn't
drink Barolo in Bari or Chianti in
Cagliari. Stick to the local grapes and
you'll find better deals and more
interesting wines. Zibibbo (Sicily), Soave
(Veneto), pignoletto (Emilia-Romagna):
all rank as some of Italy's most underrated.

08

DIGEST LIKE AN ITALIAN

Add bitter spirits to the long list of
Italian contributions to the world of
food and drink. *Amari* are ideal for late-
afternoon sipping or as a *digestivo* after
a big meal. Pick your poison: Campari
and Aperol are good gateways, but try
minty Fernet-Branca, artichoke-based
Cynar, and syrupy-sweet Averna.

ANATOMY
of a dish

CAFFÈ

A SHOT OF HISTORY

Muslim traders brought coffee to
Venice in the sixteenth century,
but true Italian coffee culture
began in 1884, when Angelo
Moriondo invented the espresso
machine. Italy's singular
dedication to espresso-based
coffee is the root of most café
culture as we know it today.

THE DARK ROAST

Don't expect subtle notes of wild
fruits in your *caffè* (the more
common name for espresso in
Italy). Italians roast beans
longer, for a dark, oily, potent
brew. As you move south, expect
caffè to get stronger and shorter;
by the time you hit Sicily, you
can nearly scrape it with a spoon.

SURE SHOT

Espresso is a complex science, requiring the proper ground (fine) and pack (tight), the right water temperature (92–95°C), and the correct length of extraction (20–25 seconds). Why is Italy's coffee so good? Decent beans, good machines, and excellent technique.

CREME DE LA CREMA

How to spot a well-pulled shot? Look for the caramel-colored layer, called *crema*, resting on top. Formed by a mixture of air bubbles and coffee's natural oils, it's a good indicator of quality. Some say a good *crema* can hold a spoon of sugar for five seconds, but who needs sugar?

Chapter Eight

LAKE COMO

For Alessandro Sala most days begin while the rest of Italy is still sleeping. Under a bank of stars, a canopy of clouds, or a sheet of rain, he settles into his small motorboat and maneuvers quietly out of the tiny port of San Giovanni and into the heart of Lake Como. Even in the dark, the outline of the mountains that guard the lake reminds you that it's not far across this wishbone of water. But it is a long way down—five football fields at its center, the deepest lake in Italy.

Alessandro starts by collecting the shallowest nets, the ones he uses to catch *persico*, perch, best dusted in flour and pan-fried in butter. From the coastline around San Giovanni he works the boat out toward Como's deeper reaches, where he hopes to find his nets filled with *agone*, freshwater shad, short and plump and swollen with fat to keep it warm so far below the surface.

He covers kilometers of Como in search of the nets, pulling them up for the better part of three hours, filling the boat with silver-green bodies that stiffen as the day grows from black to brown to gray, until the sun from behind the Grigna mountains pokes the first holes through the wall of darkness and the lake begins to reveal itself.

By the time he parks the boat and off-loads the catch, the 8 A.M. bells of San

321

Giovanni will just begin to sing their good-morning missive, setting the rest of the village's forty-two souls in motion.

✦ ❧ 🍸

Some places stick to your bones. They burrow beneath your skin, slip silently into your marrow. You find yourself overtaken by their energy, some life-affirming magic built into its DNA. Sometimes the triumphing factors are as clear as a mountain stream (Antoni Gaudí's genius! Kyoto's ancient magic!), but once in a while an unknowable force wins you over, some opaque combination of light and angle, flesh and pheromones. And when it does, it has the alchemic effect of making everything feel special. Those screaming voices suddenly sound like songbirds; that run-down B&B glows with rustic charm. If you've traveled much, you no doubt have found a few of those places, the ones that live on as little islands of happiness in the turbulent waters of your mind.

San Giovanni is one of those towns. We came here by accident, the result of poor planning and the rest of northern Italy being overbooked. Laura and I found a room available at a hotel just above the village and wandered down for dinner, then the next morning for coffee. The church bells rang and light snaked through the narrow streets, bathing two perfect cappuccinos and two dumbstruck humans in an autumn-morning glow. We were in love.

Twice we tried to leave San Giovanni. Twice we failed.

The first time we tried to leave San Giovanni was after dinner at Ristorante Mella, a low-lit, family-run place a few steps from the water. It was a cold Tuesday night in late October, and we shared the restaurant with a young Italian-German couple and their new baby. Dinner was as simple as it was striking: whitefish, fried crisp in butter and dressed with a vibrant salsa verde, followed by a risotto of pike and autumn squash, the rice suffused with the double-edged sweetness of roasted gourd and simmered fish. I spoke with Rosy, the co-owner with her husband, for

Alessandro works with up to a dozen
specialty nets when fishing Lake Como.

the better part of an hour about everything I could conjure up in my middling Italian: the fragrant court bouillon used to make the risotto, the types of lake fish that make a hearty ragù, the nocturnal habits of her husband the fisherman.

The next day, we made it all the way to Verona, to a fancy pizzeria pit stop, just before heading into Venice to meet a group of fishermen from the outer islands of the sunken city. As I chewed on the yeasty, €30 crust, all I could think about was the charming little restaurant and the sparkling body of water beyond it. I excused myself from the table, walked out into the courtyard, and dialed the restaurant. Rosy picked up. "Of course. No problem. I haven't touched the place since you left."

I should tell you now that you won't find much in San Giovanni. There are no general markets, no cute little shops, no wood-burning pizza ovens, no ancient salumeria with a mustachioed butcher selling suckling pig and reciting Dante. You won't even find a place to buy a lightbulb or a head of garlic. Technically it's a part of Bellagio, the self-proclaimed "pearl of Lake Como" found a mile down the shore, but it's very much a village of its own—ask any of the residents, and they'll emphatically agree that the pizzerias, souvenir shops, and glitzy hotels of its neighbor have nothing to do with life in San Giovanni. There are two small bed-and-breakfasts, a miniature museum of esoteric animal sculptures and modern art, a single café that serves coffee and croissants in the morning, wine and cheese in the early evening. A small port with generous views across the narrow lake. And there is Ristorante Mella, the only restaurant in San Giovanni and the real reason we keep coming back.

Mella is owned by Alessandro and his wife, Rosy, a couple in their late forties with deep roots in the Como area. Mella was one of Italy's first *ittiturismi*, the aquatic analog of Italy's massive *agriturismo* industry, a restaurant and lodging where at least 40 percent of the business comes from fishing. It is located in a small two-story building a block from the water, with a wooden sign that announces the

Mella mantra: *Pesce dalla rete alla padella,* Fish from the net to the pan. Alessandro is the fisherman; Rosy manages the front of house and the two apartments that they rent out to visitors. It's a small, unassuming operation but one that says as much about the greatness of Italy's regional food culture as any of the flashier, fancier outposts of fine dining found around Lombardy.

The menu at Mella is a crash course in Como's underwater ecosystem: *persico* (perch), the omnipresent whitefish of the lake; *trota,* brown trout that funnel into the lake from the rivers that feed it; *salmerino* (char), spotted and plump and ready for a sear. You won't find any shrimp, any salmon, anything that comes from the ocean or a body of water beyond. Yes, there is a handful of meat and vegetable dishes for land lovers, but 90 percent of the menu is fish, and 100 percent of the fish served at the restaurant comes directly from Alessandro's boat.

It was Alessandro's catch I had on my mind the second time we tried to leave San Giovanni. We were halfway to the airport—flights purchased, car rental due back within the hour—when I pulled over on the side of the lake, turned off the car, and turned to my wife. "I can't leave." A look of relief broke out across her face. "Me, neither." We flipped the script, broke plans with friends and family, and shouldered the steep cost of our spontaneity. For a few long minutes after rebooking the tickets, I felt a tinge of buyer's remorse, but the moment we wound our way around the lake and back into the village, it dissipated like Como's layer of morning fog. When I called Rosy, she didn't sound surprised when I asked, "You think I could come back and spend a few days on the boat with Alessandro?"

🗡 🍃 🍷

Lake Como was formed just after the last ice age, when retreating glaciers left a long, jagged body of water in their place. One of seven lakes in Lombardy, the northern region of Italy, which ranks as the country's wealthiest, Lake Como is smaller and deeper than Lake Garda and Lake

SOME PLACES STICK TO YOUR BONES, SLIP SILENTLY INTO YOUR MARROW.

Maggiore, the other so-called great lakes of Lombardy. From above it looks like an inverted Υ. Como and Lecco, the lake's two biggest cities, guard the southern points, with Bellagio positioned right at the vertex. The poet William Wordsworth called it "a treasure which the earth keeps to itself." Indeed, the wall of forested mountains that surround the lake lend it an air of breathtaking isolation, which helps explain one of its most enduring characteristics: its reputation as a hideaway for the world's rich and powerful.

For most people around the world, Lake Como is synonymous with star power. Even if they couldn't point it out on a map or spot it in a photo, they can recite the roster of titans who have sought solace from the spotlight on its shores, people so famous they require only one name: Madonna, Ronaldinho, Versace, Branson, Clooney.

But long before the *Star Wars* scenes of Natalie Portman strolling the palace gardens of Villa del Balbianello, before the music videos by Gwen Stefani and John Legend, the bad-guy showdowns in *Casino Royale* and the Clooney-Roberts canoodling of *Ocean's 12*, before Saint George purchased his lakeside villa in Laglio and created what is called by ambivalent locals the "Clooney Effect," Lake Como was a retreat for the stars of the Roman Empire, when senators and high-ranking military officials found sanctuary along its shores. Its shimmering beauty continued to attract the elite for centuries to come, as Lake Como served as muse and refuge for writers and composers, counts and cardinals. One by one, the famous villas were constructed around the lake: Villa d'Este, once the residence of religious brass and British royalty, today one of the world's top hotels; Villa Serbelloni, around the bend from Bellagio, home of the Rockefeller Foundation; and Villa Carlotta, the mother of them all, a seventeenth-century, seventeen-acre pleasure palace built by a *milanese* marquis. More than high-calorie eye candy for visitors and locals alike, it's the presence of those sprawling estates that has protected the most coveted lakefront property from an endless line of development.

(Not all Como history is so peaceable. On April 27, 1945, Benito Mussolini and his mistress, Claretta Petacci, were captured on the northwestern shore of the lake, part of a convoy of fifty Fascists heading for the Swiss border. After holding them overnight, their Communist captors executed the couple against the wall of a villa the next afternoon.)

One thing Como is not famous for is its food. When locals and foreigners wax poetic about the wonders of regional Italian cuisine—the truffles and Barolo of Piedmont, the bread and burrata of Puglia—the lake district doesn't register high on the excitement list. That's not to say you will eat poorly here. This is Italy, after all, where bad meals are as rare as honest politicians. You'll find plenty of excellent restaurants and beautiful markets and even a handful of farms and artisanal producers making the type of small-scale, high-quality ingredients that drive Italy's regional gastronomy.

The core staples of far-northern Italian food have a strong role around the lake. Polenta shows up in forms both soft and creamy, firm and crispy, serving as a base for meat, vegetables, and fish. Most of Italy's rice production takes place fifty miles to the south, in the sunken paddies surrounding Vercelli, and fittingly, it's not hard to find excellent risotto made with arborio or carnaroli rice in almost any restaurant you stop into. But don't come here expecting rib-sticking red-sauce fare, delicate seasonal vegetable dishes, or a catalog of regional pasta creations.

Lake Como sits just below the Swiss border, and at times it looks, sounds, and tastes more central European than Italian. The local dialect has the hard, guttural edge of German; the architecture is a mix of soaring Baroque and Swiss mountain chalet. Butter trumps olive oil, cakes and baked goods are often more German than Italian in spirit, cheese tastes as though it's made for melting over a fondue flame. The most Italian part of the cuisine of Lake Como is the insistence on local, high-quality ingredients as the foundation for everything that comes out of the kitchen. And nothing is more local and of higher quality than the schools of fish swimming just beneath the lake's surface. (You'll see them everywhere—the waters of Lake Como are so crystal clear you that could read a book through them.)

For most of Lake Como's history, fishing has been a fundamental form of survival for the local population. Commercial fishing has never been big on the lake; the market for lake fish beyond those who live here is tiny. But throughout much of the twentieth century, adult males took up rod and net, catching enough to feed their families, perhaps enough to barter with. After World War II, when food supplies dwindled dramatically, fishing became a means of survival for nearly everyone on the lake.

Today, in San Giovanni's tiny port, you'll still find twenty-five fishing boats— about one for every adult male resident. But most of those boats don't go out daily, or even weekly anymore. During the 1970s and '80s, as a handful of Lake Como's largest industries shuttered, many of the poorest residents fled to Milan and other urban areas in search of opportunity. Fishing slowly evolved from a form of survival to a pastime for all but a handful of the lake's 200,000 residents.

There are just eighty licensed commercial fishermen on all of Lake Como, a number carefully calibrated to keep the stocks of fish sustainable year after year. Not all eighty fishermen work the waters consistently, but they treat the licenses like family heirlooms, passing them down from one generation to the next.

Alessandro keeps two fishing boats in San Giovanni's port, one an eighteen-foot cruiser with a center console for longer trips on the lake, the other the one he uses most often, a stripped-down fifteen-footer with nothing but an outboard motor and a steering wheel and accelerator in the nose of the boat that allow him to maneuver from either end of the vessel. The most vital equipment is the nets themselves, which come wound onto metal poles and spools that he mounts to the nose of the boat for easy release and collection.

Alessandro commonly fishes around

Alessandro and the
morning's catch.

a dozen of the lake's twenty-eight species of fish—from the small, fatty *alborella*, a freshwater sardine of sorts; to *luccio*, pike, spotted and sleek; to the bulky *tinca*, tench, a peculiar species with a whiskered face and a plump, pale green body. All serious fishing done on the lake is with vertical hanging nets cast, cast and collected by hand. Each type of fish requires its own net—the size of the holes in the net and the depth at which it floats are fine-tuned to target one fish and one fish only. Bycatch happens here as it does anywhere, but the fishermen of Lake Como rightly take pride in their careful and calculated net deployment.

On our first afternoon on the water, the clouds hang menacingly overhead, thick and swirled with dark rivulets, like cappuccino foam. Today we're after two different species, a standard strategy for Alessandro on the lake. Perch is a bottom-feeding species, fattening on the ecosystem of plankton and larvae that line the lake bed. At €60 for a kilo of cleaned fillets, it's the most expensive species pulled from Como, competing with top-tier saltwater fish in terms of price. Part of the price is driven by its star role in Como's most ubiquitous restaurant dish, *riso e filetto di pesce persico*: fillets of whitefish, floured and lightly fried, served over boiled rice goosed with butter and sage.

We start close to the shore with *persico* nets. Each net comes wound onto a metal pole, which Alessandro hangs from a wooden frame at the nose of the boat. He then inches the boat forward so that the net unspools on its own and falls into place in the water. On an average day, Alessandro will unspool seven or eight nets, nearly a kilometer of nylon stitched across Como's surface.

Next, he turns to a more challenging task. *Agone* (freshwater shad) is a small, fatty fish that feeds in deeper waters, requiring nets that float three meters below the surface and move freely with the current. Before setting the nets, Alessandro calculates the current, then gets a reading on the wind—velocity and direction—and begins to do the math to figure out just how far upshore he needs to travel to ensure that the nets will be close to San Giovanni when he comes back tomorrow morning to collect them. The numbers matter; a strong current and wind working in tandem can carry the *agone* nets more than seven kilometers overnight.

Fishing used to be a two-man job: one man would row the boat or work the sail, while the other handled the nets. Starting in the 1970s, when outboard motors became common among Lake Como's small fishing fleet, it transformed largely into a one-man operation. In Alessandro's case, it's not an entirely one-man operation—more like a one-man and one-man's-best-friend operation. His ten-year-old golden retriever, Ice, goes out with him most days, keeping him company on the lake as he sets and collects nets. He's even trained the dog to handle a few key parts of the daily operations— fetching a buoy, carrying the keys from the boat to the restaurant in his mouth.

When the last shad net is cast, I turn to Alessandro. "Now what?"

"We come back at dawn and hope for the best."

🌱 🍖 🍷

When Rino and Graziella Sala first took over at Mella in 1958, the menu was two dishes long: *riso e filetto di pesce persico* and *arborella fritta*, fried carp. They'd run specials from time to time—*pollo alla cacciatora*, polenta with wild mushrooms—but the cooking and the economy of the restaurant relied entirely on what the lake provided. They had a steady trickle of loyal customers, but it was never an easy business: the couple worked seven days a week, twelve months a year, and still took on debt for years.

Back in those days, nearly every man in San Giovanni was a fisherman—if not commercially, then one who used the lake catch to feed his family. They used nets made of silk and cotton and hung them out to dry on the stone walls—a giant, continuous spiderweb of purple, white, and red that ran through the town.

Alessandro comes from a long line of fishermen—as best as he and his mother can remember, at least four generations of

Sala men have fished these waters before him. Photos on the wall document the Sala family's time working the Lake Como waters: his grandfather pulling into port, his father on the docks of San Giovanni, a wall of plump shad behind him, drying under the midday sun.

Alessandro first learned to fish as a young boy on trips with his grandfather. He loved lake life—getting lost in the sprawling villa properties around San Giovanni, climbing through the forests that carpet the mountains, cooling off on the rocky shores after a day of mischief making. When he graduated from high school, he did twelve months of military service, then came back to San Giovanni to help his parents run the restaurant. Graziella had five sisters, each with three or four kids of her own, and everyone in the family worked at Mella at one point or another. But the job wasn't big enough to sustain a family, so Alessandro traveled around Como with his catch, selling perch, whitefish, and bleak to other restaurants. He didn't plan to be a professional fisherman, but when his

dad unexpectedly passed away in 1991, he quickly recalculated his life plans.

Rosy Castelli was born and raised up the road in Civenna, a mountain village about five kilometers behind and above San Giovanni. She knew Alessandro as the good-looking guy who rode his Vespa through town from time to time, always fast, always without a helmet—a lakeside James Dean looking for a cause. On one of those trips, he told Rosy that he and his parents needed help at the restaurant. Rosy was timid, not the type to ride off into the sunset on the back of a stranger's Vespa, but the prospect of a steady job lured her down to San Giovanni and into the lives of the Sala family. When asked all these years later if the job offer was a ploy to bring them together, Alessandro only smiles.

Rosy runs the dining room at Mella with a quiet grace that allows her, like all great hosts, to adapt to her guests: if they have come to San Giovanni for a quiet lakeside lunch, she serves them their food and gives them their space; if they have come to learn

From net to table: a fillet of char, seared on the flattop at Mella.

what makes Mella a special outpost of regional Italian cookery, she fills their minds and bellies with the information they crave. "Sometimes you use four words to speak to a guest. Other times, two will do."

Alessandro isn't the chef; that distinction belongs to Bruno Mainetti, a hard-smoking, shoulder-shrugging *napoletano* with a wry sense of humor and a love of slow-simmered sauces. It's no secret that Bruno prefers stirring red sauce to boning and browning perch, but he handles both with the skill and respect of a serious cook. Alessandro is never far from the kitchen activity, and during a busy service, he's likely to trade his fishing jacket for a chef's coat and take a position at the flattop. "He has a hard time staying out of the kitchen," says Rosy. "He wants to make sure his fish is being handled with care."

Education is a fundamental part of the work at Mella. That's why there are clipboards available with an encyclopedic rundown of the principal species of lake fish. That's why Rosy takes the extra time to explain the origin of dishes to curious clients. That's why Alessandro takes school classes, curious guests, and persistent journalists out on the lake for a closer vantage on the life of a Como *pescatore*. The first lesson, on the water and in the restaurant, is understanding the difference between lake fish and ocean fish.

People think of lake fish as inferior. It's what Alessandro's neighbor Cristian Ponzini, the owner of Silvio, calls "the war of lake fish versus ocean fish," a lifelong attempt to prove to diners that freshwater fish has a place on the table. "You can ask people in Milan if they think there are professional fishermen in the lakes, and they'll tell you no," says Alessandro. "The only people who eat lake fish are lake people or the tourists who visit us here."

To be sure, lake fish is more subtle than saltwater fish—the flavor less pronounced, the range more limited. What matters most is the quality of the water they live in. Catch a fish in a small, murky pond dense with dirt and sediment and you'll be eating fish with an undertow of earth in its flesh. "Think of it like the concept of *terreno* in wine," says Alessandro. "A fillet of *lava-rello* from Lake Como tastes different from a fillet from Lake Garda." Lake Como is known for the purity of its water, and the fish that Alessandro catches reflects it: mild, meaty, a near-blank canvas for a variety of flavors and techniques.

If Alessandro and Rosy are working from a disadvantage in terms of product recognition, they have put generations of accumulated experience into practice to fill the menu with dozens of little tastes of Como. They make fragrant, full-flavored stocks from the bones and bodies of perch and chub. They cure whitefish eggs in salt, creating a sort of freshwater *bottarga*, ready to be grated over pasta and rice. Shad is brined in vinegar and herbs, whitefish becomes a slow-cooked ragù or a filling for ravioli, and pigo and pike form the basis of Mella's *polpettine di pesce*. Pickled, dried, smoked, cured, pâtéd: a battery of techniques to ensure that nothing goes to waste. If you can make it with meat, there's a good chance Alessandro and Rosy have made it with lake fish.

And then there's *missoltino*, the lake's most important by-product, a staple that stretches back to medieval times and has been named a *presidio* by Slow Food, a designation reserved for the country's most important ingredients and food traditions. The people still making *missoltino* can be counted on a single hand. Alessandro guts and scales hundreds of shad at a time, salts the bodies, and hangs them like laundry to dry under the sun for forty-eight hours or more. The dried fish are then layered with bay leaves, packed into metal canisters, and weighed down. Slowly the natural oils from the shad escape and bubble to the surface, forming a protective layer that preserves the *missoltino* indefinitely.

It can be used as a condiment of sorts, a weapons-grade dose of lake umami to be detonated in salads and pastas. In its most classic preparation, served with *toc*, a thick, rich scoop of polenta slow cooked in a copper pot over a wood fire, it tastes of nothing you've eaten in Italy—or anywhere else.

"Tastes are changing," says Alessandro.

"If we tried to cook the menu that my parents cooked twenty years ago, we wouldn't be able to do it. Back then, it was all whole fish: grilled, fried, in the oven." Mella's few concessions to contemporary tastes—the blini with the purple swoosh of caramelized onions, the herb-strewn lake "paella"—may seem like a small distance to travel in a sixty-year journey, but to Alessandro and Rosy, they mark an entrance into a world their parents would only vaguely recognize. "People want options now, dozens of them, and they want clean fish: no bones, easy to eat. We try to respect that but keep the traditions in place."

"Our type of food will never be competitive with the big restaurants of Italy," says Alessandro. Even the big restaurants surrounding Lake Como. Down the road, at Silvio, diners pack in by the dozens for a taste of lake cuisine with cheffy flourishes. In Bellagio, a mediocre pizzeria sees more customers in a day than Mella sees in a week. Its location in one of Como's tiniest villages, an unlikely place to search for greatness, means that people come to Mella not by default but by decision. It's one of the only restaurants on the lake listed in Slow Food's guide to Italy's best osterie, a bible for the country's serious eaters. When I mention that to Alessandro and Rosy, they seem genuinely perplexed.

"Really? That can't be," says Rosy. I pull the book out of my bag, turn to the dog-eared page, and pass it across the table. "Huh. There we are." Alessandro continues to stare at the page, as if seeing is not believing. Finally he closes the book and leaves it on the table. "To be honest, I'm allergic to guides. They make you do things you don't want to do. I want to be left alone to do this as we decide to do it."

My short, unhappy life as a fisherman is one of humiliation and defeat, of failures so pronounced they feel cartoonish in hindsight: hooked boot, broken rod, shattered ego. At nineteen, after a decade of disappointment, I found myself on the verge of my first catch, a sparkling bass from a pond in Southern California, three pounds if it was an ounce, but just as the fish was within my grasp, the line snapped and my catch vanished, leaving me to wallow in my ineptitude. It would be another nine years before I finally reeled in a fish, which I bathed in brown butter and capers and devoured with a vengeance.

I worry that my shortcomings as a fisherman will seep into Alessandro's daily work on Lake Como. But on our first early morning out collecting the perch and whitefish nets we dropped yesterday afternoon, it's immediately clear that his skill far exceeds any troubled past I drag onto the boat. The nets are plugged everywhere with small silver fish with bright orange fins, one every few feet of net to be plucked from the hole and placed into a large Styrofoam container. Within thirty seconds, he knows he'll pull in fifteen kilos of perch before the morning is out.

Alessandro scoops up a large green fish among the catch, its jaw locked around a perch trapped in the net, a rare instance of bycatch in a process carefully calibrated to keep the lake sustainably stocked. "We set the net sizes so that the fish we catch are at least three years old—old enough to have reproduced at least once. Small fish pass right through, larger ones hit the net and keep going." A crew of fifty wardens, a mix of government employees and volunteers, works the waters, holding commercial and casual fishermen to the lake's strict quotas.

"The system is set up to be sustainable for eighty of us. If you add any more, either the lake goes hungry or we do."

In other parts of Italy, the struggle to save fishing traditions is very real. On the island of Burano, in the Venetian lagoon, *pescatori* and clam diggers struggle with the impact of global warming and mass tourism. In Liguria, the stunning stretch of coast that houses some of Italy's most charming hamlets, including the five villages of the famed Cinque Terre, tourism has proven more lucrative than fishing, and many have traded their nets for jobs on terra firma. *Ittiturismo*, an idea the Sala family helped pioneer in Italy, addresses both threats, providing education

THE FIRST NET COMES UP
SLOWLY, WEIGHED DOWN BY
A WEB OF WRITHING BODIES.

_____

about and awareness of the environmental threats to sustainable fishing while offering tourists a chance to partake in an ancient tradition.

By 8 A.M., yesterday's nets are in and the catch is accounted for. By 9 A.M., Alessandro has unloaded the boat and taken the fish to the prep kitchen below Mella. By 11 A.M., twenty kilos of perch and whitefish have been gutted, scaled, and filleted and are ready for a searing flattop or a pan of risotto.

Over the next week, Alessandro and I fall into a rhythm: out in the late afternoon to drop the nets, back at dawn to collect the fish. I've always believed fishing to be a mixture of manual labor and Zen-like patience, but with each passing day, I come to appreciate a more nuanced picture, one filled with little tricks and moments of intuition and raw intelligence. Fishing at this level is part science, part art. If anything, Alessandro leans toward the latter. His boat has no electronic equipment to speak of—no radar, no depth finder, no next-generation nets or reels. He knows the depth of the lake at any given spot from years of practice. He makes constant calculations and recalculations based on the emerging evidence—a shift in the wind, a change in water temperature—and generally makes a strong argument that the key tool in a fisherman's kit is an active mind and a sharp intellect.

Every morning I come home wet and frozen. Every morning my wife greets me at the door with a warm towel and a cool grin. *"Ciao, mio pescatore!"* It becomes a running joke in San Giovanni. Marco, the cheery barista at Nenè Food Bellagio, the village's lone café, serves every spritz with an inquiry about the day's catch. The old men who gather at the port in the afternoons eye me with a mix of wonder and suspicion. Chef Bruno waits by the docks, smoking cigarettes, ready to question my competency. "What, no fish today?" For her part, Mamma Graziella appears ready to make us members of the family. "Stay as long as you like."

I indulge in the fisherman fantasy, though secretly I fear that Alessandro would prefer his regular fishing companion, Ice, back on the boat. The regal retriever carries keys and fetches buoys and probably speaks better Italian than I do.

But Alessandro's patience with me never wavers. Most days, we fish in the rain, normally a light, persistent drizzle that clings to our bodies and seeps into our bones. Alessandro knows this lake better than most people know themselves, and behind every inch of shoreline, every distant villa, every quiet cove is a memory. He tells fishing tales, but of a different stripe than the ones I'm used to—about the first time he took his son out to teach him how to fish and how the young boy counted the fish like sheep until he fell asleep. Or the wealthy couple from Milan who went out dressed to the nines and came back with fish guts fermenting on their Armani threads. Or the time a police boat pulled him and a fellow fisherman over close to Clooney's compound in Laglio, concerned that they were paparazzi. "I'm trying to work, and he's talking to me about photos of George Clooney!" (The police concern wasn't un-

founded; paparazzi have been known to dress up like fishermen in the hope of snapping a shot of Lake Como's gods.)

One afternoon, the drizzle turns into a deluge. We race to collect the nets, but the rain comes down in thick sheets that swallow the lake whole. Alessandro gives up on the nets, calmly steers the boat along the coast until he finds the mouth of a cave, and maneuvers us under its rocky roof. At first we just float there, saying nothing, listening to the thunderous collision of water. Finally Alessandro speaks up.

"A few years back, I got a phone call from a couple from Milano. They had just been on vacation where their teenage son fell in love with fishing, and they wanted to know if I'd be open to taking him out on the lake to show him a few things. 'He's disabled,' the mother told me, 'but he's very active and all he talks about now is fishing.' They came up a few weekends later, and I took all three out in the afternoon on the boat. As soon as we're out of the port, the boy gets anxious: 'When can we throw the nets? When can we throw the nets?' I taught him a few of the basic techniques, pulled up a net or two to show him the catch, but left the rest in the water as I would on any other day. Later, they came in for dinner. At the end of the meal, the dad pulled me aside: 'I'm wondering if you could find a place for us to stay tonight. We'd really like to go back out again when you pull up those nets.' Rosy put them up in one of our rooms, and at 4 A.M., the father and son loaded into the boat and off we went. Again the boy was anxious to get involved. You know what it's like—these nets are heavy and hard to handle, and the boy had a serious disability, but that didn't stop him. He insisted on pulling up all the nets. We had a huge morning—about fifty pounds of *persico* and *tinca*. You can't imagine the smile on his face as we pulled into port. That was years ago, but the boy still calls the restaurant to see how the fishing is going."

The sound of the storm crashing into Lake Como fills the cave with a white noise that nearly drowns out the little cracks in his voice. "You don't do this job to make money."

After four days of rain, the sky finally breaks on our last morning in San Giovanni. I meet Alessandro in the port at 6 A.M., our routine now so ingrained that we slip wordlessly into our positions on the boat. The sun won't rise for another two hours, and the vast darkness swallows us the moment we leave the port. An orange sickle moon hovers just above the bell tower of Saint John the Baptist, smirking, as if it knows something we don't.

Last night in the driving rain we dropped seven nets—four for perch, three for shad. The weekend is coming and, with it, more mouths to feed. Soon Mella will shutter for the winter and life around the lake will go quiet. Alessandro and Rosy like to travel when the restaurant is closed—to Spain or Portugal or Mexico, places where Rosy can relax and Alessandro can fish.

The first net comes up slowly, weighed down by a web of writhing bodies. We pluck the perch from their place in

Alessandro's nylon wall and deposit them in a hard-plastic bucket. The morning looks promising.

It's too early to talk, so we work in silence, the only noise the rattle of the engine and the patter of Alessandro's lessons replaying in my mind.

Keep the nets clean. Wrap them carefully. A tangled net or a broken net can ruin you.

The work is in the nets: cast them in the evening, reclaim them in the morning. Fishing is an act of faith—like running a restaurant in a tiny village, raising a family on a boat, or riding a Vespa up the mountain in search of the one girl who will make you whole. With every cast of the net, Alessandro's life on Lake Como grows a few inches deeper.

Another net, another wall of fish. Alessandro flips a perch into the bucket, and the undead contort on contact. A large spotted char comes up with the last piece of *persico* net, its mouth wrapped around a small perch. An unexpected passenger, the kind that could feed a family of *milanesi* later tonight. Alessandro pries it from the

perch and throws it back in the water, just as he does every time there's a doubt.

Treat the lake as though your children will need it to survive.

We move toward the center of the lake, searching for the *lavarello* nets. The few clouds in the sky have turned to cotton candy, meaning the sun isn't far behind. Across the water in San Giovanni, the bells begin to sing their morning song, the last I will hear at Alessandro's side. Our plane departs from Milano in four hours; my time in Italy is coming to an end.

Keep your mind active. Pay attention to everything. Every detail can impact the catch.

The first two *lavarello* nets come up empty, save for a few feisty crayfish. Maybe we worked this area too hard earlier in the week. Maybe the current shifted in the night. Maybe the whitefish decided to swim deeper.

Alessandro keeps after the net, pulling it up piece by piece, his face fixed on the nylon.

It doesn't matter what we catch right now. The nets are already set. What matters is what we learn about tomorrow.

MATT GOULDING is a James Beard Award–winning writer and the cofounder of Roads & Kingdoms. He is also the coauthor of the *New York Times* bestselling series *Eat This, Not That!* He divides his time between the tapas bars of Barcelona and the barbecue joints of North Carolina.

DOUGLAS HUGHMANICK is director of design for Roads & Kingdoms. He is also a cofounder of Roads & Kingdoms, as well as ANML, a digital design studio he operates in the San Francisco Bay Area.

NATHAN THORNBURGH is a cofounder of Roads & Kingdoms, where he puts all his previous careers—as a musician, a foreign correspondent for *Time* magazine, and an accomplished drinker—to good daily use.

ACKNOWLEDGMENTS

I have always been slightly uncomfortable writing about Italy—a culture this old, this revered, this well documented by wonderful writers, cooks, and scholars scarcely needs another foreigner opining on what makes its cuisine special. But everywhere I turned in Italy, I found people willing to share—a family recipe, a bottle of wine, the last bite of something delicious and meaningful. It's thanks entirely to the heroic generosity of the Italians that this book was even possible.

I met Alessandro Martini at a Parmigiano-Reggiano factory outside Bologna and we became fast friends. His enthusiasm and knowledge of all things Italian changed my perspective on this remarkable country, and his spirit touches every one of these pages. DOP for life.

Along the way, I met dozens, if not hundreds, of people who shared in Alessandro's boundless energy, the dozens of people who welcomed me into their lives: Roberto Petza and Domenico Sanna, who cracked Sardinia wide open for me; Massimo Bottura and his extraordinary team, including Enrico Vignoli, who showed me the full potential of what Italian food can be; the AVPN and Roberto Di Massa, for teaching me the true nature of pizza; Paola Nano and the people at Slow Food for introducing me to so many of Italy's most passionate food fighters. To the Dicecca siblings, who welcomed me into their burrata bubble with the gusto of a long-lost family. Katie Parla made Rome her home and her muse, and has been generous with her considerable knowledge of the local scene. Few people know Rome quiet like Andrea Sponzilli, Alessandro Bocchetti, and Elisia Menduni—thanks for deepening my faith in the Eternal City. And to Luciana Squadrilli, one of the most passionate pizza nerds in the world—thanks for all that you've taught me.

Back in Brooklyn, where the red sauce simmers, Nathan Thornburgh proves himself year after year, book after book, to be the best partner, editor, and friend a roving writer could hope to have. And the crew behind him at Roads & Kingdoms, including executive editor Cara Parks and photo editor Pauline Eiferman, are the ones who make us look good day in and day out.

Douglas Hughmanick continues to set the bar ever higher for designers of all stripes with his work on this series—we never forget how lucky we are to have you on our side. And to Laura White, our secret weapon, who dots our i's and crosses our t's with incredible skill and grace.

To our photographers: Michael Magers, whose Italian might not be as good as his Spanish, but his lens speaks a universal language that has formed the aesthetic backbone of this book seies; Alfredo Chiarappa, who bounded from Bologna to Rome to Puglia in pursuit of the Italian culinary soul; and Martina Albertazzi, the master of the *mamme*.

Anthony Bourdain has done incredible work in Italy for fifteen years, and along the way has built around him an ever-growing Italian family. I hope the book lives up to the lofty expectations set by your adopted country. In any case, thanks for all that you do to make these books, and a world full of inspiring, exhilarating opportunities, happen.

To Kim Witherspoon, the bridge between so many of the people involved in these books. Your collaboration on all fronts makes all the difference.

To Karen Rinaldi, an editor, publisher, and consigliere par excellence. Your friendship and guidance mean the world to me. And to her crack team at HarperCollins, including Hannah Robinson, Leah Carlson-Stanisic, and John Jusino, for helping to shepherd these books to the finish line.

I've benefitted from any number of enthusiastic ambassadors of Italian food culture—writers and cooks who filled my mind with the beauty of Puglian bread customs and central Italian ragù traditions. To all the unwitting professors over the years: Marcella Hazan, Elizabeth David, Mario Batali, Pellegrino Artusi, Apicius, Lidia Bastianich, Faith Willinger, Fred Kaplan, and Waverley Root, among others—thanks for a life's worth of lessons.

And, above all, to my wife, Laura: There is no one I'd rather share a plate of pasta and a bottle of Barolo with than you, *amore mio*.

ROADS & KINGDOMS

Roads & Kingdoms is a digital media company at the intersection of food, travel, politics, and culture. Named the 2017 Publication of the Year by the James Beard Foundation, R&K works with partners such as CNN and Anthony Bourdain to expand the definition of food and travel journalism. Check out our work at roadsandkingdoms.com.